ORIGINAL SIN

CRITICAL AMERICA

Richard Delgado and Jean Stefancic
GENERAL EDITORS

ORIGINAL SIN

Clarence Thomas and the Failure of the
Constitutional Conservatives

SAMUEL A. MARCOSSON

NEW YORK UNIVERSITY PRESS
New York and London

NEW YORK UNIVERSITY PRESS
New York and London

Library of Congress Cataloging-in-Publication Data
Marcosson, Samuel A.
Original sin : Clarence Thomas and the failure of the constitutional
conservatives / Samuel A. Marcosson.
p.   cm. — (Critical America)
Includes bibliographical references and index.
ISBN 0-8147-5640-9 (alk. paper)
1. United States. Supreme Court—History. 2. Constitutional law—
United States—Interpretation and construction—History.
I. Title. II. Series.
KF8742 .M27 2002
347.73'26—dc21   2001008462

New York University Press books are printed on acid-free paper,
and their binding materials are chosen for strength and durability.

Manufactured in the United States of America
10   9   8   7   6   5   4   3   2   1

For my Mother—

*Some small repayment, I hope, for a lifetime of lessons
in love, courage, and perseverance.*

CONTENTS

It is late on a June Washington evening, the cool air carrying only the slightest hint of the oppressive Potomac summer to come. Clarence Thomas, the youngest and most junior Justice on the Supreme Court, sits alone in his chambers. After two years maintaining the relatively low profile common to new members of the Court, Thomas is facing the most crucial decision of his young tenure. The moment of decision is at hand in the most important case in which he has yet participated, *Loving v. Virginia*.[1] *Loving* is the latest suit arguing that a state law barring marriage between men and women of different races violates the Constitution. Though the Court has avoided addressing this question in the past,[2] Thomas's fellow Justices have decided that the time has come, and have unanimously voted to strike down the Virginia antimiscegenation statute. All the Justices have signed off on Chief Justice Warren's short opinion. All, that is, save Thomas. All that remains before the decision is issued is for Thomas to take his stand. Though his position will not change the outcome of the case, he agonizes.

Before him are two drafts. At his left hand is a proposed dissent,[3] arguing that the framers of the Fourteenth Amendment neither believed nor intended that their handiwork would invalidate state antimiscegenation laws. For a committed originalist, Thomas argues in the draft dissent, this is the end of the inquiry, whatever any twentieth-century Justice may think.

Glancing to his right, he sees his other option: a concurrence. It argues that antimiscegenation laws employ a racial classification, in violation of the color-blindness principle that lies at the core of the Fourteenth Amendment.[4] This principle is every bit as important to him as the originalism contained in the dissent. Yet application of the two principles yields contrary results. Hence his dilemma: dissent as an originalist, or concur on the basis of color-blindness?

The considerations that have been occupying his thoughts since oral argument vie again for attention. Try as he might, Thomas cannot ignore his personal discomfort with the notion of dissenting in *Loving*. The state has discreetly avoided enforcing its law against Ginnie and him since they moved to Virginia after his confirmation to the High Court. So upholding the law would not place them in direct jeopardy of prosecution. Still, dissenting from a decision guaranteeing the right of interracial couples to enter into lawful marriages in Virginia—he cannot help but wonder how a dissent from someone in his unique position would be used in the hands of racists who believe antimiscegenation laws are not only constitutional, but a good thing.

And he thinks of Ginnie. Their love is as real, and as entitled to respect, as that of any all-white or all-black couple. With a fierceness bordering on rage—an absolute moral outrage, of the intensity possible only for people like Thomas who believe in moral absolutes—he knows it is wrong for anyone to deny them that respect, especially on the basis of the color of their skin. It is worse still for the state to lend its official voice (and the weight of its criminal law) to that disrespect. The Court is doing the "right" thing, Thomas knows. How much better it would be, though, if Virginia would do so itself, or if the nation would use the political process to amend the Constitution to compel it to do the right thing.

Then, too, there are the jurisprudential implications. A dissent would become a central part of his legacy. It is not that Thomas is shy about vigorously advancing the uncompromising originalism in which he believes. He purposely has laid low for most of his first two terms on the Court, even quietly joining the majority opinion in *Miranda v. Arizona*, the self-incrimination case in which he was first tempted to express his discomfort with the Warren Court's non-originalist methods. But as this second year comes to a close, the time seems right to emerge from the shadows and express his own, originalist judicial identity. In fact, Thomas is proud of the originalist analysis he has penned, knowing that it is the only stance he can take consistent with his unbending fidelity to the Originalist School of constitutional interpretation.

And that is what bothers him. The Court would be upholding the antimiscegenation statute were it employing the Originalist School's methods—*his* methods. Thomas views it as his mission, perhaps even his destiny, to eventually bring the Court around to a committed, consistent originalism.[5] He also knows that his dissent, should he issue it, would be misinterpreted in the mass media as an endorsement of antimiscegenation laws. A linkage between originalism and racism would be inimical to his goals. He wonders how long it would be (if ever), and how many law review articles and speeches it would take, before the public would grasp the difference between finding a practice constitutional, and approving of it. In the meantime, the originalist cause would have been set back by years.

Thomas suddenly becomes aware that he is growing increasingly irritated with himself. He prides himself on his decisiveness, but on this case he seems unconquerably hesitant; he senses no course which he can confidently follow. Damn it, he thinks, this will not do. Tonight, I will decide, and tomorrow I will circulate one of these opinions. He resolves to read each opinion, one last time, then make his choice. He begins with the dissent. . . .

INTRODUCTION

Day by day, case by case, the Court is busy designing a Constitution for a country I do not recognize.[1]

Recognize: 1. to be aware of as something or someone known before, or as the same as that known . . . 3. to be aware of the significance of [to *recognize* symptoms] 4. to acknowledge the existence, validity, authority, or genuineness of (to *recognize* a claim]. . . .[2]

Questions of constitutional interpretation are ultimately questions about recognition. This is most obviously so with reference to Webster's fourth definition of *recognize*: a court "recognizes" the validity of the plaintiff's claim or it does not, hence deciding the case. But it is also true, perhaps in less obvious ways, that the first and third definitions reflect competing visions of constitutional interpretation. That competition is the subject of this book.

The first definition: "to be aware of as something or someone known before, or as the same as that known." One could hardly hope for a better description of *stare decisis*, the legal doctrine by which judges commit themselves to defer (more or less rigidly, depending on a number of factors) to previous decisions, in the hope that society can be governed by reasonably predictable rules so that every case need not be considered as if no one ever thought about the issues before. *Stare decisis* cannot function unless judges can recognize the present case as "the same as that known"—that is, the same as the earlier cases that demand deference. This requires an ability to weigh the sameness of the facts giving rise to each case, and then determine whether the legal rule that decided the first case applies to the facts of the second.[3]

But this type of recognition also works at a deeper, doctrinal level. A court may credit an argument because it is one that the legal system has "known before." In the United States, a person can file a lawsuit claiming that her "freedom of speech" has been abridged, because the courts recognize that sort of claim as one the legal system exists to adjudicate.[4] In Malaysia, the government can file charges against a newspaper reporter because he has "scandalized the court," because the courts recognize such charges as ones the legal system exists to adjudicate.[5]

This first definition, then, represents recognition at a literal level: One cannot *re*-cognize that which she has not encountered and been aware of before. Under this definition, re-cognition is dependent on the past, and is a function of tradition. Both at the factual level ("Are these the circumstances in which this traditional rule governs?") and at the doctrinal level ("Is this claim available based on the traditional rules?"), a judge who makes decisions on the basis of re-cognition is bowing to tradition.

This link between re-cognition and tradition is present in Justice Antonin Scalia's dissenting opinion in *Board of County Commissioners v. Umbehr,* which contains the passage quoted at the chapter opening. The Court in *Umbehr* held that the First Amendment constrains governments from terminating contracts or discharging at-will employees because the contractor or employee criticizes the government. In other words, the authority of government officials to reward their loyal supporters with government contracts or jobs (after having created the openings by getting rid of pesky opponents) is limited. Justice Scalia's dissenting opinion emphasized the long American tradition of political patronage,[6] implicitly asserting that this tradition made it self-evident that those practices could not be unconstitutional. Its closing reference to recognition should be understood as first-definition recognition, as re-cognition.

This is the core premise of originalism: Judges cannot recognize what has not been seen before. To be valid in Justice Scalia's eyes, a constitutional claim must be one he re-cognizes because it has been "seen" before, and by very specific sets of eyes: those of the people who wrote and ratified the constitutional provision at issue. Or, if we're not sufficiently sure whether *they* validated the claim, it is acceptable to turn to the eyes of generations of people who have lived under the Constitution long enough to establish a tradition either acknowledging the claimed right or refusing to do so.[7] Either way, it is not much of an exaggeration to say that to originalists, any truly innovative constitutional argument is fatally flawed precisely because it is innovative.

Webster's third definition of "recognition" provides a competing vision of constitutional interpretation. It means "to be aware of the significance of." The work of Justice Harry Blackmun, perhaps the most passionately expressive writer on the Court in the twentieth century, best exemplifies this very different approach. In *DeShaney v. Winnebago County Department of Social Services*,[8] four-year-old Joshua DeShaney was beaten

> into a life-threatening coma [by his father]. . . . [He] suffered brain damage so severe that he is expected to spend the rest of his life confined to an institution for the profoundly retarded.[9]

The Court held that even though the state had failed to act after receiving reports of the ongoing abuse, it could not be held liable because it had no constitutional duty to protect Joshua. In dissent, Justice Blackmun said:

> Poor Joshua! Victim of repeated attacks by an irresponsible, bullying, cowardly, and intemperate father, and abandoned by respondents who placed him in a dangerous predicament and who knew or learned what was going on, and yet did essentially nothing except, as the Court revealingly observes, . . . "dutifully recorded these incidents in [their] files." It is a sad commentary upon American life, and constitutional principles—so full of late of patriotic fervor and proud proclamations about "liberty and justice for all"—that this child, Joshua DeShaney, now is assigned to live out the remainder of his life profoundly retarded. Joshua and his mother, as petitioners here, deserve—but now are denied by this Court—the opportunity to have the facts of their case considered in the light of the constitutional protection that 42 U.S.C. §§ 1983 is meant to provide.[10]

DeShaney was characteristic of Blackmun; his passionate focus on the consequences of the Court's rulings is on display in *Webster v. Reproductive Health Services*,[11] and his unwillingness to abide injustice resounds in *Richmond v. J.A. Croson Co.*[12]

3

Even beyond Justice Blackmun's passionate approach, interpretation guided by a mandate to be "aware of the significance of" a decision —third-definition recognition—is the core of much of the Court's constitutional work of the last half-century. The Court based many of the key rulings constituting the criminal procedure revolution of the 1960s on discussions of the real-world significance of confessions obtained in violation of the right to remain silent,[13] admitting the fruits of unreasonable searches,[14] and a criminal defendant's lack of legal representation.[15]

Two paradigms, then, each based on a different definition of "recognition." They are separated by asking whether the judge re-cognizes the claim (the first definition), or whether she recognizes it (the third definition). There should be no doubt about the wide and unbridgeable divide between these approaches. If we were to ask Justices Thomas and Scalia whether the contemporary significance of a provision of Article I, or the Bill of Rights, ought to matter when the Court interprets that provision, their answer would be that it does not.[16] If it has undesirable consequences, it may be changed by others—Congress, the states, the people directly, working in some combination—but not by judges. First-definition recognition—originalism—demands that its champions ignore the forward-looking significance of their decisions, and say:

> Though the heavens may fall before the ink is dry on this decision, it is the outcome dictated by the original understanding of the Constitution. The burden of producing the amendment needed to permit the sun to rise tomorrow is committed by the fifth of its Articles to the infinitely greater wisdom of the body politic rather than to the humble devices housed in these poor Chambers.[17]

Justice Scalia demonstrated this sort of steely tunnel vision in his majority opinion *Employment Division v. Smith*.[18] There, the Court rejected the claim that the Free Exercise Clause of the Constitution protects the right of members of a Native American church to use peyote as a sacrament, overriding Oregon criminal law banning the use of peyote as a controlled substance. In ruling in favor of the state, the Court acknowledged,

> It may fairly be said that leaving accommodation to the political process
> will place at a relative disadvantage those religious practices that are not
> widely engaged in; but that unavoidable consequence of democratic gov-
> ernment must be preferred to a system in which . . . judges weigh the so-
> cial importance of all laws against the centrality of all religious beliefs.[19]

Undesirable consequences? That appeal has no currency here, Justice
Scalia answers. Go tell it to the legislature.[20]

The first part of this book, consisting of the first five chapters, will ask
whether the judicial originalists are living up to their own lofty standards. Have they recognized only principles, arguments, and understandings that were "seen" by the eyes of the founding generation, re-
fraining from resort to non-originalist methods to avoid painful outcomes? In these chapters I will demonstrate that the current generation
of judicial originalists has repeatedly recognized the contemporary significance of their decisions and acted accordingly.

Chapter 1 will take up the story of the Clarence Thomas introduced
in the preface, the one appointed to the Supreme Court in 1965 by President Lyndon Johnson. This odd counter-historical story permits us to
understand better the central paradox of the judicial performance of the
real-life Clarence/Justice Thomas: his devotion to an interpretation of
the Equal Protection Clause dictated by recognition, despite his constant, thunderous protestations in other cases that only re-cognition is a
legitimate basis for constitutional decision-making.

Others have remarked about this, some in passing and some at length,
without trying to explain it. In Chapter 2 I will try to provide that explanation. It is not simply that Justice Thomas is a hypocrite; something
much more important is at work here. Much as Justice Thomas may be
devoted to re-cognizing only what the founders saw, that devotion is
swept away by something he *hears* when it comes to the Fourteenth
Amendment: the voice of Clarence Thomas, relating the awful significance of the originalist answer to the questions raised in cases of race
and equality. In those cases, first-definition re-cognition gives way to
third-definition recognition.[21]

Chapter 3 will move the discussion beyond the Fourteenth Amendment and address the judicial originalists' infidelity to their method
when it comes to the takings and compensation requirements of the

Fifth Amendment, and the search-and-seizure requirements of the Fourth Amendment. Each of these areas has been the subject of considerable scholarly scrutiny in recent years, much of it focused on the original understanding of the two amendments. In these areas, the judicial originalists have, at best, selectively picked out facets of the original understanding that support their favored conclusions while ignoring less helpful aspects of the historical record.

From these examples, together with the Fourteenth Amendment record compiled by the originalists, a picture begins to take shape, one of jurists whose positions bear a closer resemblance to those taken by the contemporary Republican Party than with those of the framers of the constitutional text involved in each case. Just as Justice Thomas recognizes what he cannot ignore when it comes to the Fourteenth Amendment, he and Scalia recognize their political ideology when private property and criminal procedure are before the Court. A scientist testing an "originalist hypothesis" and a "political hypothesis" would find in the opinions of Justices Thomas and Scalia substantial evidence to support the latter.

In Chapter 4, I will address the more complex area of federalism. In this area, a committed, consistent, and narrow conservative majority made up of Justices Thomas, Scalia, O'Connor, and Kennedy, and Chief Justice Rehnquist, has been engaged in a decade-long campaign to redraw the lines between the federal government and the states, limiting the former while carving out areas of exclusive authority and autonomy for the latter. Across this swath of cases, the "Federalism Five" have been inconsistent originalists. When they have tried to build an originalist argument for their vision of federalism, they have focused exclusively on the *original* original understanding, rather than consider the effect two centuries of constitutional amendments have had on that design. Once again, the contemporary politics seem to matter more than a straightforward assessment of the original understanding.

Chapter 5 will assess the originalists' performance in what history will undoubtedly mark as the Rehnquist Court's signature case: *Bush v. Gore.*[22] The case was distinct from any in the Court's jurisprudence, in that it presented an unprecedented opportunity for the Court to influence not only the nation's destiny but its own future roster and direction. Never before had the Court held the power to select the President, much less one who almost certainly would nominate replacements for some of the Justices. The handiwork of the Justices in the majority, from federalism to affirmative action and beyond, may well have been at stake in the choice represented by the name of the case: Bush versus Gore. The temptation to recognize the significance of the outcome, rather than to re-cognize the original understanding of the issues, could never have been greater.

And, history will judge, never have judges given in so completely to that temptation. Justices Scalia and Thomas joined both the *per curiam* majority opinion and Chief Justice Rehnquist's concurrence. The reasoning of those opinions provides the strongest evidence of the non-originalism, and the results-orientation, of the Court's conservative wing. The majority opinion contained equal protection analysis that would, if applied generally, radically transform Fourteenth Amendment jurisprudence, reshaping it in ways that are unrecognizable to its framers, unsupported by any precedent, and directly contradictory to the positions taken by Scalia and Thomas in the past. And the concurring opinion violated the core principles of federalism, so much the heart of the conservatives' project for the last decade, by refusing to accept a state Supreme Court's interpretation of state law. It made a deeply unconvincing attempt to transform a routine difference of opinion over how to read state law into a problem of constitutional dimension. There is no way to read the majority and concurring opinions in *Bush v. Gore* as anything other than confirmation, when the Court might well have been facing the highest stakes and the greatest responsibility in its history, that the current crop of "originalists" is anything but. Their commitment instead was to their own personal and political hearts; when they could not ignore their own desire to produce the presidency for which they yearned, they adopted a jurisprudence of recognition.

The second part of the book, encompassing Chapters 6–8, will examine originalism itself in light of the dismal performance of its champions. In Chapter 6, I will assess the costs associated with the method, mindful of the originalists' failure to deliver the benefits they claim on behalf of their method. In particular, we must be wary of the serious loss of interpretive flexibility inherent in originalism. The era in which we live is so distant from that of the original framers that binding us to their priorities and perspectives cannot help but render us less able to address our problems and meet our collective goals. We must seriously reckon with the implications of Justice Kennedy's comments in *Clinton v. City of New York,* the case in which the Court struck down the "line-item veto" power Congress had given to the President. In concurring, but expressing barely disguised regret over having to do so, Kennedy wrote:

> Whether or not federalism and control by the electorate are adequate for the problem at hand, they are two of the structures the Framers designed for the problem the statute strives to confront. The Framers of the Constitution could not command statesmanship. They could simply provide structures from which it might emerge. The fact that these mechanisms, plus the proper functioning of the separation of powers itself, are not employed, or that they prove insufficient, cannot validate an otherwise unconstitutional device.[23]

A remarkable confession, really: Even if our constitutional structures are inadequate to meet contemporary problems, that's just the way it is, unless and until a constitutional amendment is enacted to save the day. This admission justifies a simple demand: If originalists agree their method leaves us with inadequate governmental structures and powers to meet problems, they should at least bear the burden of proving that they deliver the gains they argue make the trade-off worthwhile.

One of the key advantages originalists claim, of course, is that their theory constrains judges not to impose their own politics, values, or whims on the country.[24] On this point, originalists fail to meet their burden of proof for two reasons. First, there is scant evidence that originalism truly and consistently constrains judges. In the hard cases—especially in the *painfully hard* cases like Justice Thomas's encounter with the voice of Clarence Thomas and the selection of a President—self-proclaimed originalists either forget entirely about providing a justification based on the original understanding, or they provide a flimsy façade of a historical argument. And second, there is little evidence that originalism is uniquely or unusually constraining. If the test is how often the judge is compelled to accept an interpretation she or he finds personally unwelcome, the careful reader finds as many examples of non-originalist judges accepting such consequences. In other words, we get the same constraining effect without the negative consequences.

What does the failure of the constraint argument mean for originalism? Everything. This constraining function is essential to originalism; it is the basis on which originalists claim that their method overcomes the famous counter-majoritarian difficulty. For at least the past 40 years, courts and constitutional scholars have been concerned with the counter-majoritarian difficulty, which challenges the democratic legitimacy of judicial review because it imposes the will of unelected, life-tenured judges on the democratically elected institutions and, hence, on the people's right to govern ourselves. Justice Scalia wrote of the common-law process of judge-made law that it "would be unqualified good, were it not for a trend that has developed in recent centuries, called democracy."[25]

Originalists claim to have resolved the problem. Their claim starts with the premise that legitimacy depends, at the very least, on a mechanism that constrains judges from imposing their own personal views on the rest of us. Originalists offer their method as that mechanism, because it commits judges to impose the views of the founders and *only* the views of the founders. The originalists' injunction to the judges is to speak for James Madison and Alexander Hamilton, but not for themselves. Their failure to obey this injunction devastates their claim to have found a solution to the counter-majoritarian difficulty.

More importantly, though, in Chapter 7 I will suggest that judicial originalists are borrowing from an empty account even when they adhere to the original understanding in their quest for democratic legitimacy. They believe that the founders are the proverbial "rich uncle" to whom they can always turn for sustenance, and whose authority—conferred by "We the People" at the moment of constitutional ratification or amendment—is unquestionable.

The problem, though, is that the rich uncle is bankrupt, and has been from the outset. Justices Thomas and Scalia and their colleagues both on and off the federal bench believe implicitly that the constitutional founders are overflowing with legitimacy. This is their core claim, and their core mistake. The Constitution as originally understood is far more anti-democratic than the Article III judges so feared by the originalists.

The counter-majoritarian objection to judicial review was never the problem. In trying to resolve the counter-majoritarian difficulty, constitutional theorists have been stuck on the trivial question while ignoring the important one. The anti-majoritarian origins of the Constitution are the true threat to the legitimacy of governance under the Constitution. The issue is not whether judicial decisions interpreting the Constitution are legitimate. The issue is whether the Constitution itself is legitimate.

Chapter 8 will wrestle with one natural response to this critique: If the anti-democratic origins of the Constitution are the primary obstacle to its legitimacy, why should we be bound by it at all? The answer, I will suggest, is that we should not be, at least not by the *original* Constitution. The originalists' way of dealing with the counter-majoritarian difficulty makes the anti-majoritarian origins problem far worse than any other interpretive method, because it "locks in" the understanding held at the anti-democratic founding as permanently binding.

But the Constitution has gained legitimacy over 200 and more years through a process of transformation *that includes non-originalist judicial interpretation.* Together with the formal, Article V amendment process, the judicial role has, over time, proved indispensable in moving the Constitution past its problematic origins. The originalists would remove this crucial mechanism providing for constitutional change and (hence) for increased democratic legitimacy.

For this reason, I will propose a different, more pro-active role for the Court. It must undertake a process of *legitimation.* Instead of simply interpreting and applying the constitutional provision at issue in a particular case, the Court should engage a logically prior question: Does the historical record provide a basis for questioning the legitimacy of the provision? The Court's responsibility under the Constitution is to minimize—and if possible eliminate—the remaining effects of those provisions that were a product of the anti-democratic origins of the Constitution.

Ironically, this approach is a fuller, more genuine originalism than the re-cognition model advanced by the constitutional conservatives. Their fixation on the text and the meaning ascribed to it by the framers omits a crucial component of complete originalist analysis: the underlying context. Article I, Section 3 of the Constitution states:

> Representatives and direct Taxes shall be apportioned among the several
> States . . . according to their respective Numbers, which shall be deter-

mined by adding to the whole Number of free Persons, including those bound to Service for a Term of Years, and excluding Indians not taxed, *three fifths of all other persons.*[26]

The originalist would examine the text of this provision and conclude that each state's number of seats in the House of Representatives would be based on its number of "free Persons" plus "three fifths of all other (i.e., not free) persons." Inquiry into the framers' understanding would confirm that slaves would be counted for purposes of determining congressional representation, but only to the extent of 60 percent of their actual numbers.

What is missing from this re-cognition style originalism is assessment of the purpose of this provision: to ensure that the southern states, with smaller populations of "free Persons," would not be overwhelmed by the northern states—and hence to preserve the South's ability to block any attempt to undermine or eliminate the slave trade. Real originalism would take account of this context.

Of course, this particular provision is of no contemporary moment; the Court need not interpret the Three-Fifths Compromise since it was rendered a nullity by the Thirteenth Amendment. But this cannot be said of other provisions, and the democratic legitimacy of the Constitution depends not on judicial restraint in dealing with these provisions but on active judicial scrutiny.

What would legitimation look like? For the most part, it would not be a radical departure from some traditional constitutional interpretation. From the outset, John Marshall enjoined us never to forget it is a Constitution we are expounding.[27] Honoring that injunction demands that, within the range of interpretive integrity (i.e., among those interpretations that plausibly read constitutional text and structure), the Court should search for the reading that leaves the provision at issue most consistent with the rest of the Constitution and the values to which it aspires.[28]

To this search for consistency the Court should bring a new degree of skepticism. Too much of our constitutional history has been marked by undeserved reverence, with too little attention paid to the underside of the Constitution's framing and its provisions. Rather than the faux originalism of Thomas and Scalia, which asks only what the framers understood, the Court should ask deeper questions about the historical context: What motivated the framers? Was the goal for which they were aiming legitimate, and if so does it remain legitimate when measured against the Constitution as it has been amended since 1789?

In place of the original understanding, the Court should interpret the provision so as to eliminate its anti-democratic elements. I will explore two examples to demonstrate how legitimation would work. The first is a remarkable 1999 decision in which the Alabama Supreme Court held that the state Constitution contains no guarantee of equal protection of the laws.[29] The Court's opinion was rigidly originalist and, if we accept originalism's legitimacy, almost inarguably correct. The original understanding of the framers of the current Alabama Constitution plainly was that it would contain no equal protection guarantee. In order to take that understanding as a given, however, the Court had to deem the historical context of the 1901 Constitutional Convention (called for the express purpose of writing white legal and social supremacy into state law) irrelevant to a proper interpretation of the Constitution the conventioneers produced. A legitimizing court would take a very different view of how to weigh the threats to legitimacy posed by non-originalist interpretation on the one hand and a racist, undemocratic Constitution on the other.

The second example I will discuss concerns a case that never was filed. For much of the twentieth century, efforts to pass meaningful federal civil rights legislation died in the U.S. Senate at the hands of implacable southern Senators willing to use their status as committee chairs to block bills from getting a hearing, and to use the filibuster to prevent legislation that did make it to the floor from being passed. What if a constitutional challenge to the filibuster rule had been filed? A legitimizing court, I will argue, would have ruled for the plaintiffs in such a suit and ordered the Senate to vote on civil rights legislation in a timely manner.

Legitimation would produce a Constitution more at peace with itself. The changes "We the People" have wrought in two centuries of formal amendment, civil war and reconstruction, civil rights and economic upheaval, are in many ways in tension with the original Constitution. To see this, however, the Court must examine not just the original understanding (originalism of the Thomas/Scalia variety), but the historical context and the underlying motives of the framers (in truth, a fuller and more accurate originalism). It must also recognize the modern-day implications of strict adherence to the narrow original understanding. To relieve the tension, in turn, the Court must identify, appreciate, and give life to the broad values animating the Constitution as it has been improved gradually since 1789. I will suggest the use of three such values (democratic governance through republican institutions, equality before the law, and respect for individual rights). Where a plausible interpretation of the text is available that would be consistent with those values, the Court should adopt that interpretation in lieu of one that is, in the Scalian sense of the term, "originalist."

The originalist engine is undoubtedly driving the Supreme Court into the twenty-first century. The inauguration of George W. Bush raises the distinct likelihood that originalist reinforcements may be joining the Supreme Court in the next several years. Even the less conservative Justices have increasingly been rendering opinions that base interpretation on a historical analysis of the original understanding of the relevant constitutional text.[30] Non-originalist scholars like Laurence Tribe[31] and Cass Sunstein[32] have written articles that accept in significant ways constrained aspirations for constitutional adjudication, articles which by all appearances seem to be a product of the originalist ascendence.

For all their seeming success, though, the originalists have failed on their own terms. Their inability to adhere consistently to the demands of the original understanding, and their failure to harmonize that original understanding with the core constitutional values we have nurtured in the Constitution's 220-year life, will ultimately bring the originalist engine to a sputtering halt. The current originalist era will, for all of that, leave an important legacy: a reminder that the task of interpreting our Constitution must begin with the effort to seek out its history. Our task is to develop a new approach which builds upon that essential, but ultimately inadequate, insight as we go about the hard work of constitutional interpretation.

There are many people to thank for their assistance, support, and advice while I worked on this book. Deans Donald Burnett and Laura Rothstein provided both emotional encouragement and financial support via summer research grants. My colleagues on the faculty at the Louis Brandeis School of Law at the University of Louisville were more than helpful; particular thanks to Enid Trucios-Haynes and Serena Williams. Jim Becker, a former student and research assistant and now everything one could ever hope for in a law/computer guru, was always there no matter how I tried to foul things up. My research assistants, Tricia Keelen-LeMeur and Jim Herr, went about their work with great skill and humor. Several colleagues at other schools helped with their comments: Bill Eskridge, Nancy Levit, and Carol Steiker were all generous and insightful, as were the participants at the Central States Legal Scholarship Colloquium. They will rightfully expect me to make clear that they are not to blame for the numerous ways in which the text suffers because I did not sufficiently appreciate their wisdom, and I do so now. Above all, my thanks to Professors Richard Delgado and Jean Stefancic. With no reason to take any particular interest in my work, they suggested and provided me the opportunity to take up this project, then encouraged me and provided cogent advice and comments along the way.

Portions of the Preface and Chapter 1 were originally published, in somewhat modified form, in my article "Colorizing the Constitution of Originalism: Clarence Thomas at the Rubicon," published in volume 16 of the journal *Law & Inequality*. That material is reprinted here with the permission of the journal.

CHAPTER ONE

I NEVER LIE

There is an old logic trick, consisting of two statements and an assumption that the first statement is true:

I never lie.
I'm lying.[1]

The listener ends up in a logical impossibility if she assumes the first statement to be true. She knows by assumption that the speaker never lies, so the second statement ("I'm lying") must be true. But if it is true, then the speaker is lying—which is impossible, because the speaker never lies. The lesson, if there is one, is to question initial assumptions.

If Clarence Thomas were compelled to decide *Loving v. Virginia*, he would face precisely the same situation. The first of his two statements would be: "I always decide constitutional issues based on the original understanding of the framers, as discerned from the available historical evidence."

Since Thomas has frequently said precisely this,[2] we are not being unfair to him if we assume for the moment that it is true. And if it is, the 1967 version of Justice Thomas would find his voice in an opinion dissenting in *Loving*. Rather than explaining why this is so, let us hear it from him directly (sort of).

Thomas, J., dissenting:

The most dangerous tendency for the members of this Court is to find in the Constitution those rights we most fondly wish were contained therein. For me, this threat has never loomed more prominently than it does today. Any reader familiar with my life as an American citizen will understand my abiding belief that no person should be prevented from marrying the love of his or her life, without regard to race or color.

But I write today not to express my views on what policies the Commonwealth of Virginia should adopt regarding interracial marriages. Nor do I express my opinion as to whether our Constitution ought to take this decision out of Virginia's hands by prohibiting the states from adopting bans on such marriages.

Rather, I write as a Justice of the Supreme Court, bound by my oath of office to interpret the Constitution faithfully according to its terms. That oath compels me to conclude that nothing in the Constitution, as written and intended by its Framers, prevents Virginia from enacting the policy it has chosen.[3] Because "[t]his case is ultimately a reminder that the Federal Constitution does not prohibit everything that is intensely undesirable,"[4] I must respectfully, and sorrowfully, dissent.

A.

The question before the Court is whether the Fourteenth Amendment's Equal Protection Clause[5] restricts the power of the States to bar interracial marriages.[6] Answering this question requires us to determine the original understanding of what the text meant in 1868 when the Fourteenth Amendment was ratified. In determining the original understanding, it is tempting to say simply that the framers intended to create a "color-blind" Constitution, and to bar the states from utilizing any racial classifications. This was, famously, the view the first Justice Harlan expressed in his dissenting opinion in *Plessy v. Ferguson*.[7] Since the Court correctly concludes that the Virginia statute at issue here classifies citizens by their race,[8] it violates this understanding of the Equal Protection Clause.

Notwithstanding Justice Harlan's views, however, the "color-blind Constitution" ideal is simply too general to constitute a basis for our decision. It represents an originalism so diluted as to be unrecognizable.[9] The ideal might be useful as a general guidepost,[10] but it cannot substitute for careful historical analysis of whether the framers of the Fourteenth Amendment intended to bar racial classifications in this particular area.[11] For this reason, our mandate is to search for the original understanding at the most specific level for which there is sufficient historical evidence to discern with confidence a relevant understanding.[12] If we knew nothing of the framers' intent with respect to antimiscegenation laws in particular, then it would be appropriate to resort to a higher level of generality,[13] perhaps even the very high level of abstraction represented by the "color-blind Constitution" ideal. That course, however, is foreclosed by the presence of evidence at the more specific level,[14] evidence I next proceed to review.

B.

One of the best indications that the framers of the Equal Protection Clause did not intend to displace antimiscegenation laws is that those laws remained undisturbed in the years immediately following ratification.[15] In the days and years immediately following passage of the Amendment, the states, both those of the former Confederacy and those that remained loyal to the Union, continued to enforce antimiscegenation statutes.[16] In light of this record, it is implausible to believe that the framers of the Fourteenth Amendment intended to end the states' power to ban interracial marriage; this weighs heavily in favor of the Commonwealth's position.

This post-ratification record is consistent with the compelling evidence that when it was ratified, the Fourteenth Amendment was not understood either to establish a general principle of color-blindness or to affect antimiscegenation laws. As for the general principle, some of the sponsors of the Amendment had earlier proposed language explicitly barring governments from using racial classifications of all kinds.[17]

> Congress repeatedly rejected such a measure, however, choosing the far more ambiguous language of the present Fourteenth Amendment. . . . Color blindness, then, was explicitly rejected as constitutional text. . . .[18]

Lest we understate the differences between pure color-blindness and what was actually enacted, it is well to recall that one of the principal advocates of color-blindness, Wendell Phillips, called the Fourteenth Amendment "a fatal and total surrender," "an infamous breach of the national pledge to negroes . . . a party trick designed only for election-eering purposes."[19] Raoul Berger puts it plainly:

> When we look to the soil from which the Fourteenth Amendment sprang, attribution to the framers of the aim of creating uncircumscribed racial equality is like insisting that roses bloom in the Sahara Desert.[20]

The majority is thus quite wrong to suggest that "[t]he clear and central purpose of the Fourteenth Amendment was to eliminate all official state sources of invidious racial discrimination in the states."[21] Perhaps color-blindness is the applicable principle in one or more particular contexts; we need not resolve that issue today. But plainly it is not the general principle guiding Fourteenth Amendment analysis.

Even if color-blindness were the governing principle intended by the framers of the Equal Protection Clause, there is yet another, insuperable difficulty with the majority's analysis. The Fourteenth Amendment was designed to provide equal protection of "the 'person and property' of blacks against violence."[22] This protection manifestly was *not* intended to extend to areas that were not at the time considered "civil rights." The framers of the Fourteenth Amendment drew what Professor Richards aptly characterizes as:

> a sharp distinction . . . between equality in basic rights like protection of life, liberty, and property and rights to social and political equality (in marriage, schooling, and voting), applying equal protection to the former *but not the latter*.[23]

More consistently with the terminology of the time, Professor Mc-Connell calls the protected category "civil rights."[24] However phrased, the crucial point is that any right deemed a matter of "social equality" is not protected by the right to equal protection of the laws.[25]

Marriage fits within the class of "social rights."[26] As a result, the Four-teenth Amendment does not guarantee equal protection with respect to a state's marriage laws.[27] Indeed, the "social rights" formulation was the primary answer given by sponsors of the Amendment to the charge that ratification would result in widespread interracial marriage.[28] It there-fore most accurately reflects the understanding of the Amendment held by those who decided to include it in our foundational document.[29] Indeed, antimiscegenation laws may represent the archetype of the racialism in "social rights" left undisturbed by the Equal Protection Clause.

The inclusion of marriage in the class of unprotected social rights provides compelling, perhaps irrefutable evidence that antimiscegenation laws were unaffected by the Fourteenth Amendment. If any more proof is required, it is supplied by the amendment's sponsors' direct, unequivocal statements on the precise question of antimiscegenation laws. Even a recent scholarly attempt to use debates regarding the Civil Rights Act of 1875 (hereinafter the "1875 Act") to build a case that the Fourteenth Amendment rendered antimiscegenation laws unconstitutional[30] concedes that prior to 1868, during debates over the Civil Rights Act of 1866 (hereinafter the "1866 Act") and the Fourteenth Amendment, Republicans *denied that antimiscegenation laws would be affected by their proposals*.[31] In response to Democratic accusations that the 1866 Act would make state antimiscegenation laws illegal, "Supporters . . . immediately sought to allay concerns that the bill would repeal" those laws.[32] In light of this, the evidence is overwhelming that the framers and ratifiers of the Fourteenth Amendment neither expected nor intended to nullify state antimiscegenation laws. For me, that is the end of the matter.

C.

I am forced to conclude that the framers of the Fourteenth Amendment did not intend to create a "color-blind Constitution," and certainly did not intend to do so insofar as antimiscegenation laws were concerned. Ratification of the Amendment was based, at least in significant part, on assurances by its supporters that these laws would *not* be affected.

The majority takes substantial comfort, I presume, in its confidence that it today reaches the "right" decision—right in terms of the moral rights of free people not to be subjected to odious government interference in their personal lives on the basis of the color their skin. I have no doubt that this is the "right" decision for our nation to make on this question. I would take greater comfort, however, had the nation actually done so, through the constitutional amendment process designed for the People to make such fundamental decisions to alter the way we govern our affairs.[33] I agree with Professor Tribe that we must reject interpretive methods "that would treat the Constitution as amendable by procedures nowhere specified therein."[34] Since I am convinced that the Fourteenth Amendment, as originally understood by those who supported and ratified it, did not alter Virginia's power to enact and enforce the law at issue today, I dissent.[35]

This opinion undeniably represents the position a staunch originalist would have taken in *Loving*.[36] If Justice Thomas took this stance, it would validate our assumption that the first statement ("I'm always an originalist") is true.

But the consistency of the *Loving* dissent with Justice Thomas's originalist judicial voice is only part of the story. We can also approach the task of assessing what Thomas might have done in *Loving* by asking what he has done in cases arising under the Equal Protection Clause. A nutshell synopsis of that position provides the second statement, parallel to "I'm lying":

> I decide issues arising under the Equal Protection Clause of the Fourteenth Amendment based on the principle that "the government may not make distinctions on the basis of race."[37]

The originalist Thomas, we have seen, would find that antimiscegenation laws are constitutionally valid. What would the Thomas who rejects racial classifications have said?

Thomas, J., concurring in part and concurring in the judgment:

The Court today gives life to the fundamental and great principle animating the Equal Protection Clause of our Constitution's Fourteenth Amendment: the government shall not classify citizens on the basis of their race. As I stated in *Adarand Constructors, Inc. v. Pena*,[38] "[U]nder our Constitution, the government may not make distinctions on the basis of race."[39] In Virginia, however, the right of residents to have their marriages recognized by the State is conditioned entirely on their race. By maintaining its antimiscegenation statute, Virginia has refused to "treat citizens as individuals, [rather than] as members of racial, ethnic or religious groups."[40]

Barring interracial marriages is, so far as the Equal Protection Clause is concerned, no different from barring intraracial marriage. A "mandatory miscegenation" law would claim the same right Virginia asserts in this case: the power to deal with people on the basis of a racial classification. A state which compels either separation or unwanted association on the basis of race violates the Constitution.

That is why the proper remedy in this case is to permit Mr. and Mrs. Loving to live the life they have chosen as man and wife, in Virginia if that is their wish, without fear of prosecution or imprisonment. Surely, it would accord with no one's understanding of the Fourteenth Amendment for the district court to attempt to frame a decree requiring a certain number of interracial marriages; merely to state the notion of judicial interference with these private decisions is to immediately see why it is repugnant. Racial separation that results from private, individual choices is no business of this Court or of the Constitution.[41]

The Court correctly rejects the state's claim that it is treating members of both races equally, in that both are limited to marrying within their race and equally are barred from marrying outside it. True or not,[42] this argument is beside the point. It is sufficient that, as the Court recognizes, "Virginia's miscegenation statutes rest solely upon distinctions drawn according to race."[43] The classification itself, and not its content, is the *sine qua non* of the constitutional violation.[44]

Finally, I add that, owing to my belief that the Due Process Clause does not contain a "substantive" component,[45] I do not join Part II of the Court's opinion, which rests on the recognition of a substantive constitutional right to marriage as an aspect of due process of law.[46] Otherwise, I concur.

I never lie. I'm lying.

I am always an originalist. The Constitution is color-blind.

The lesson of the second pair of statements is the same as it was for the first: Be careful about assumptions. The foregoing opinions reveal that an originalist judge and a color-blind judge considering *Loving* would have been on opposite sides of the fence. If Justice Thomas would have adopted the color-blind position set forth in the second opinion, if he would have concurred in *Loving*, it belies our assumption that the statement "I am always an originalist" is true.

So: Whither Justice Thomas in *Loving*? This question is provocative because the fictional Thomas considering *Loving* would have been able to find ample support for each of the opposite results in Thomas's own jurisprudence. Scan the notes; both the dissent and the concurrence contain numerous citations to opinions the real-life Thomas has written. The problem is that they *cite different opinions*. The dissent refers to his frequent professions of fidelity to a jurisprudence of original understanding, while ignoring his Fourteenth Amendment writing. The concurrence, meanwhile, is full of references to Thomas's Fourteenth Amendment cases, but mentions neither originalism in general nor the original understanding of the Fourteenth Amendment in particular.

I did not create this pattern of parallel omissions and attribute it to Justice Thomas. Instead, it is the single most striking feature of the jurisprudence he has crafted for himself. It is true, without exception, that Justice Thomas has never cited an Equal Protection Clause case in support of one of his frequent assertions of his originalist philosophy. More crucially, he has never done any of the following with reference to an Equal Protection Clause issue: included a reference to any opinion, written by Thomas himself or any other judge, stating that original understanding is the basis for constitutional interpretation; included any discussion of the original understanding of the Fourteenth Amendment; explained why the Fourteenth Amendment alone is different from the rest of the Constitution in a way that renders originalism inapplicable.

Instead, when it comes to the Equal Protection Clause, Justice Thomas has spoken in the manner of a proponent of a "living Constitution," one whose interpretation is guided in large part by contemporary social conditions and evolving understandings of majestic (but often vague) constitutional language. Consider, for instance, his concurring opinion in *Missouri v. Jenkins*,[47] a school desegregation case testing the limits of a federal court's authority to remedy prior discrimination. Thomas simply asserted color-blindness as the operative constitutional principle,[48] while citing no history, statements by the framers, or any other evidence that this was, in fact, the framers' design.[49]

Instead, Thomas provided a personalized invocation of the children he believes have been ill-served by judicial efforts to integrate schools. He criticized the district court for "tak[ing] upon itself to experiment with the education of [Kansas City's] black youth,"[50] and attributed to it "the idea that any school that is black is inferior, and that blacks cannot succeed without the benefit of the company of whites."[51] Thomas lauded all-black schools, so long as they are not produced by State action, because they "function as the center and symbol of black communities, and provide examples of independent black leadership, success, and achievement."[52]

Of course, none of this has anything whatsoever to do with the original understanding of the Fourteenth Amendment. Coming from a self-described originalist, this language is jarring. And it's not as if Justice Thomas doesn't know how to invoke original understanding when he wants to. Indeed, another section of his opinion in *Jenkins* demonstrates as much. In that section, Thomas addressed the separate issue—also relevant to the decision but not involving the Fourteenth Amendment—of the equitable authority of the federal courts. He provided a detailed historical defense of the position that "the Framers did not intend federal equitable powers to reach as broadly as we have permitted."[53] Originalism is a trick: now (equity) you see it, now (equal protection) you don't.

And there are myriad other examples. Thomas's opinions in cases such as *U.S. Term Limits, Inc. v. Thornton*[54] and *Rosenberger v. Rector and Visitors of Univ. of Va.*[55] fairly bristle with historical detail supporting his vision of the Qualifications Clause[56] and the Establishment Clause.[57]

This astonishing disconnect between two lines of cases from the same Justice makes obvious which of the two opinions he would have chosen in *Loving*: the concurrence. If Thomas did not find it necessary to address the original understanding of the equal protection clause in *Jenkins*, nor be guided by it in *Adarand* or any other Fourteenth Amendment case he has considered, there is no reason to suppose things would have been different in *Loving*.

To the contrary: *Loving* is the case in which the factors that make the Fourteenth Amendment different for Thomas resonate most powerfully. The framers believed that equal protection would permit assignment of students to public schools on the basis of race; this was intolerable to Thomas in *Jenkins*. They believed that equal protection would permit race-conscious government programs; this was intolerable to Thomas in *Adarand*. And they believed that equal protection permitted race-based restrictions on marriage—an outcome more intolerable to Thomas than any other, as I will show in the next chapter.

CHAPTER TWO

MULTITUDES IN ME

Do I contradict myself?
Very well then I contradict myself,
(I am large, I contain multitudes.)[1]

The explanation for Justice Thomas's departure from originalism where the Fourteenth Amendment is concerned is quite simple. Originalism is a jurisprudence of deafness. Its practitioners must shut out all voices but those of the framers, or at least those heard by the framers. But when it comes to the Equal Protection Clause, and especially antimiscegenation laws, a voice speaks which *Justice* Thomas cannot ignore: that of *Clarence* Thomas.

Originalism is the extreme case in which "the legal system 'silences' certain stories."[2] The stories it silences, of course, are those told by individuals and groups who were not represented during the framing and adoption of the constitutional provision at issue.[3] If the law generally reduces the stories of under- or unrepresented minorities to a whisper, originalism does more. It requires them to be silent.[4]

Originalism's deafness is on display in Justice Thomas's dissenting opinion in *Hudson v. McMillian*,[5] one of his most rigidly originalist opinions. *Hudson* raised the issue of whether an inmate's beating in a state prison constituted cruel and unusual punishment under the Eighth Amendment. The majority opinion expansively reckoned with—heard —Hudson's voice. It described details of how guards "placed Hudson in handcuffs and shackles," "punched Hudson in the mouth, eyes, chest, and stomach, . . . held [him] in place and kicked and punched him from behind," resulting in a "cracked partial dental plate."[6] In contrast, Thomas's dissent barely mentioned Hudson's story, saying only, "The magistrate who found the facts in this case emphasized that petitioner's injuries were 'minor.'"[7] The majority spoke of Hudson by name; Thomas depersonalized him by referring to "petitioner." In place of Hudson's story, Thomas substituted the originalist narrative he related in formulating the general principle (the Eighth Amendment does not apply to the prison conditions to which a convicted felon is subjected)[8] he believes governs the Cruel and Unusual Punishment Clause.[9]

The contrast between this performance and his concurrence in *Jenkins* is jarring.[10] Shielded by originalism, Justice Thomas refused to hear Hudson's story, rendering his personal narrative of abusive treatment in prison irrelevant. As I explained in the preceding chapter, in *Jenkins* Thomas stepped out from behind that shield, passionately relating the personal stories of the schoolchildren of Kansas City. For Justice Thomas, *Hudson* was about re-cognizing the Eighth Amendment. He heard only the story told, heard, and understood by the framers. But the Fourteenth Amendment case, *Jenkins*, was about recognizing the story of the contemporary individuals denied justice by a color-conscious remedial order.

Thomas's need to recognize the implications of race-based classifications resonates with particular force in the crucible of *Loving*. The originalist Constitution—even including the post–Civil War amendments—silenced the story of an African-American man who emerged from the cradle of American apartheid, rose from poverty, achieved the pinnacle of power and success in his chosen profession, and married a white woman with whom he lives in the Commonwealth of Virginia. Upholding antimiscegenation laws fundamentally denies the equal citizenship of Clarence Thomas, the man.[11]

The lesson is that Clarence Thomas matters to Justice Thomas, even if he should not matter to a genuine originalist. But that lesson is not unique to *Loving*. Instead, it sheds light on Thomas's puzzling performance in the equal protection cases he has considered since actually joining the Court in 1991. Clarence Thomas's life, experiences, and voice have mattered in those cases, too.

I am aware of the risk of slipping into psychobabble in attempting to establish the connection between Thomas's personal experiences with issues of race and his judicial performance. For this reason, and because it's really rather pointless, I will not attempt to suggest that any particular psychological mechanism is at work here, that Thomas is expressing some internal racial self-loathing, or compensating for some insecurity. Instead, I propose simply to remark on aspects of Thomas's life experiences that are—for whatever reasons—reflected in his judicial treatment of racial issues. It is that reflection, inevitably non-originalist, that deserves attention.

SCHOOL DESEGREGATION

The views Justice Thomas expressed in *Jenkins* about all-black and integrated schools were those one could expect to hear from Clarence Thomas. Thomas benefitted from the superior education he received attending all-black parochial elementary and secondary schools.[12] More importantly, he has expressed the pain he experienced when, starting in the tenth grade, he began to attend school with white students. While at the Immaculate Conception Seminary College (where Thomas was one of three African-American students), he was subjected to daily racial taunts.[13] A white student drew a knife on him, characterizing it as a joking "welcome." Another student exclaimed on the day Dr. Martin Luther King, Jr., was assassinated, "Good—I hope the SOB dies."

Fast-forward nearly three decades. When Justice Thomas was faced with a remedial decree based on the premise that integrated public schools in Kansas City would offer a superior education compared to the nearly all-black schools that gave rise to the lawsuit in the first place, he could have (an originalist would have) heeded the framers' voices telling him that racial classifications in public education are not a matter of constitutional concern. Instead, he heard and acted on the belief that allegedly superior integrated schools are a cruel illusion. Recall his criticism of the trial court's rationale: It was based, he said, on "the idea that any school that is black is inferior, and that blacks cannot succeed without the benefit of the company of whites."[14] Originalist re-cognition gave way to third-definition recognition.[15]

If anything is surprising about Thomas's performance in *Jenkins*, it was its honesty. Thomas could not have been more direct in expressing the basis for his views, and it had nothing to do with the original understanding of the Equal Protection Clause. He might at least have mounted an originalist line of argument, along the lines suggested by

Professor Michael McConnell.[16] The fact that he did not discloses much about what actually drove Thomas to his conclusion, and about the power of that driving force.

AFFIRMATIVE ACTION

Clarence Thomas also has experience with affirmative action, having benefitted from it in being admitted to Holy Cross College and Yale Law School. However, he also found these opportunities a mixed blessing.

According to Thomas's college classmate Lester Johnson, their experience at Holy Cross included the knowledge that "the white students were looking at us, suspecting there's another dummy who doesn't deserve to be here."[17] Thomas had almost the same feeling about his years at Yale Law School, where he felt that because of affirmative action, "You had to prove yourself every day because the presumption was that you were dumb and didn't deserve to be there on merit."[18]

Thomas has cited these experiences as the reason he came to oppose affirmative action. And since that early lesson in the cost of being stigmatized as less-than-deserving of the honors he has achieved, Thomas has seen it reinforced by subsequent repetitions—including most crucially his nomination to the Supreme Court. When President George Bush asserted that Thomas was "the best qualified" candidate, it triggered substantial skepticism that he was instead the most qualified conservative *black* candidate.[19] Even in the moment when Thomas achieved the pinnacle of success for an attorney in the United States— nomination to the Supreme Court—it was tainted by the lingering doubt people expressed about whether he had gotten there because of his race rather than his accomplishments.

Thomas has taken his position on affirmative action, forged in the crucible of his own experience, with him onto the Supreme Court. In this area as well, the voice of Clarence Thomas echoes in the anti-affirmative action rhetoric of Justice Thomas, even though it is obvious that his personal views (much less his personal experience) are irrelevant to an originalist inquiry into the constitutionality of affirmative action. He has focused heavily on the stigmatizing effect affirmative action has on its "beneficiaries." In *Adarand*, Thomas wrote:

So-called "benign" discrimination teaches many that because of chronic and apparently immutable handicaps, minorities cannot compete with them without their patronizing indulgence. Inevitably, such programs engender attitudes of superiority or, alternatively, provoke resentment among those who believe that they have been wronged by the government's use of race.[20]

This, of course, is a pure policy argument; it speaks to whether affirmative action is a good idea, not whether it is constitutional. And it speaks straight from the heart and life experience of Clarence Thomas, whose voice Justice Thomas simply cannot ignore, even at the expense of the original understanding of the Equal Protection Clause.

VOTING RIGHTS

Justice Thomas's views of the Voting Rights Act of 1965 also carry echoes of the personal story of Clarence Thomas. Professor Scott Gerber has already remarked on the striking similarity between his judicial position and the *political* views Thomas espoused before becoming a judge. Gerber points to a speech Thomas delivered in 1988, in which he said of the Act, "Unfortunately, many of the Court's decisions in the area of voting rights have presupposed that blacks, whites, Hispanics and other ethnic groups will inevitably vote in blocs."[21] Then, in *Holder v. Hall*,[22] Thomas brought this critique with him, saying in his concurring opinion:

[W]e have given credence to the view that race defines political interest. We have acted on the assumption that members of racial and ethnic groups must all think alike on important matters of public policy and must have their own "minority preferred" representatives holding seats in elected bodies if they are to be represented at all.

As Gerber noted, these pronouncements differ "in word choice alone."[23]

But if we search only a bit deeper, and look for the common roots of the political and the judicial, we find the personal: the Clarence Thomas who was by his own admission deeply hurt by the hostile reception he encountered from the mainstream civil rights community when he came to Washington, D.C. as one of the few high-ranking African-American officials in the Reagan administration.[24] Mayer and Abramson quote Thomas in a telling passage: "The harangues to which we [black conservatives] were subjected," he said in one such speech, "were considerable. There was no place any of us who were identified as black members of the administration could go without being virtually attacked." The hazing from other African-Americans in particular was so vicious, he said, even his friends were attacked. One friend, according to Thomas, was forced to leave a party just because he was known to associate with him.[25]

Thomas reaffirmed the continuing impact of those years in a 1998 speech at the Washington and Lee University School of Law, saying, "Throughout the 1980s, many Blacks who dared to disagree with the conventional paradigm were attacked. These Blacks were called 'Uncle Tom's,' 'sell-out's,' and a myriad of other names."[26]

Thomas's perception of his treatment in this respect dovetails perfectly with his judicial chafing at the notion of a uniform identity of political interests and views shared by members of a racial group. It is not very difficult to imagine Thomas's reaction if the lines of his congressional district were drawn to create a majority-black district and produced a representative such as Maxine Waters of California or Cynthia McKinney of Georgia. He certainly would not view that outcome as making his vote meaningful or producing a member of Congress likely to represent his views on matters of national policy, and he would resent the contrary assumption as a stereotype based solely on his race.

The problem with all of this is not that it makes Justice Thomas unique in that his personal experiences with race have affected his jurisprudence. It would be easy to show that the same is true about Justice Thurgood Marshall, and it would be only slightly more difficult—because in our culture we do not easily perceive "whiteness" as a race unless we force ourselves to do it[27]—to do the same for most of the white Justices who have populated the Court. Chief Justice Warren's experience as a key advocate of the internment of Japanese-Americans during World War II very likely shaped his judicial views of racial issues, for example.[28]

But unique or not, Thomas's record presents an insoluble problem. To remain on the interpretive "high ground" originalism claims for itself, its self-professed devotees are compelled to be consistent about it. The advantage claimed for originalism is that it prevents judges from descending onto the terrain of their own personal or political preferences. Once originalists cede this high ground and join the rest of us in the valley below, their advantage is irretrievably lost.

One final point, less about originalism than about the color-blindness principle Justice Thomas has championed. If I am right that recognition of contemporary consequences and of his own life experience explains the non-originalism of Justice Thomas's Fourteenth Amendment views, it is the equivalent of saying that race explains his performance. Here then is the great irony of Justice Thomas: By saying that under the Fourteenth Amendment "the government may not make distinctions on the basis of race," Thomas himself is making a distinction on the basis of race.[29] In other words, race has substantial force in explaining much of Thomas's performance in his decade on the Court.

CHAPTER THREE

HYPOTHESIS TESTING

Up to this point I have focused primarily on the ultimate reckoning Justice Thomas would have faced in dealing with *Loving v. Virginia*, and secondarily on his performance in the actual Fourteenth Amendment cases he has helped decide. Shining the light so specifically on Thomas runs the considerable risk of making my argument seem personal to him. It is not. *Loving* and Thomas are simply the most stark and compelling example of a phenomenon that has become almost endemic to the "originalists"— their inability to ignore their personal and political views when the original understanding conflicts with those views. In other words, the supposedly originalist jurists have been interpreting the Constitution in light of decidedly non-originalist considerations. By looking beyond the Equal Protection Clause, and bringing Justice Antonin Scalia's work into the mix, we find an unmistakable pattern of recognitive interpretation.

In this chapter, I will introduce Exhibits B and C: the originalists' performance when it comes to the Takings Clause of the Fifth Amendment and the Search and Seizure Clause of the Fourth Amendment. Moving beyond the Equal Protection Clause is essential to my implicit purpose: to test two contrary hypotheses. The "originalist hypothesis" posits that we can explain the positions Justices Thomas and Scalia have taken by reference to the original understanding of constitutional provisions. The second, the "personal/political hypothesis," is that their positions instead can be explained by reference to individual experience and values and/or contemporary conservative political views.

In interpreting the Takings Clause, the originalists have championed the "regulatory takings" doctrine, a jurisprudence that fits comfortably with conservative political disdain for federal government regulation. The problem is that it bears no resemblance to anything the founders of the Takings Clause would recognize. After assessing the originalists' Takings Clause performance, I will pause to discuss the doctrine of *stare decisis* as a basis upon which they might attempt to excuse their non-conformity to the original understanding, and explain why that excuse would be unavailing.

The originalists' performance in deciding cases under the search-and-seizure provisions of the Fourth Amendment tells a similar story. The original meaning of this constitutional language has been the subject of a swirling academic debate in the last decade, and it is fair to say that the original understanding is unsettled. It is clear, however, that the Scalia-Thomas position on search-and-seizure issues at best has been only selectively consistent with the original understanding.

THE TAKINGS CLAUSE OF THE FIFTH AMENDMENT

The Fifth Amendment to the Constitution permits government to take private property, but with a catch: "[N]or shall private property be taken for public use, without just compensation."[1] Interpretation of this language involves (among other steps) an assessment of what constitutes a "taking," for which "just compensation" must be provided. Consider two different government actions affecting property. In the first, Cook County seizes half of Mrs. O'Leary's 100 acres of land, intending to tear down her farm and build a fire station in its place. In the second, the city of Chicago passes an ordinance barring the use of cows for dairy production within city limits.

Cook County plainly has "taken" Mrs. O'Leary's property, in the most literal sense: It has physically taken away half of her land. No one doubts that the Fifth Amendment requires that she receive compensation. If her 100 acres were worth $100 before the County's action, and the value of the remaining acreage holds steady at $1.00 per acre afterward, the County must compensate Mrs. O'Leary to the tune of $50.

But what about Chicago's regulation? It has not physically "taken" anything; Mrs. O'Leary still has her 100 acres. But her lucrative dairy operation (Mrs. O'Leary's cows are known far and wide) must be shut down. As a result, let us assume that her valuable acreage is rendered worthless. It was good for dairy farming or for nothing at all. As far as Mrs. O'Leary is concerned, the bottom line in this case is far worse than the County's seizure: Here, government action has robbed her property of all value instead of just half.

But is the regulation a "taking" as far as the Fifth Amendment is concerned? Professor William Treanor threw down the gauntlet for an originalist answer to this question when he said categorically:

> The original understanding of the Takings Clause of the Fifth Amendment was clear on two points. The clause required compensation when the federal government physically took private property, but *not when government regulations limited the ways in which property could be used.*[2]

The framers were well aware that regulations often diminish the value of private property. Instances of this effect were neither unheard of nor even rare in the late eighteenth century.[3] Had the Fifth Amendment been intended to mandate compensation for such regulations, it would appear in the historical record, whether in the form of cases brought by property owners obtaining compensation or commentators describing this notion of what constitutes a "taking." To the contrary, however, there were no such cases,[4] and James Madison made plain his view that compensation was due only when government physically takes private property.[5]

The Supreme Court in the nineteenth century took the same view. The first Justice Harlan, writing for the Court in *Mugler v. Kansas*,[6] rejected the claim that a Kansas statute mandating that places where liquor was produced be closed was a taking, writing:

> A prohibition upon the use of property for purposes that are declared, by valid legislation, to be injurious to the health, morals, or safety of the community, cannot, in any just sense, be deemed a taking or an appropriation of property for the public benefit.[7]

It was not until 1922 that the Supreme Court veered off the path suggested by the original understanding of the Fifth Amendment. In *Pennsylvania Coal v. Mahon*,[8] the Court substituted for the clear rule that regulations could never constitute a taking the amorphous declaration,

"[W]hile property may be regulated to a certain extent, if regulation goes too far it will be recognized as a taking."[9] From that single moment of originalist sin, an immense body of case law began to grow trying to define what "too far" means in this context.

The *Pennsylvania Coal* moment was significant in another respect as well. In addition to jettisoning the original understanding of the Takings Clause, the Court engaged in explicit recognitive interpretation. Justice Holmes's aversion to the impact regulations could have on property rights (and values) was, as Professor Treanor has argued, a "career-long" cause, a close cousin of the substantive due process cases in which the conservative Court invalidated police power regulations because they interfered with property rights. As Justice Stevens wrote:

> The so-called "regulatory takings" doctrine that the Holmes dictum kindled has an obvious kinship with the line of substantive due process cases that *Lochner* exemplified. Besides having similar ancestry, both doctrines are potentially open-ended sources of judicial power to invalidate state economic regulations that Members of this Court view as unwise or unfair.[10]

The Court based its decisions during the pre–New Deal era on economic theories favoring sacrosanct property rights, predicting all sorts of horrific economic consequences if it tolerated governmental interference with property rights. Justice Holmes's approach to protecting property rights, however, survived the 1937 overthrow of its substantive due process counterpart, and has thrived in the 60 years since.

Pennsylvania Coal, no less than the substantive due process body of cases, was marked by recognition of contemporary consequences as the basis for decision. Justice Holmes referred to the central purpose of protecting property rights: so that they "can be exercised with profit."[11] For the government to invade the profit-generating potential of property, even if it did not physically invade the property itself, had the same inimical effect of "mak[ing] it commercially impracticable to" use the property.

Of course, the framers of the Fifth Amendment had not seen that concern as relevant in the case of government regulations. For an originalist, then, interpretive re-cognition should render it irrelevant. And, unsurprisingly, that case has been made in the pages of the United States Reports since the modern-day originalists have joined the Court. The dissenting opinion in *Lucas v. South Carolina Coastal Council*[12] carefully considered the historical evidence, reaching the same conclusion I described above: "The Fifth Amendment's Takings Clause originally did not extend to regulations of property, whatever the effect."[13] Further:

> Most state courts agreed with this narrow interpretation of a taking. "Until the end of the nineteenth century . . . jurists held that the constitution protected possession only, and not value." Even indirect and consequential injuries to property resulting from regulations were excluded from the definition of a taking.[14]

The irony is that this originalist salvo was fired by Justice Blackmun, criticizing the non-originalist majority opinion penned by Justice Scalia. Somewhat amazingly, Justice Scalia even conceded the lack of originalist support for his conclusion, saying:

> Prior to Justice Holmes's exposition in *Pennsylvania Coal Co. v. Mahon,* . . . it was generally thought that the Takings Clause reached only a "direct appropriation" of property . . . or the functional equivalent of a "practical ouster of [the owner's] possession. . . ."[15]

One might have expected the next sentence to be something like:

> Justice Holmes's exposition was, therefore, a fundamental departure from the original understanding of the Takings Clause, one we should correct absent an overriding reason to adhere to the error made in *Pennsylvania Coal.*

Instead, Scalia simply accepted the *Pennsylvania Coal* revolution, applying it to hold that any regulation that "denies all economically beneficial or productive use of land" constitutes a taking.[16] Justice Scalia, but not the founders, would be Mrs. O'Leary's ally in her fight against Chicago.

It is true, as Justice Scalia commented,[17] that not even Justice Blackmun was willing to go so far as to abandon *Pennsylvania Coal* and be constrained by the original understanding.[18] But that should be cold comfort to the originalists. In areas in which they trumpet the original understanding as the key to constitutional interpretation, Justices Scalia and Thomas make a habit of criticizing just that sort of unwillingness of other judges to be constrained by the original understanding. When it comes to regulatory takings, however, they blithely join the non-originalists in casting off the founders' shackles.[19]

One commentator, Andrew Gold, has recently come to the originalists' defense. Gold's argument is inadequate. First, he explicitly disavows the regulatory takings regime of *Pennsylvania Coal*, conceding, "There is little evidence that [Holmes's] pragmatic doctrine of when a regulation 'goes too far' is historically supported."[20] But that is precisely the regime Justices Thomas and Scalia and accepted and championed; Gold's own argument indicts them as non-originalist on this front. Second, Gold claims no more than that:

> the text and historical record of the Takings Clause *arguably support* a just compensation requirement for regulatory takings. The existing evidence, however, is sufficiently ambiguous to preclude a clear sense of the original understanding.[21]

If that is the best an originalist can offer, it is not enough. Remember, originalism is touted as the basis upon which it is legitimate for the unelected judiciary to overturn the democratic decisions of the peoples' representatives. Where there exists a lack of clarity in the historical record, an originalist is compelled to respect the benefit of that doubt and stand clear of the operation of a statute or executive decision. Gold is thus quite wrong to suggest that since "the original understanding cannot serve as a guide for the courts. . . . [t]he riddle of regulatory takings may be resolved only through the common law and stare decisis."[22] It can also be solved through democratic decision-making.

There is yet another inconsistency inherent in Justice Scalia's unquestioning acceptance of *Pennsylvania Coal*. Remember, Justice Holmes provided little guidance in how to determine when a regulation constitutes a taking, saying only that "if regulation goes too far it will be recognized as a taking." The ambiguity of such a "too far" test runs afoul of the admonition that the Court should avoid "conclusion[s] that can not be demonstrated true or false by factual inquiry or legal reasoning," and should eschew tests that call on the Court to answer "the pure policy question whether [a] limitation . . . *goes too far.*"[23] That warning was sounded by Justice Scalia, dissenting from the Court's application of the "undue burden" standard in assessing abortion regulations in *Stenberg v. Carhart.* He has not, to date, explained why the Court is better equipped to judge when an environmental regulation goes "too far" (and thus becomes a taking) than it is to judge when an abortion regulation goes "too far" (and thus becomes an undue burden).

The similarity between the originalists' performance in the realm of regulatory takings and their disregard of the original understanding of the Fourteenth Amendment runs deep. In both areas, there are compelling arguments that the framers' understanding was simply wrong and ought to be abandoned. Their notion of "property," and hence what could constitute a "taking" of property, "is either incoherent or outdated in the modern economy."[24] In an age of virtual reality and Websites and the intangible notions of property wrapped up in the information age, the notion that an owner's property rights can be "taken" only by physical invasion or dispossession makes little sense—*to us.* But if originalism is to actually constrain judges, the conclusion that the framers were wrong, or even that their concepts are outmoded, cannot be a sufficient reason to ignore their views.

A QUICK DETOUR: STARE DECISIS AS THE ORIGINALISTS' "OUT"

As I implied earlier, the originalists might be able to justify their stance in cases like *Lucas* if they identified an overriding reason to adhere to the non-originalist precedent (*Pennsylvania Coal*) rather than the original understanding (regulatory effects on property values are not takings). One such reason might be found in the concerns animating the doctrine of *stare decisis.* As between upsetting the settled expectations that have arisen from over 75 years of transactions under the regulatory takings regime of *Pennsylvania Coal* and restoring the original meaning of the Fifth Amendment, the jurist might argue that an otherwise ironclad commitment to originalism must give way to the impossibility of re-ordering the entire property law system.[25]

Three difficulties undermine this defense, however. First, the originalists have not used it; the Scalia-led resurgence of the Takings Clause has not been marked by apologetic professions of the unfortunate necessity that makes it impossible to return to the original understanding. Instead, these cases have been the occasion for vigorous, nearly self-righteous declarations of the constitutional validity of *Pennsylvania Coal* and its progeny.

Second, the originalists cannot rely on *stare decisis* because a constitutionally discernible basis for doing so is lacking.[26] The harmful consequences of upsetting settled precedent, while real, are no more presumptively controlling than any other categories of harmful consequences that might lead a judge to disregard the original understanding. Compare those consequences with slavery, for example. If the inimical consequences of upsetting precedent-induced expectations are sufficient justification for an originalist to stray, then surely the consequence of reinforcing the evil of slavery should have been sufficient. But for a "real" originalist like Chief Justice Taney in *Dred Scott v. Sandford*,[27] such consequences don't matter: To take account of them he would have to *recognize* them, and constitutional interpretation demands a jurisprudence of *re-cognition*. As Professor Eisgruber explained, Chief Justice Taney's infamous opinion effort was "an originalism indifferent to justice."[28] And that is the essential point: Originalism is and must be indifferent to justice, precisely to the extent that the framers promoted, sanctioned, or tolerated injustice.

Rather than being guided by re-cognition, the originalist who compromises in the direction of *stare decisis* is engaging in selective recognition. And when she does so primarily when it protects non-originalist decisions that fit a particular political agenda—whether they be *Brown v. Board of Education*, *Loving v. Virginia*, or *Pennsylvania Coal v. Mahon* —then virtually nothing is left of the claimed constraining power of originalism.

Finally, even if the originalists interposed *stare decisis* as an obstacle to applying the original understanding of the Takings Clause, we could not let them off the hook until we raise an additional question: Are they consistent in the way they use *stare decisis*? The concern being expressed, remember, is about the ramifications of returning to the original meaning of the provision. We know, generally, that when it comes to the Takings Clause, the "ramifications" we're talking about are also ones anathema to the conservative political agenda of the Republican Party: government regulation, often in the service of environmental protection.[29] So the question naturally arises: Are the neo-originalists consistently concerned about the effects of overturning precedent, or only when those effects happen to be harmful to the conservative political agenda?

Our effort to answer this question is aided by the presence of an almost perfect parallel case, also involving the authority of government to regulate economic activity. I have already noted that the Takings Clause "wrong turn" in *Pennsylvania Coal* was a close relative of the property rights-driven agenda of the substantive due process era that came to a close in 1937. It was then that the Court reinterpreted the Commerce Clause to authorize substantial regulation of the economy by the federal government.[30] This "switch in time" was bitterly criticized at the time as a gross departure from the original understanding of the Commerce Clause.[31] For present purposes, I propose to assume that those criticisms were well taken.

Hence, we have two constitutional provisions, both directly affecting the authority of government to impose regulations on private economic actors and activity. The original understanding of the first (the Takings Clause) is favorable to extensive regulation, while the judicial precedent (*Pennsylvania Coal*) is not. The originalists have chosen to follow the precedent, a position perhaps defensible on the basis of *stare decisis*. The original understanding of the second (the Commerce Clause) imposes severe limits on regulation, while the precedent (*Jones & Laughlin*) removes those limits.

So what do the originalists make of *stare decisis* when it comes to the Commerce Clause? Recently, they have launched an attack on Congress's authority under the Commerce Clause. While the Court has professed to act in concert with the modern broad reading of the Commerce Clause, that profession is dubious at best. In *United States v. Lopez*, a slim conservative majority "interpreted" the post-1937 Commerce Clause jurisprudence to permit Congress to use its power to regulate activities having an effect on interstate commerce only if the activities are "economic" or "commercial" in nature.[32] It imposed this limitation even though the Court had, in *Wickard v. Filburn*, held that:

if appellee's activity be local and though it may not be regarded as commerce, it may still, *whatever its nature,* be reached by Congress if it exerts a substantial economic effect on interstate commerce. . . .[33]

In *United States v. Morrison,*[34] the Court reiterated and extended the *Lopez* misreading of precedent, overturning a portion of the Violence Against Women Act as exceeding Congress's powers under the Commerce Clause and perpetuating the Court's diminishment of the Commerce Clause. This is not the work of a Court careful to heed the demands of *stare decisis.* (I shall have much more to say about *Lopez* and *Morrison* in the next chapter.)

Nevertheless, we can take the Court at its word and assume for current purposes that *Lopez* and *Morrison* are not the start of a complete return to the pre-1937 state of affairs. However, Justice Thomas penned a revealing one-paragraph concurring opinion in *Morrison*:

> I write separately only to express my view that the very notion of a "substantial effects" test under the Commerce Clause is inconsistent with the original understanding of Congress' powers and with this Court's early Commerce Clause cases. By continuing to apply this rootless and malleable standard, however circumscribed, the Court has encouraged the Federal Government to persist in its view that the Commerce Clause has virtually no limits. Until this Court replaces its existing Commerce Clause jurisprudence with a standard more consistent with the original understanding, we will continue to see Congress appropriating state police powers under the guise of regulating commerce.[35]

Justice Thomas's position is that we should return to something very close to the original understanding of the Commerce Clause, even though the jurisprudence of the past 60 years has led the federal government to act as if "the Commerce Clause has virtually no limits," and despite the enormous consequences such a change would have on the national economic and social landscape. This is not the stance of an originalist willing to bend even a bit in the direction of *stare decisis* in the interest of avoiding turmoil. It is not, then, the stance of an originalist who could point to *stare decisis* to justify adhering to the non-originalist regulatory takings doctrine.

The Takings Clause presents a troubling case for the originalists. They have adhered to (and extended) the jurisprudence of regulatory takings, even though it is non-originalist. Since neither Justice Scalia nor Justice Thomas has explained why, we are left to speculate. If *stare decisis* is an unsatisfying answer, and if we place their Takings Clause jurisprudence side-by-side with their (especially Justice Thomas's) nascent Commerce Clause revolution, a strong answer begins to suggest itself: the conservative disdain for extensive government regulation.

Ah, but they might say, you have us wrong: It is not our disdain for government regulation that is important; it is the *founders'* disdain for (and fear of) "big government" that is important. On this reasoning, the originalists would claim that if a theme of mistrust of government power lurks in their opinions, and explains their Takings Clause and Commerce Clause views, it is a theme with a firm foundation in the views of the framers.[36] Justice Scalia has made a related point, arguing that modern doctrine has "gutted" the constitutional prohibition on impairment of the obligation of contracts because "we value property rights less than the Founders did."[37]

In other words, the originalists would defend their non-originalist interpretation of a specific provision (the Takings Clause) by reference to a general principle (limited government and respect for property rights) which the framers did share. But that will not do, since we know for certain that however strong the framers' worries about big government might have been, and however much they respected property rights, they did not go so far as to believe that compensation is due when government regulations diminish or even wipe out the value of private property. In this sense, Justice Scalia's criticism of contemporary Contract Clause doctrine (that it undervalues property rights relative to the founders' beliefs) is the mirror image of my critique of his Takings Clause position: He overvalues property rights relative to the founders' beliefs.[38]

Indeed, the simplicity of this rejoinder makes it difficult to believe the originalists would even attempt to raise the discussion to the more general level of "big government" when faced with the specific non-originalism of their position on regulatory takings. But that is precisely what Justice Scalia has tried to do when it comes to the Equal Protection Clause. In an important passage explaining his position that antimiscegenation laws violate the Fourteenth Amendment even though they were supported by a long, post-ratification tradition, Scalia wrote that that tradition "was contradicted *by a text*—an Equal Protection Clause that explicitly establishes racial equality as a constitutional value."[39] The general "value" of equality, according to Scalia, trumps mountainous evidence of the framers' understanding that—if in fact they meant to write such a value into the Constitution—they did not mean it to include a constitutional right to enter into interracial marriage.

Of course, Justice Scalia cannot really mean this seriously, except as an escape hatch to avoid the unacceptable result of arguing that *Loving* was wrong. We know he isn't serious about it because he said so himself. In a reply to Professor Ronald Dworkin's critique of his originalist arguments, Scalia reckoned with the question of whether it is a "denial of equal protection . . . to have segregated toilets in public buildings, or to exclude women from combat?"[40] Scalia's answer is that these things do not violate equal protection, an answer he provides *"on the basis of the 'time-dated' meaning of equal protection in 1868."*[41] So much for "constitutional values." If we're "time-dating" when it comes to women in combat or unisex toilets, why aren't we "time-dating" for antimiscegenation?

The answer is simple. Antonin Scalia believes creating unisex toilets and/or assigning women to combat duty are ridiculous ideas. But he can't say that, because what Antonin Scalia thinks is ridiculous is not supposed to matter. So instead, he pretends to care that the framers of the Fourteenth Amendment would have thought them ridiculous ideas. He must not really care about their notions of ridiculousness, though, because they thought the idea that they were creating a constitutional right to interracial marriage was just about as ridiculous, and Justice Scalia tells us their position on that question must give way to a constitutional "value."

Neither *stare decisis* nor generalized expressions about the value the founders placed on limited government or property rights can rescue the originalists' Takings Clause jurisprudence. Rather than taking up the task of restoring the original understanding and jettisoning the regulatory takings doctrine, they have extended the non-originalist move the Court made in *Pennsylvania Coal.* Their work constitutes considerable evidence in support of the political hypothesis.

THE SEARCH AND SEIZURE REQUIREMENTS
OF THE FOURTH AMENDMENT

On the basis of recent scholarship, it is fair to say that the search and seizure provisions of the Fourth Amendment are the constitutional provisions as to which the original understanding is most in dispute. The Supreme Court's treatment of these provisions has been called an "embarrassment," and worse.[42] If there is any area in which the originalists should be called upon to ply their trade and rescue modern doctrine from the morass, it is the Fourth Amendment.

In fact, Justices Scalia and Thomas have brought about a gradual transformation of the Court's framework for consideration of Fourth Amendment questions, and it has been in the general direction of an originalist, or at least historical, inquiry. So far, so good. The problem has been in the execution of their campaign; more specifically, with their limited willingness to accept the originalist design even when it does not suit their political views.

There can be little doubt that the originalists have transformed the terms of the Court's engagement with the Fourth Amendment. Professor David Sklansky traced the gradual shift in the cases from 1987, when Justice Scalia wrote the majority opinion in *Arizona v. Hicks*[43] and showed "apparent comfort . . . with received interpretations of the Fourth Amendment,"[44] to 1999, when he wrote for the Court in *Wyoming v. Houghton*[45] that the proper question in a Fourth Amendment case is whether the government's actions were "regarded as an unlawful search or seizure under the common law when the Amendment was framed."[46] This process represents a "doctrine developed and promoted over a period of years by a justice [Scalia] particularly attentive to linguistic nuances, and then explicitly embraced by the Court."[47]

Whether this approach is really originalist depends, of course, on whether the framers of the Fourth Amendment understood it to require a common law-based analysis of the reasonableness of a search or seizure. After all, it is not enough (for an originalist) to look at the common law of 1791 to discern the original understanding of the Constitution—which could, after all, have been intended to repudiate or depart from the prevailing common law. Professor Sklansky makes a compelling argument based on the text, the evidence of the framers' intent, and the constitutional structure, that the Fourth Amendment was not intended to codify the then-existing common law rules.[48]

Having said that, though, I am inclined to credit Justices Scalia and Thomas with trying to move Fourth Amendment doctrine in an originalist direction, at least when it comes to deciding how the Court will go about answering Fourth Amendment questions. In other words, they have tried to pose the questions so that they require originalist inquiry. The more important issue, though, is whether their answers really match those of the framers, or whether they have simply provided originalist language to disguise a non-originalist substance.

The ongoing debate over the meaning of the Fourth Amendment is well known. Professor Akhil Amar of Yale Law School set the kettle brewing with his 1994 article, *Fourth Amendment First Principles*. There, besides calling the current state of Fourth Amendment affairs an embarrassment, Amar called it a "sinking ocean liner—rudderless and badly off course."[49] He advanced the radical notions that searches do not require warrants and need not be supported by probable cause, and took the controversial position that evidence seized pursuant to a warrantless search need not be excluded from subsequent criminal trials.[50] Instead, Amar posited, the Fourth Amendment means what its literal words say: that the people are entitled to be "secure in their persons, houses, papers, and effects, against *unreasonable searches and seizures.*"[51] Searches must, in other words, be reasonable, without regard to the question of whether government officials have obtained a warrant. If they are not reasonable, the remedy sounds in tort, as Amar argued in his 1998 book, *The Bill of Rights: Creation and Reconstruction*:

> Virtually any search or seizure by a federal officer would involve a physical trespass under common-law principles. An aggrieved target could use the common law of trespass to bring suit for damages against the official. . . . If the search or seizure were deemed lawful [i.e., reasonable] in court, the defendant would prevail; but if . . . the search were found unlawful, the defendant government official would be held strictly liable. There was no such thing as "good faith" immunity.[52]

In instances in which a warrant is sought and issued, it must be supported by probable cause, as the text goes on to state.[53] But the validity of a search is not contingent on the warrant, nor on the presence of probable cause.

Amar's regime, of course, bears almost no resemblance to current Fourth Amendment law. And it gets worse: Amar would jettison the exclusionary rule fashioned by the courts to enforce the very requirements he argues are ill-conceived, and he would dramatically increase the availability of tort remedies against governments and officials who violate the Fourth Amendment's core "reasonableness" requirement. All in all, it is fair to say that in nearly every important way, Amar believes we have gotten the law of searches and seizures exactly backwards.

If we assume for a moment that Professor Amar is correct, what can we say about the performance of the constitutional conservatives? At best, they get a mixed grade. It is clear that they approve of the move away from the centrality of the warrant and toward an inquiry into the reasonableness of a search (again, an inquiry they believe must be guided by the common law rules extant in 1791). As Justice Scalia wrote in *California v. Acevedo*:

> The Fourth Amendment does not by its terms require a prior warrant for searches and seizures; it merely prohibits searches and seizures that are "unreasonable." What it explicitly states regarding warrants is by way of limitation upon their issuance rather than requirement of their use.[54]

So far, so good. Indeed, Justice Scalia cited Amar's work in that opinion,[55] and more recently, Justice Thomas (in a concurring opinion joined by Justice Scalia) relied explicitly on Professor Amar's position.[56] At the very least, the originalists have surpassed their Fourteenth Amendment performance by addressing the original understanding of the search and seizure language, as they did at length in Justice Scalia's concurring opinion in *Minnesota v. Carter*[57] in 1998.

The rest of the story, however, is disturbing and revealing. Rather than fighting to invigorate the tort remedies available to victims of unconstitutional searches, the originalists have been on the front lines reinforcing the barriers plaintiffs must overcome to prevail in such actions. In *Anderson v. Creighton*,[58] Justice Scalia wrote the majority opinion holding that government officials may not be held liable if a "reasonable officer could have believed that the search comported with the Fourth Amendment."[59] That is, no liability attaches to some searches conducted in violation of the Fourth Amendment even if they were not, in fact, reasonable.[60] This result seems markedly in contrast to the text of the Fourth Amendment and the original understanding of the framers.[61]

The majority's answer to this critique unmasks its non-originalism. Justice Scalia acknowledged the "surface appeal" of the argument that "It is not possible . . . to say that one 'reasonably' acted unreasonably." But, he said, this surface appeal "is attributable to the circumstance that the Fourth Amendment's guarantees have been expressed in terms of 'unreasonable' searches and seizures."[62] Of course. On his better days, Justice Scalia calls this "circumstance" the "text" of the Constitution. The text says an unreasonable search violates the Fourth Amendment, and it is thus an oxymoron to speak of a "reasonable violation."

Far from emphasizing the role of damages in remedying Fourth Amendment violations, Scalia expressed concern that "fear of personal monetary liability and harassing litigation will unduly inhibit officials in the discharge of their duties."[63] But as Professor Amar (and even some of his most severe critics) have pointed out, the framers wanted to inculcate precisely this fear. The common-law regime at the time provided the polar opposite of *Anderson*-style qualified immunity in search-and-seizure cases. Officials were liable (often for heavy punitive damages) in trespass for warrantless searches if their search *was in fact unreasonable*, regardless of whether they "reasonably" thought otherwise.[64] Whatever else one might say about Justice Scalia's rule, it is inconsistent with the original vision, and his is a mighty contribution to the deterioration of the tort remedy Professor Amar urged is the best (and originalist) way to enforce the Fourth Amendment.

There is a deeper irony in this performance. On the issue of the reasonableness of a search or seizure, Justices Thomas and Scalia have crafted a regime under which the Court looks to the founding-era common law rules. But their affinity for the common law does not extend to the issue of tort suits and immunity, for in 1791 "the victim of an unreasonable arrest or search could sue the offending officer for trespass damages. The common law recognized no broad doctrine of official immunity."[65] It is difficult to understand why the framers would on the one hand want to codify the *rules* of the common law on reasonableness, but not the *remedies* of the common law when it came to unreasonable conduct—and the originalists have not troubled themselves to explain the mystery.

In sum, the originalists' work on the Fourth Amendment is more defensible than their performance on the Fourteenth only to the extent selective originalism is superior to non-originalism. This selectivity confirms a point I made in discussing the Takings Clause: The present-day judicial originalists are more interested in a conservative political agenda than they are in the actual original understanding. Suppose we take as a working thesis the proposition that Justices Scalia and Thomas cut their originalist cloth to tailor a politically conservative suit. Would the evidence of their work on the Fourth Amendment confirm or contradict this hypothesis? Professor Amar supplies the answer:

> I would resist partisan or ideological efforts to pick and choose. . . . For example, "conservatives" might be tempted to use this essay to gut the exclusionary rule further while ignoring the need to build up civil remedies. But this "conservative" move would break faith with constitutional text and history. It would also leave the people less "secure in their persons, houses, papers, and effects."[66]

An ideologically driven, conservative judge would, in other words, do precisely what Justices Scalia and Thomas have done in these aspects of their Fourth Amendment writing. This does not prove that they are ideologically driven, of course; it may simply be that their originalism is muddled.

That possibility is supported by the admirable willingness of the originalist justices to hold particular searches or seizures unreasonable in numerous cases. Most recently, Justice Scalia wrote the Court's 5–4 decision (a majority that included Justice Thomas) in *Kyllo v. United States,*[67] holding that police use of a thermal imaging device to measure heat radiating from a home constituted an unlawful search. And in *County of Riverside v. McLaughlin,*[68] Justice Scalia dissented from a holding that, in cases of warrantless arrests, delays of less than 48 hours before a judicial determination of probable cause are presumptively reasonable.[69]

But we should not make too much of these cases. They do tend to undermine the ideological explanation somewhat, but not as much as might appear at first glance. Justice Scalia was careful in *Kyllo* to limit the reasoning to the use of heat imaging devices directed at private homes,[70] and his position in *McLaughlin*, had it been adopted, would simply have rejected a presumption of reasonableness for delays of less than 48 hours. It would still have permitted government officials to demonstrate that any delays were reasonable. And even to the extent these cases do show Justices Scalia and Thomas will not always vote that any conduct by police and prosecutors conforms to the requirements of the Fourth Amendment, they hardly show that their votes are dictated by the mandates of the original understanding.

In any event, all of this is the *best case scenario* for Thomas and Scalia. It credits their common-law approach to determining what constitutes a "reasonable" search with being the approach the framers intended, and it assumes that they are on firm ground when it comes to substance where they have found common cause with Professor Amar, since these are the only arguably originalist fragments of their Fourth Amendment work. Even this "good" news half of the story requires that Amar's account be reliable and accurate on the issues as to which he and the judicial originalists agree (the reasonableness focus, and the "wackiness" [Amar's word][71] of the exclusionary rule). If, however, Amar got it wrong on those points, then Justices Scalia and Thomas have been untrue to the original understanding across the board.

In fairness to them, the evidence is unsettled and open to more than one reasonable interpretation. Amar combines elegant prose with considerable historical evidence to support his views. Justices Scalia and Thomas certainly employed an undeniably originalist approach in *Minnesota v. Carter*, at least as to the narrow question of whether a person has a right to object to a warrantless search of *someone else's* home.

On the other side, Professor Davies has launched a withering historical broadside at Amar, arguing that "framing-era common law never permitted a warrantless officer to justify an arrest or search according to any standard as loose or flexible as 'reasonableness.'"[72] Instead, he argues, the framers were concerned with and sought to ban "general warrants"; they did not intend to authorize warrantless searches.[73] Other scholars have made this debate a rousing one in the pages of the nation's law reviews.[74]

We are left with two possibilities. Either Thomas and Scalia are non-originalists who have utterly and consistently failed to protect the right of the people to be free of unconstitutional exercises of governmental authority, or they are selective originalists who have adhered to the framers' understanding where it lets loose government power but not where it reins in that power and remedies excesses. Whichever it is, the thread that binds their Fourth Amendment jurisprudence is not the original understanding; it is conservative political ideology.

CHAPTER FOUR

STATES OF GRACE?

In the prior chapter I showed that the inconsistency of Justices Thomas and Scalia's devotion to originalism extends beyond the Equal Protection Clause, encompassing the Takings Clause of the Fifth Amendment and the Search and Seizure Clause of the Fourth Amendment. When we examine an even broader area, however, we see even deeper problems with originalism. When it comes to the "New Federalism," inconsistent originalism is only part of the problem. Of perhaps even greater concern is that the originalist vision of federalism is myopic, narrow, and shallow. And, it is no surprise, this performance has again come in the service of a conservative political agenda.

This story is largely told in the 1990s, but it has a prologue. Between 1976 and 1985, the Supreme Court fought a skirmish over an issue whose significance hardly seemed to warrant the bitterness with which the Justices waged the battle. In hindsight, though, the dispute over whether Congress could enforce the minimum wage and overtime provisions of the Fair Labor Standards Act (FLSA) against the states was a precursor of the more wide-ranging battle over federalism that has erupted in the last ten years.

The FLSA front in the federalism war opened with the Court's 1977 decision, *National League of Cities v. Usery*.[1] The Court held in that case that Congress could not apply the FLSA to the states when they are performing "traditional governmental functions." When it comes to private employers, there is no doubt that the Commerce Clause provides ample authority for the FLSA provisions involved in *National League of Cities*. Thus, the majority had to identify something in the Constitution that limited that authority when it came to state governments. That something was the Tenth Amendment: "The powers not delegated to the United States by the Constitution, nor prohibited by it to the States, are reserved to the States respectively, or to the people."[2] Since the majority in *National League of Cities* was unwilling to go so far as to say that Congress could never subject the states to Commerce Clause regulation, it was compelled to establish a standard distinguishing areas of state immunity from those where the states stood in the same position as private employers. In the years following *National League of Cities*, the Court made its best attempt at drawing this line, pointing not only to "traditional governmental functions" but to "matters that are indisputably 'attribute[s] of state sovereignty.'"[3]

Ultimately, however, the Court brought this Tenth Amendment controversy to a close, overruling *National League of Cities* in the 1985 case, *Garcia v. San Antonio Metropolitan Transit Authority*. In *Garcia*, the Court rejected as:

> unsound in principle and unworkable in practice . . . a rule of state immunity from federal regulation that turns on a judicial appraisal of whether a particular governmental function is "integral" or "traditional."[4]

Any federalist-inspired limits on Congress's Commerce Clause regulation of the states, the Court held, exist not through judicial enforcement of "predetermined notions of sovereign power," but through "the structure of the Federal Government itself," which offers opportunities for the states to assert and protect their sovereignty and interests.[5]

In hindsight, *Garcia* was less an end than a beginning. Then-Justice Rehnquist's dissent was prophetic, if undiplomatic:

> I do not think it incumbent on those of us in dissent to spell out further the fine points of a principle that will, I am confident, in time again command the support of a majority of this Court.[6]

Two of the *Garcia* dissenters—Rehnquist and O'Connor—have been joined by Justices Scalia, Kennedy, and Thomas, and these five spent the 1990s carrying forward the principles to which Rehnquist referred, vindicating his prediction. On issues of state prerogatives and federal limits, this narrow majority has been consistent, cohesive, and resolute. Discussion of the relationship between New Federalism and the original understanding is complicated by the fact that multiple constitutional provisions have been at issue in the debate, including the Commerce Clause, the Tenth and Eleventh Amendments, and Section 5 of the Fourteenth Amendment. Nevertheless, a brief recounting of the many fronts in the federalism wars tells the essential story. Every one of the following cases was decided by a 5–4 vote with the same Justices in the majority (Rehnquist, O'Connor, Scalia, Kennedy, and Thomas) and in dissent (Stevens, Souter, Breyer, and Ginsburg) each time:

United States v. Morrison (2000)—The Court limits Congress's power under the Commerce Clause and Section 5 of the Fourteenth Amendment, holding unconstitutional a provision of the Violence Against Women Act creating a cause of action for gender-motivated violence.

Kimel v. Florida Board of Regents (2000)—The Court holds that Congress's attempt to give private individuals a right of action against the states for age-based employment discrimination is not a valid exercise of Congress's power to enforce the Fourteenth Amendment.

Alden v. Maine (1999)—The Court holds that a state may not be sued by a private individual in its own courts for a violation of federal law, because state sovereign immunity cannot be abrogated by Congress when it acts pursuant to the Commerce Clause and because that immunity extends beyond the actual text of the Eleventh Amendment, which refers only to state immunity from suit in federal courts.

Printz v. United States (1997)—The Court strikes down a provision of the Brady Handgun Violence Prevention Act requiring state law enforcement officials to perform background checks on individuals attempting to purchase handguns.

Seminole Tribe of Florida v. Florida (1996)—The Court strikes down a provision of the Indian Gaming Regulatory Act authorizing suits against states who do not negotiate in good faith with Indian tribes in certain contexts, because Congress may not abrogate state sovereign immunity when acting pursuant to the Commerce Clause.

United States v. Lopez (1995)—The Court strikes down as beyond Congress's Commerce Clause authority a provision of the Gun-Free School Zones Act of 1990 making it a federal crime to possess a firearm in a school zone.

These cases fall into three categories: those where Congress attempted to regulate private conduct but encroached into areas reserved for the states (*Morrison, Lopez*); those where Congress attempted to abrogate the states' sovereign immunity (*Alden, Kimel, Seminole Tribe*); and cases where Congress attempted to compel state authorities to perform federally mandated tasks (*Alden* [adjudicate federal law claims against the state], *Printz* [perform background checks on gun buyers]). Each category reveals something important about originalism as Justices Scalia and Thomas have been practicing it.

REGULATION OF PRIVATE CONDUCT: THE COMMERCE CLAUSE

There is an inherent difficulty in evaluating the originalists' performance in Commerce Clause cases: Justices Scalia and Thomas have parted company. True, they both joined the majority opinions in *Lopez* and *Morrison*, but Thomas wrote concurring opinions arguing that although he liked the direction in which the majority was heading—enforcing what he sees as the inherent limits on Congress's Commerce Clause powers—it was not going far enough. Thomas conceded in *Lopez* that, after 60 years of the expansive, post–New Deal reading of the Commerce Clause, it might be too late in the day to abandon the doctrine that it vests Congress with power to regulate activity having a "substantial effect" on commerce.[7] However, he went further in *Morrison* and called on the Court to jettison the "substantial effects" test, *stare decisis* be damned, and return to the original understanding so that Congress would stop "appropriating state police powers under the guise of regulating commerce."[8]

These concurrences were not joined by Scalia or any of the other members of the "Federalism Five." In effect, Justice Thomas has said that Justice Scalia's position is insufficiently faithful to the original understanding. For his part, Scalia has not indicated whether his stance is dictated by his view of the original understanding or by the doctrine of *stare decisis*. In either case, we cannot judge which position—the sweeping change called for by Justice Thomas, the milder departure from the post-1937 jurisprudence reflected in the *Lopez* and *Morrison* majority opinions, or the position of the dissenters in those cases—is actually originalist until we decide where we stand on this continuum:

ANTI-FEDERALISM ↔ FEDERALISM ↔ NATIONALISM

Plainly, *Lopez* and *Morrison* moved us somewhat to the left on this continuum from where we had been before, and Justice Thomas would move substantially farther in that direction. But where were we before *Lopez*? If we were consistent with the federalist design, then a move to the left (especially on the scale proposed by Justice Thomas) would be non-originalist, since it would align us with the anti-federalists who opposed the Constitution on the ground it gave too much power to the new, untested, and potentially tyrannical national government. On the other hand, if we had strayed too far in the nationalist direction, then the moves made in *Lopez* and *Morrison* would represent an originalist correction, and Justice Thomas would either move us back where we belonged or over-correct.

So we know that either Justice Thomas or Justice Scalia is being non-originalist here, and it is possible both of them have strayed. But this aspect of the debate over *Lopez* and *Morrison*, while important, is not the one I want to consider. Instead, I propose to assume for the sake of the discussion that the outcome was right in both cases (regardless of whether the majority or Justice Thomas offered the correct rationale) in this sense: The framers of the Commerce Clause would have agreed the federal government lacked the powers Congress purported to exercise.

The originalist reader will no doubt say: If that is so, then Justices Thomas and Scalia got it right. If that is what the framers believed, then Congress does not have those powers. What the originalists did not consider, however, and what they virtually never consider with the necessary care and attention, is what has happened since the framers of the Commerce Clause did their work.

Originalism does not demand that the Court interpret the original Constitution as a museum piece. While originalists reject the idea of a "living Constitution," they agree that it does change by virtue of, and must be interpreted in light of, subsequent amendments. An easy illustration of the difference: Assume that Bill Clinton had sought re-election in the year 2000, and a challenge was brought in one or more states to keep his name off the ballot. If the Court was interested only in the *original* understanding, it would have nothing to say about a re-election bid by a two-term President. Nothing in the Qualifications Clause[9] disqualifies an individual because of the number of terms he has previously served. Think Franklin Roosevelt.

But the Twenty-Second Amendment changed all that. So the inquiry must examine the original understanding, as altered by subsequent amendments. Justice Scalia accepted this self-evident point, agreeing with Professor Tribe that "'constitutional provisions sometimes acquire new meanings by the very process of formal amendments to other parts of the Constitution.'"[10] Similarly, Justice Thomas's concurrence in *Printz v. United States* recognized the need to consider the original design in light of subsequent amendments, saying that the limited national powers conferred in 1789 might have been further limited by a subsequent amendment—in that instance, the Second Amendment.[11]

In my view, this point explains why the Court was probably right (or at least was well within the range of defensible originalist choices) in *Lopez* but deeply wrong in *Morrison*. The contrast reveals much about the emptiness of originalist thought as currently practiced on the Court.

As for *Lopez*, it is difficult to quarrel with the majority's key premise that the framers of the Commerce Clause would have been startled at the notion its grant of authority ran sufficiently far as to permit the federal government to criminalize gun possession. Even some ardent defenders of a broad interpretation of Congress's Commerce Clause authority have conceded that the provision at issue in *Lopez* pushed the limits of Congress's powers to, or even past, the breaking point of a credible connection to interstate commerce.[12]

But what about subsequent amendments? Neither the majority nor Justice Thomas considered the matter, but it was a relatively harmless omission in *Lopez*. Nothing in the subsequent amendments to the Constitution demonstrably expands Congress's Commerce Clause authority when it comes to gun possession. If anything, the Second Amendment might arguably restrict that authority, the point Thomas made with respect to a different federal gun restriction in *Printz*.

Perhaps the best argument for an expansion that would affect *Lopez* was made in Justice Breyer's dissent in *Morrison*. Breyer argued that expanded Commerce Clause authority results from the transformed economic world of our century in which "virtually every kind of activity, no matter how local, genuinely can affect commerce . . . outside the State. . . ."[13] But since that argument says only that more things affect commerce, it is persuasive only if we assume the validity of the "substantial effects" test in the first place—which is precisely what Justice Thomas disputes. In any event, Justice Breyer's economic transformation argument is not the same thing as a formal constitutional amendment expanding Congress's authority over the subject matter.

But when we turn to *Morrison*, the error that was harmless in *Lopez* becomes meaningful indeed. At issue in *Morrison* was Congress's authority to provide a cause of action for women who are victims of gender-based violence—a cause of action, in other words, for victims of a particularly pernicious form of unequal treatment. In this area, Congress's authority changed in 1868 with ratification of the Fourteenth Amendment, particularly section 5, which empowered Congress to enforce the amendment's provisions "by appropriate legislation." Unlike gun regulation, we cannot excuse the originalists' failure to consider the possible impact of that change, arguably the most meaningful in our history, on the Commerce Clause.

At first glance, this may seem odd. The Fourteenth Amendment undoubtedly empowered Congress, but how did it change the reach of the Commerce Clause? The answer lies first in understanding how the limits of constitutional authority are marked, and second in understanding the relationship between the Commerce Clause and the Fourteenth Amendment. As with other delegations of power, Congress's authority to regulate interstate commerce is limited in two distinct ways: by virtue of its own scope (regulations must apply to "Commerce . . . among the several States"), and by virtue of *the existence and force of the states' reserved powers*. The powers not delegated to the federal government are, in the words of the Tenth Amendment, "reserved to the States. . . ." The Reservation Clause exerts an "inward pressure" against expansion of federal powers:

Every time a new power is delegated to the federal government, it is removed from the list of reserved powers. And when it is removed, the inward pressure eases.

It might be said, however, that I am mixing apples and oranges, that the inward pressure on the interstate commerce power consists of state reserved *commerce* power. Under this reasoning, only a subsequent amendment reducing state power to regulate commerce might produce a corollary expansion of federal commerce power. In other words, the prior illustration must be refined:

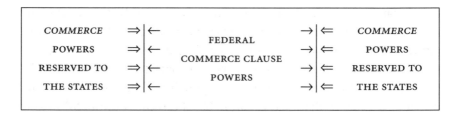

But this is obviously wrong. The reserved state powers that limited the federal government's interstate commerce powers do not consist solely of state powers over commerce. Critics of a too-expansive interpretation of the Commerce Clause have argued that it would infringe on the states' general police powers, which is the equivalent of saying that state police power authority defines, at least in part, the space into which the federal government may not move. Of course, state police powers encompass far more than simply regulation of commerce. State power over commerce is not the only type of state power that helps to mark the limits of the federal power to regulate commerce.

The first distinction, then, between *Lopez* and *Morrison* is that *Lopez* involved a subject matter (gun possession) over which the federal government's authority has not expanded since the original Constitution—and arguably might have been reduced when the Second Amendment was ratified—but *Morrison* involved a subject matter (protection against inequality) over which the federal government's authority has increased since 1789. Prior to the Fourteenth Amendment, the entire question of whether and how to secure equality before the law was entrusted to the states; that is, since it was not one of the powers delegated to the federal government it was one of the powers reserved to the states under the Tenth Amendment. Yet, while Justice Thomas indicated in *Printz* that an originalist should consider the effect a subsequent amendment might have on the original understanding (conveniently, when that effect might be to reduce federal authority in a way consistent with a present-day conservative political agenda), he ignored the possible relevance of an amendment (the Fourteenth) when it came to the federal government's authority to use its Commerce Clause power to provide women equal access to justice.

In practice, this distinction should have led the Court in *Morrison* to question the applicability of a key element of its

Lopez analysis. The Court said in *Lopez* that Congress can regulate activity that is not itself interstate commerce under the post-1937 "substantial effects" test only if the activity is commercial or economic (the Court used these terms interchangeably).[14] In explaining why the distinction between commercial and non-commercial activity is determinative, the Court said little more than that it had never before applied the substantial effects test to non-economic activity. This was false,[15] but never mind. Even if the Court had never done it before, that fact standing alone is not a reason not to do it. The Court had also never *refused* to do it, so precedent was neutral on the issue. Unfortunately, the Court did not explain its rationale for not taking the additional step in *Lopez*, and then simply cited *Lopez* as the reason not to do so in *Morrison*.

One potential explanation could be that commerce, even if entirely local, is at least the general subject matter of the Commerce Clause. It is only one step removed from the "interstate commerce" power: the "interstate" part, a gap that logically can be filled by looking to the interstate effects of the activity. Non-economic activity, being neither interstate nor commercial, must pass through two levels of indirection, and nothing about the interstate effects of an activity logically suggests why they should substitute for "commerce."

On this reasoning, we have a starting point, an understanding of Congress's Commerce Clause power *circa* 1789. Congress can regulate commercial activity that is either itself interstate or has a substantial effect on interstate commerce. But that cannot be the end of the inquiry. We must consider whether the post–Civil War constitutional revolution expanded the scope of Congress's power to regulate activity affecting interstate commerce to include at least some non-commercial activity. That inquiry should have led the Court in *Morrison* to section 5 of the Fourteenth Amendment, which entrusts Congress with the power to enforce the requirement that no person be denied equal protection of the laws. After ratification of the Fourteenth Amendment, Congress was empowered to regulate not just a specific activity (commerce), but *activity, whether commercial or non-commercial, resulting from or producing unequal protection of the laws.*

So the Court in *Morrison* needed to consider a dimension it ignored: Does Congress have power to regulate activity (non-commercial, to be sure) having a substantial effect on interstate commerce *and* resulting in substantial part from an unequal protection of state laws? Gender-based violence against women may be non-commercial activity, but it is non-commercial activity over which Congress has an express grant of authority. Section 5 of the Fourteenth Amendment entrusts Congress with the power to enforce the requirement that no person be denied equal protection of the laws. To be sure, the Court in *Morrison* examined and rejected separately the argument that section 5 itself was a sufficient source of authority for the VAWA. But that is not the same question I suggest the Court, and especially the originalists, should have asked, which is whether the Fourteenth Amendment expanded Congress's power to regulate activity affecting interstate commerce.

An originalist needed to ask that question, but neither Scalia nor Thomas did so. To do so would have required examining the original understanding not of the Commerce Clause, but of the Fourteenth Amendment. As Professor Nowak explained:

I do not care very much about what the drafters and ratifiers of the Constitution of 1787 thought about the structure of our federal system. . . . If the Civil War did anything, it changed the structure of our nation from one where political and economic power resided in certain localities to one truly unified nation.[16]

The framers whose vision of federalism mattered were those of 1868, not 1789. Had the Court bothered to look, it would have found that the framers of the Fourteenth Amendment intended to authorize Congress to step in and provide equality before the law when the states failed to do so. Professor Douglas Laycock argued, slightly more broadly, "The War and the amendments made the federal government responsible for the protection of liberty in the states."[17] For reasons I shall explain, I am somewhat less certain that the framers of the Fourteenth Amendment meant for Congress to be responsible for the "protection of *liberty* in the states." But I am certain they intended Congress to be responsible for the protection of *equality* in the states.

This is not to say this view is enshrined in the early precedents interpreting the Fourteenth Amendment. Indeed, the Supreme Court from 1873 to 1883 eviscerated Congress's authority to guarantee equality before the law by overturning federal laws criminalizing race-based violence and private conspiracies to deprive people of equal protection of the law ,[18] as well as the Civil Rights Act of 1875, which barred private discrimination.[19]

But the truth is that the rulings of the post–Reconstruction Court bear false witness to the original understanding of the Fourteenth Amendment. Even though the framers of the Fourteenth Amendment intended that these groups not be left to the whims of the states for their protection, the Court said in *The Civil Rights Cases* with respect to private discrimination, "if it is violative of any right of the party, his redress is to be sought under the laws of the state. . . ."[20]

When the post-Reconstruction jurisprudence is juxtaposed with *Morrison*, the resulting picture is striking: Congress has been left powerless at the intersection of perhaps its two most important sources of constitutional authority, the Commerce Clause and section 5 of the Fourteenth Amendment. It has no place in regulating private, non-commercial activity which has a substantial effect on interstate commerce *and* is intended to infringe the equal status of vulnerable minority groups. What activity might that be? Ironically—tragically—the very activity that proved most devastating for the aspirations of freed slaves to political equality and economic opportunity: violence, murder, and mayhem designed to intimidate them in the exercise of their new constitutional rights.[21] And to that we must now add the very activity, violence against women, that Congress found keeps them from full and equal participation in the educational, social, and economic life of the nation.

The originalists focused exclusively on the framers' understanding of the Commerce Clause, particularly when it came to the federalist-inspired limits on that congressional power. It was this aspect of the Commerce Clause that should have set off alarm bells, however, because the lines federalism established in 1789 were redrawn in 1868. It is to the lasting shame of the Supreme Court that in the ensuing twenty years it erased the new line, and it is to the lasting shame of the contemporary Court that it continues to look only at the originalist line, as if the faded line that should have been never was.

By its reasoning in *Lopez* and *Morrison*, the Court treated all non-commercial activity the same for purposes of the substantial effects test: It does not suffice. But if we are to make any sense of these cases, a more sensitive lens is required: Subsequent constitutional development must be brought to bear. It is precisely this alteration-by-subsequent-amendment that the Court failed to consider in *Morrison*. The originalists never examined the effect the Fourteenth Amendment might have had on the scope of Congress's power to regulate commerce. This is empty originalism, looking at what the framers of the Commerce Clause intended as if the subsequent 200 years of constitutional change did not change its meaning for us.

STATE SOVEREIGN IMMUNITY

Morrison is heir to *Lopez* in its Commerce Clause analysis, but it also has roots in another line of the Court's neo-federalist jurisprudence. Just as the Court found the Commerce Clause an inadequate source of authority to support the VAWA, it reached the same conclusion with respect to section 5 of the Fourteenth Amendment. In that analysis, the Court echoed statements it has made in a series of cases limiting Congress's authority to abrogate state sovereign immunity. Those cases, like *Morrison*, have substantially limited the scope of Congress's section 5 powers.

The breadth of section 5 is relevant to the sovereign immunity issue because the Court has held that when Congress acts to enforce the Fourteenth Amendment, it has the power to abrogate the state sovereign immunity provided for in the Eleventh Amendment. If it is acting with only the Commerce Clause (or any other source of power vested by Article I) behind it, the regulation might be valid as to private actors but not as to the states. Think of it as a game of constitutional rock-paper-scissors: Article I beats private conduct, the Eleventh Amendment beats Article I, the Fourteenth Amendment beats the Eleventh, and private conduct beats the Fourteenth Amendment.

In 2000, the Court decided *Kimel v. Florida Board of Regents*, a collection of cases brought by employees alleging that their employers—all state governments or agencies—had discriminated against them on the basis of their age in violation of the federal Age Discrimination in Employment Act (ADEA). The states, in turn, interposed the defense that the suits ran afoul of their sovereign immunity, as recognized by the Eleventh Amendment. Since it was established (and unchallenged) law that Congress could abrogate this immunity if it was acting pursuant to section 5 of the Fourteenth Amendment, the question for the Court to consider was clear: Is application of the ADEA to the states an exercise of section 5 power?

The Court's answer: No. Its reasoning, not to put too fine a point on it, was astonishing. The Court noted that, in past age discrimination cases brought under the Equal Protection Clause itself, it determined that age-based classifications are to be subjected only to the lowest level of judicial scrutiny available in an equal protection case. That is, "States may discriminate on the basis of age without offending the Fourteenth Amendment *if the age classification is rationally related to a legitimate state interest*." This is distinct from the scrutiny to which the Court subjects classifications based on gender and race, characteristics as to which a "tighter fit between the discriminatory means and the legitimate ends they serve."[22]

The Court has been at pains to emphasize that this difference in the level of scrutiny is not outcome-determinative.[23] Instead, it is but the framework through which the Court will evaluate governmental classifications. But in *Kimel* the Court gave the level of scrutiny substantive effect by holding that when rational basis scrutiny applies to a constitutional claim, it bars Congress from abrogating state sovereign immunity via statutory anti-discrimination protections such as those contained in the ADEA:

> The Act, through its broad restriction on the use of age as a discriminating factor, prohibits substantially more state employment decisions and practices than would likely be held unconstitutional under the applicable equal protection, rational basis standard.[24]

In other words, section 5 of the Fourteenth Amendment functions as little more than a license for Congress to say, "Yeah, and that goes double!" Enforcement under section 5 is limited—not entirely, but very nearly so—to conduct already rendered illegal by the Constitution.

In case the Federalism Five had not been sufficiently clear in *Kimel* about the limits of section 5 and the primacy of the level of scrutiny, it put an exclamation point on its reasoning in 2001, ruling that states are immune from private suits under the Americans with Disabilities Act, despite voluminous evidence of widespread discrimination by state governments against people with disabilities.[25] The Court emphasized its quarter-century-old holding that classifications based on disability are subject only to rational basis scrutiny under the Constitution, and that in the ADA Congress had imposed requirements substantially wider than merely barring irrational classifications.[26] Under the majority's view of section 5, that meant Congress had gone too far.

The vehicle by which the Court accomplished this transformation of an analytical device into a substantive limitation was its view of the difference between "enforcing" a right, which Congress is empowered to do, and defining a right, which it is not. By this reasoning, if Congress subjects the states to greater regulation than would be permissible under the Fourteenth Amendment itself, it is not "enforcing" the Fourteenth Amendment but defining its scope.

The difficulty with this logic is that prior to *Kimel* the Court had permitted Congress substantially greater leeway in legislating pursuant to section 5. In *South Carolina v. Katzenbach*, the Court upheld a statutory ban on literacy tests as a condition for voting, even though the Court had held seven years before that literacy tests do not, on their face, violate the Constitution. And in *Fitzpatrick v. Bitzer*, the Court upheld application of Title VII of the Civil Rights Act of 1964 to the states as exercise of section 5 enforcement power, even though it makes illegal practices that do not themselves violate the Fourteenth Amendment.[27]

More important, that leeway on display in the earlier cases had reflected the original understanding of the relationship between Congress and the judiciary in enforcing the Fourteenth Amendment. As Professor Laycock pointed out:

> Judicial supremacy to set both the floor and the ceiling on federal rights in the states does not reflect the original meaning of the Fourteenth Amendment. Congress did not entrust the fruits of the Civil War to the unchecked discretion of the Court that decided *Dred Scott v. Sanford....*[28]

The framers were prophetic in believing that "Congress needed enforcement powers because judges might not enforce the new Amendments."[29]

So if the results in *South Carolina v. Katzenbach* and *Fitzpatrick v. Bitzer* recognized those points, what happened in *Kimel*? Actually, it is not *Kimel* to which we must look, for the evisceration of Congress's authority to enforce the Fourteenth Amendment did not begin there. Rather, it can be traced to a case having little to do with equal protection, and everything to do with the Court's legitimate need to protect its institutional authority. In *City of Boerne v. Flores*, the Court rejected Congress's attempt to reverse by legislation an interpretation of the Free Exercise Clause the Court (per Justice Scalia) had rendered only a few years earlier, in *Employment Division v. Smith*.[30] Because the Religious Freedom Restoration Act (RFRA) was so overt a challenge to *Smith*, the Court saw it as a direct challenge to its power to interpret the Constitution. If it had been upheld, the Court feared, RFRA-like statutes could proliferate in reaction to every unpopular decision, transforming section 5 into the means by which the authority to define the scope of the Bill of Rights would be transferred from the Court to Congress. Assuming its long-standing role as the guardian of the separation of powers between the branches, and with the special need to do so when the perceived incursion was into its own realm, the Court struck down RFRA.

In other words, *City of Boerne* was really about the Court defending its authority to interpret the *First* Amendment. But that defense did collateral damage to a proper understanding of section 5 of the Fourteenth Amendment. Though RFRA was in substance about the First Amendment right to free exercise, it was defended as an exercise of Congress's power to enforce the Fourteenth Amendment. Why? Because the Fourteenth Amendment is the vehicle by which the First Amendment has been held applicable to the states.

In other words, the argument made in defense of RFRA was that Congress's section 5 power to enforce the Fourteenth Amendment includes the power to enforce all the rights incorporated through the Fourteenth Amendment. I do not quarrel with that proposition, one the Court explicitly adopted.[31] But that does not mean there is no difference between the deference due Congress when it uses its section 5 powers to enforce a provision of the Fourteenth Amendment itself and when it uses those powers to enforce a provision appearing elsewhere in the Constitution but incorporated through the Fourteenth Amendment.

When it comes to incorporated rights, a strong case can be made that Congress must take a back seat to the Court in defining the scope of the right. Indeed, that strong case was made by the Court in *Marbury v. Madison,* where Chief Justice Marshall proclaimed the Court's prerogative to "say what the law is."[32] While the Fourteenth Amendment changed the balance between the states and the federal government, it did not similarly change the balance between Congress and the Court when it came to interpreting pre-existing constitutional provisions, including the Bill of Rights.

The Court's 2000 decision in *Florida Prepaid Postsecondary Educ. Expense Bd. v. College Savings Bank* is consistent with this distinction. Besides guaranteeing equal protection of the law, the Fourteenth Amendment bars the states from depriving a person of life, liberty, or property without due process of law. This is not an incorporated right; it is directly in the Fourteenth Amendment itself. Under my theory, this should have been an area in which the Court would recognize and defer substantially to Congress's authority to provide a remedy pursuant to section 5. The Court in that case agreed that Congress's section 5 powers permit it to extend a remedy for a state's violation of an individual's property right (property being one of the things of which an individual cannot be deprived without due process of law).

However, since the violation Congress may remedy is not of the property right itself but of the failure to provide due process, its section 5 authority permits a federal remedy only when the state has failed to provide one. In short, Congress's authority is triggered not by the violation itself, but by the failure to provide adequate process to remedy the violation. Thus, it is the guarantee contained in the four corners of the Fourteenth Amendment itself (due process) that puts Congress's section 5 power at its apex.

Because RFRA pertained to an incorporated right, the arguments made in its defense would have represented a sweeping expansion of legislative prerogatives across virtually the entire swath of the Bill of Rights. The pre-*City of Boerne* cases recognizing a broader congressional role pursuant to section 5 had involved enforcement of the substantive equality guarantee of the Fourteenth Amendment, and they could have stood untouched, until the Court brought them more directly into its line of federalist fire in *Kimel.*

Professor Amar implicitly rejects this distinction, saying that the issue of congressional power in *City of Boerne* was "obviously about the meaning of Reconstruction."[33] But I don't think *City of Boerne* was about the meaning of Reconstruction, at least not in the same way the *Civil Rights Cases* and *Kimel* were about the meaning of Reconstruction. The framers of section 5 undoubtedly wanted to empower Congress to enforce the equal protection and due process norms embodied in section 1. It is not as clear that they meant to empower Congress to the same degree in enforcing the religious freedom norms of the First Amendment. The careful approach I suggest would have protected the Court from the direct challenge RFRA represented without doing unnecessary collateral damage to section 5.

I should emphasize here that I agree with Amar that the Court was wrong even in *City of Boerne.* It should have upheld Congress's power to enforce the incorporated right just as it should uphold Congress's power to enforce rights contained directly in the Fourteenth Amendment. My point is simply that if the Court felt itself institutionally compelled to reject the congressional attempt to overrule *Employment Division v. Smith,* it could have done so without doing incalculable damage to Congress's section 5 powers.

How does all of this relate to a critique of the originalists? If we adopt the narrow focus implicit in this argument, the outcome is clear: Within the substance of the Fourteenth Amendment itself, the framers envisioned a level of legislative supremacy the Court has ignored, with the unfortunate complicity of the self-proclaimed originalists. Their crabbed view of Congress's authority under section 5 bears little resemblance to the framers' emphasis on Congress's role. Numerous scholars have traced the Court's hostility to the framers' vision of section 5. Consider Akhil Amar's summary, rendered in typically vivid style:

> The Reconstructors also explicitly empowered a politically powerful and permanent institution—Congress—to "enforce" the values of liberty and equality at the heart of Section 1. . . . But Section 5 was basically neutered by—you guessed it—the Supreme Court itself, which has repeatedly refused to accept the broad power the document gives Congress to help vindicate the rights of blacks and other civil rights claimants. From the infamous *Civil Rights Cases* of 1883 . . . it has been the Supreme Court that has rendered the Fourteenth Amendment more institutionally anemic than its framers intended.[34]

The other sovereign immunity cases the Court has decided did not require it to ignore the original understanding of section 5 of the Fourteenth Amendment to the degree the majority did in *Kimel*, since those cases did not implicate the guarantees of the Fourteenth Amendment itself and Congress's authority to enforce them. Nevertheless, they do provide additional evidence of the originalists' failure to engage the impact of the Civil War on the federalist structure.

Justice Kennedy delivered the Court's opinion in *Alden v. Maine*, in which the five-member majority held that the Constitution gives the states sovereign immunity against suits alleging violation of federal law, even when those suits are filed in the states' own courts. This conclusion ran into an immediate difficulty: the apparent absence of any support for it in the text of the Constitution. The provision of most obvious relevance, the Eleventh Amendment, carves out a zone of immunity only from the "Judicial power of the United States." In other words, in federal courts. No wonder, then, that the Court quickly disclaimed reliance on the Eleventh Amendment in explaining the basis for its discovery of immunity from suit in a state's own courts:

> We have . . . sometimes referred to the States' immunity from suit as "Eleventh Amendment immunity." The phrase is convenient shorthand but something of a misnomer, for the sovereign immunity of the States neither derives from nor is limited by the terms of the Eleventh Amendment.[35]

Having eschewed reliance on the Eleventh Amendment itself, one might have expected the Court next to find another textual foothold for state sovereign immunity. More to the point, we would expect that if the Court did not move to find an alternative textual basis, our resident originalists Thomas and Scalia would raise up their voice in protest against this amendment-by-judicial-fiat. After all, while originalism is not identical to textualism, the originalists do frame their inquiry as a search for the original understanding *of the text* of the Constitution. But the Court did not search the text, and Thomas and Scalia silently concurred. Instead, the Court asserted that "sovereign immunity derives not from the Eleventh Amendment but from the structure of the original Constitution itself." In other words, state sovereign immunity "is demarcated not by the text of the Amendment alone but by fundamental postulates implicit in the constitutional design."[36]

In fairness, however, the Court in *Alden* did engage in a historical examination of the framers' vision of the states' position in the original federalist framework, rendering its approach at least plausibly originalist.[37] The problem is that it replicates in a less direct way the same mistake that attends the Court's section 5 jurisprudence: It ignores the impact of the Civil War on that original federalist framework.

Justice Kennedy's rendition of the antebellum structure is open to considerable doubt, as Professor Chemerinsky has shown.[38] But even if Kennedy was right, the fact remains that the Civil War forever altered the relationship between the states and the federal government. Justice Kennedy declared in *Alden*:

> The constitutional privilege of a State to assert its sovereign immunity in its own courts does not confer upon the State a concomitant right to

disregard the Constitution or valid federal law. The States and their officers are bound by obligations imposed by the Constitution and by federal statutes that comport with the constitutional design. *We are unwilling to assume the States will refuse to honor the Constitution or obey the binding laws of the United States. The good faith of the States thus provides an important assurance that "[t]his Constitution, and the Laws of the United States which shall be made in pursuance thereof . . . shall be the supreme Law of the Land."*[39]

Perhaps the original founders, who saw the states as the best line of defense against the possibility of a tyrannical central government, trusted those states to obey their obligation to respect federal law. Perhaps. But the Reconstruction framers, hard off the attempted secession of the southern states and the tragedy that followed, manifestly did not.

The originalism practiced by the Court in *Alden, Kimel,* and the other sovereign immunity cases of the 1990s[40] suffers from its failure to integrate the changes the framers of the 1860s made to the framework of the 1780s. The explanation traces back to the same pattern we saw with respect to the inconsistency of the originalists' fidelity to their method when it comes to color-blindness, regulatory takings, and unreasonable searches and seizures: Like those others, federalism is a pet cause of contemporary conservative political thought. It should come as no surprise that the judicial originalists have focused on the first generation of framers' devotion to local governance and a national government of limited powers, to discover an original understanding that encompasses this plank of the conservative political platform. Of course their historical review settles in the favorable era when the constitutional architecture was framed. But they ignore the lessons of an era in which the Constitution was redesigned, an era in which the architects saw the states not as the protectors of liberty and equality but as the threats to those values. Though the originalists fail to recognize it, neither the Eleventh Amendment nor the Commerce Clause escaped the 1860s unaltered.

Lest we doubt that the originalists' approach to the sovereign immunity cases reflects a results-oriented fixation with states' rights rather than a consistent application of interpretive principles and methods, consider the contrast between the way *Alden* framed the sovereign immunity question and the way *Kimel* framed the section 5 question. When it advanced a pro-states' rights outcome in *Kimel,* the Court resorted to a hyper-textualist concentration on the specific word "enforce" to find a limitation on the powers section 5 of the Fourteenth Amendment bestows on Congress—even though it is evident that the framers of that amendment envisioned a much broader role for Congress in protecting civil rights and guaranteeing equal protection of the laws. But equivalent literalism would lead to a less happy outcome for the states under the Eleventh Amendment. Should we be surprised, then, that the originalists (by now, it should be plain "federalists" is the more accurate description) look to broader structural imperatives they have discovered in the constitutional framework, even though those imperatives appear nowhere in the text of the Constitution?

COMMANDEERING OF STATE OFFICIALS

Finally, the third category of neo-federalist cases places off-limits a particular means (utilization of state resources) by which Congress might seek to exercise its powers effectively. This is an odd group of cases, because the issue is so far removed from the core federalism concerns one can actually detect in the originalist framework. It is also a revealing group of cases, because in it the Federalism Five play a game of "now you see it, now you don't" originalism which unmasks their deep results-orientation in this area.

Before turning to each of these points, it is worth observing that, as with the Court's sovereign immunity jurisprudence, the anti-commandeering cases place the originalists in the odd position of advancing a doctrine for "there is no constitutional text speaking to [the] precise question." Again, as the Court did in *Alden,* Scalia's opinion in *Printz* looked instead to the relevant "historical understanding and practice," as well as "the structure of the Constitution."[41] That is a decidedly non-textual version of originalism, but let us credit it with being originalist in approach, at least.

The problem, though, is that when it comes to the other fronts in the federalism wars, there is a textual basis for the Federalism Five's concerns, if not for their interpretations. The actual text of the Constitution does reveal a number of concerns that animated the framers. One of those was fear of the potential misuse of centralized power, a concern reflected in the principles that the federal government would be one of limited, enumerated powers, and that those powers not delegated would be reserved to the states. Even if we question the current Court's application of those notions in its Commerce Clause cases, it cannot be denied that in performing the function of defining and enforcing the limits of federal powers, the Court is doing a job the framers thought was important.

Similarly, the framers' concern about state sovereign immunity can hardly be doubted. The Eleventh Amendment was the swift reaction to the Court's decision that states could be sued in federal court by the citizens of other states in *Chisholm v. Georgia*,[42] which was seen as an infringement of the appropriate zone of state autonomy. Whether the five federalists who make up the current majority are right in how they are defining that zone, the framers' concern with it is apparent.

Not so with "anti-commandeering." It is not just that Justice Scalia was wrong on the merits in *Printz*; he was making up the concern itself. None of the concerns that actually have a textual basis were implicated in the Brady Handgun Violence Protection Act (the "Brady Act"). The states' sovereign immunity was not on the line, since Congress was not regulating the states as such. Instead, the Brady Act barred private merchants from selling guns until a five-day waiting period had expired.[43] The assistance of the states was enlisted in making that period serve its intended purpose, to check the criminal background of would-be gun buyers in an effort to keep weapons out of the hands of convicted felons. But the states were not themselves the target of the regulation. Nor was Congress intruding into an area reserved to the states for regulation, since it was undisputed that the sale of handguns to convicted felons has a "substantial effect" on interstate commerce.[44]

The anti-commandeering rule stretches originalist fidelity beyond the breaking point. In *Printz*, Justice Scalia never pointed to a single line of constitutional text that established even the concern he says animated the framers. First he authored a long (but necessary) opening section distinguishing the many instances in our history (many hard on the heels of the Constitution's founding) where it appeared the federal government had commandeered state officials.[45] Next Scalia turned to "the structure of the Constitution, to see if we can discern among its 'essential postulate[s]' . . . a principle that controls the present cases."[46] Justice Scalia's reliance in *Printz* on the structure of the Constitution outside its text differed from the non-originalist use of "penumbras" by Justice Douglas in the seminal privacy rights case, *Griswold v. Connecticut*,[47] only in Scalia's tactically wise choice not to use the word "penumbra," though I confess I would have delighted in a citation to *Griswold* had Scalia decided to include one.

Absent reliance on *Griswold*, and in apparent determination to do what he could with the text, Scalia built the best case he could, which consisted of showing "that the Constitution established a system of 'dual sovereignty.'"[48] Well, of course it does. The parameters of each sovereign's status, though, requires examination of the text establishing that system. *Lopez* and *Morrison* were at least about the Commerce Clause, and *Seminole Tribe* and *Alden* were at least about the Eleventh Amendment. *Printz* was about . . . nothing.

The second point to be made about the anti-commandeering principle the Court has fashioned is that it has included the single most blatant results-oriented abuse of originalism seen to date. Rarely if ever has the Court contradicted itself as blatantly, and in as short a time, and with the same five Justices forming the majority, as it did from *Printz* in 1997 to *Alden* in 1999. In *Printz*, the Court overturned the portion of the Brady Act which compelled local law enforcement officials to perform background checks on would-be gun buyers during the five-day waiting period mandated by the Brady Act. Writing for the Court, Justice Scalia found that such a "commandeering" of local officials for federal purposes was inconsistent with the framework envisioned by the framers, concluding, "The power of the Federal Government would be augmented immeasurably if it were able to impress into its service—and at no cost to itself—the police officers of the 50 States."[49]

To reach the conclusion that such use of state officials and resources violates the framers' design, Justice Scalia had been forced to distinguish a series of early statutes which appeared, on their face, to "commandeer" state officials. He did so by observing that those laws yoked only state *judges* into federal service:

> These early laws establish, at most, that the Constitution was originally understood to permit imposition of an obligation on state judges to

enforce federal prescriptions, insofar as those prescriptions related to matters appropriate for the judicial power.[50]

In other words, the Court in *Printz* explicitly acknowledged that state judges are not subject to this principle in the same way that state executive branch officials are. This is unsurprising; state judges must, after all, apply federal law in cases arising before them. Even Spencer Roane, the Virginia judge who battled John Marshall's Court on behalf of state autonomy in *Martin v. Hunter's Lessee*,[51] agreed that state courts were obliged to decide questions of federal law. His complaint was only that the Supreme Court had no jurisdiction to review those decisions.

And yet, in *Alden* the Court proceeded as if this distinction had never been drawn. The Federalism Five, this time speaking through Justice Kennedy, opined that a state's courts have "always been understood to be within the sole control of the sovereign itself."[52] Lest there be any doubt that *Alden* is an anti-commandeering case masquerading as an Eleventh Amendment case, Justice Kennedy removed it by writing that the position advocated by the United States in the case would allow the national government to "press a State's own courts into federal service. . . ."

To be sure, the Court was concerned not just about the use of state courts but also about the notion of states as unwilling defendants; the sentence just quoted continues with Justice Kennedy decrying the idea that state courts would be pressed into service "*to coerce the other branches of the State.*"[53] But it is plain that commandeering of state courts, and not coercion of the state governments, was what the Court was really concerned about in *Alden*.

Alden tells us that Congress may not compel the states to make their judges available to resolve claims by individuals that the state has violated its federal law obligations. It did not preclude Congress from imposing the obligations; to the contrary, the Court went out of its way to emphasize that there are alternative mechanisms (e.g., lawsuits filed by the federal government itself) by which those obligations can be enforced.[54]

Nor did the Court overrule its holding in *Nevada v. Hall* that one state can be sued in the courts of another state.[55] In *Hall*, the California courts adjudicated Nevada's obligations under California law (over Nevada's stern objection). But what if the plaintiff had also brought a pendent federal claim? The answer (it would appear) is that Nevada would have had no more immunity from that claim than it did the California law claim.

To be sure, the availability of this avenue for redress is highly contingent. It probably depends on the willingness of a state to open its courts to hear federal law claims against sister states, since it appears unlikely after *Alden* that Congress could compel the states to do so. If Congress cannot "commandeer" Maine's courts to hear claims against Maine, it probably cannot commandeer Maine's court to hear claims against Vermont (or vice-versa). The plaintiff might also have to clear a number of jurisdictional hurdles, as my colleague John Cross has noted with respect to patent and copyright cases.[56] Nevertheless, the problems involved are not constitutional ones; if Vermont chooses to open its courts to Alden and its courts have jurisdiction over his cause of action, there is no constitutional barrier blocking the courthouse door.

Since Alden could turn around and sue Maine in Vermont, raising the same federal claim, the immunity recognized in *Alden* does not serve to insulate Maine. The only thing it gives Maine is the right to keep its own courts from hearing that suit, and from declaring and enforcing its liability: in other words, to keep its courts from advancing the purposes the federal law seeks to achieve. That is an application of the anti-commandeering rule, to the very context Justice Scalia had said it did not apply in *Printz*.

Federalism itself is a principal goal of conservative political ideology. The Federalism Five's ongoing campaign to cut deep gashes in the federal government's authority under the Commerce Clause and section 5 of the Fourteenth Amendment, while at the same time carving out broad areas of state autonomy, serves that ideology. Much of their work has been either marginally connected to the constitutional text or wholly unsupported by it. To the extent that their efforts are at all originalist, it is an originalism that pretends that the framework of Madison and Hamilton has survived the ensuing two centuries virtually intact. But even the *original* original understanding is not impervious to the political agenda of the Federalism Five. When ignoring the last 220 years doesn't protect state autonomy sufficiently to suit their agenda, they ignore the original design as well, adding an "anti-commandeering" feature to the design in *Printz*. With a breathtaking disregard for consistency, they then extend that rule in *Alden* even though doing so contradicts what they said in *Printz*. In that sense, the conservatives are well on the way to completing their self-fulfilling prophecy: By pretending the Fourteenth Amendment had no real impact on the state/federal balance, they are building a jurisprudence under which it will not.

From the Equal Protection Clause to the Takings Clause and the Search and Seizure Clauses, and extending into the federalism campaign of the last decade, the same pattern emerges. Where it is personally painful or ideologically inconvenient, Justices Thomas and Scalia abandon the original understanding. Sometimes they do this without even addressing the matter, almost as if they have shifted, mid-conversation, from one language to another without explanation.

We can say one thing, though, about Thomas and Scalia's non-originalist opinions; they could have been written by the drafters of the 1996 Republican Party platform. It opposed affirmative action as a violation of the "color-blindness" principle, endorsed the ongoing reinvigoration of the Takings Clause, decried criminal procedure "technicalities" such as the exclusionary rule,[57] and called for the devolution of authority from the federal government to the states.[58] The non-originalist positions taken by the conservative wing of the Supreme Court have far more in common with the 1996 Republican Party than they do with the 1789 Federalists.

If their non-originalist moments are not sufficient to demonstrate the ideological men hiding behind the originalist curtain, consider for a moment the areas of constitutional law in which Scalia and Thomas *are* faithful originalists. The death penalty is an excellent example, one Scalia himself has pointed to in writing both on the Court[59] and off.[60] Abortion, of course, is another.[61]

What do all of these have in common? Again, they are consistent with a modern-day conservative political agenda, reading like planks in the 1996 Republican Party platform. That platform, for example, took the position that:

> The unborn child has a fundamental individual right to life which cannot be infringed. We support a human life amendment to the Constitution and we endorse legislation to make clear that the Fourteenth Amendment's protections apply to unborn children.[62]

It also endorsed expansion of the death penalty.[63]

Which is unsurprising. A similar analysis would likely show that the positions taken by the most liberal Justices—probably Ruth Bader Ginsburg and John Paul Stevens—resemble those of the latter-day Democratic Party and not (other than haphazardly) those of the framers. The difference is that the non-originalists make no claim of fidelity to the original understanding, at least not at the same level of textual specificity and historicism as Thomas and Scalia. There is no double standard at work here. I am simply judging the originalists on their own terms. It is a test they have repeatedly failed. And, as the next chapter shows, the pattern extends to the case upon which history will judge the Rehnquist-Scalia Court: *Bush v. Gore.*

CHAPTER FIVE

THE SMOKING GUN

Imagine, if you will, the unimaginable. The seemingly stable American democracy faces an almost unprecedented scenario, a political crisis over the question of who rightfully should serve as President. Troubling issues unconfronted for over a century are before us; constitutional and legal mechanisms unused for that long or longer must be dusted off and utilized.

Remarkably, it appears that the answer ultimately may be provided not by the voters in the normal, quadrennial election, but by Congress. In a political atmosphere already characterized by bitter partisanship, fears of complete gridlock are peaking around increasing use of the dreaded term: constitutional crisis.

Just when it appears the strange set of circumstances could not be any more complex, the man who fears his grasp on the presidency may be loosening turns turmoil into chaos by filing a lawsuit, asking the federal courts to determine once and for all the validity of his claim to the Oval Office.

Confounding virtually all predictions, the Supreme Court steps in to avert the unrushing constitutional collision. Despite doubts about the validity of the decision, or even the basis for its intervention, the Court ends the process before it can go any further.

The result? Supporters of the plaintiff-cum-President applaud the Court for its wisdom, for recognizing the inevitably divisive weeks ahead and stepping in to relieve the nation of having to pay so high a price. The defendants, convinced that the constitutional process has been short-circuited by an activist Court with political motives, angrily decry the illegitimate President before reluctantly conceding the need to obey the rule of law.

Who are the supporters praising the Court? Not James Baker and

Trent Lott, but James Carville and Tom Daschle. Who are the opponents forcing themselves to accept what the Court has done? Not the Congressional Black Caucus, but Henry Hyde and Bob Barr. For the case I have in mind is not *Bush v. Gore*, [1] though it may have seemed so from the facts I related. Instead, I have in mind *Clinton v. Gore*, the fanciful but revealing lawsuit never filed by Bill Clinton in 1999 to block a trial of his impeachment by the Senate (perhaps making Vice President Gore the ironic, nominal defendant in his role as President of the Senate) after articles of impeachment had been passed by the House of Representatives in 1998.

Such a suit would hardly have lacked a legitimate legal foundation. Plaintiff Clinton could have raised Bruce Ackerman's argument that the articles of impeachment died with the end of the 105th Congress.[2] He also could have challenged on due process grounds a number of the actions taken by the House, including the reliance by dozens of members on evidence the President's attorneys had never seen, much less had an opportunity to rebut.[3]

Of course, the defendants (the real ones, presumably the House managers, rather than Vice President Gore) would have moved to dismiss the lawsuit on the ground that resolution of those issues—regardless of their merit—is committed to the Senate when it tries the impeachment, rather than to the federal courts. Surely, the originalists on the Court would have found that argument persuasive; after all, both Justices Thomas and Scalia joined Chief Justice Rehnquist's opinion for the Court in *Nixon v. United States*,[4] which turned away an impeached federal judge's challenge to the constitutionality of the rules by which the Senate was conducting his trial.

If that is so, however, it makes their willingness to intervene in *Bush v. Gore* puzzling, if not indefensible. The underlying context in that case was the selection of electors to represent Florida in the electoral college. To be sure, the substantive issues involved equal protection and statutory interpretation, issues that ordinarily are grist for the Court's mill. But the same would have been true of the hypothetical impeachment case: The issues would have been ones of due process and constitutional interpretation. Nevertheless, in the impeachment context the Court would have withdrawn in deference to the Senate, even though the Court rather than the Senate ordinarily decides such issues.

It is true that the Senate's power to try impeachments comes with a "kicker." The Constitution states that the Senate "shall have the sole Power to try all Impeachments,"[5] which makes it especially clear that impeachments are the Senate's turf. The language might not be quite that clear when it comes to determining the validity of electors, but there can be no doubt that this is just as exclusively a legislative prerogative. The detailed provisions of the Twelfth Amendment—all involving the steps the House and the Senate are to take in conducting the count of the Electoral College—make the absence of a constitutionally prescribed judicial role undeniable.

The question that remains, of course, is why the Court's conservative majority was unable to resist the temptation to involve itself in a dispute in which the federal courts almost certainly had no place, and in which (as I shall discuss presently) prevailing doctrine under the Equal Protection Clause should have made the Bush team's substantive case nearly hopeless. As with their agenda when it comes to takings and federalism and the rest, their dramatic moves in *Bush v. Gore* fit far more comfortably with the "political hypothesis" than with an "originalist hypothesis," and they are entirely inconsistent with the judicial conservatives' professed inclination to defer to democratic institutions and preserve the Court's limited role in our political system.

Start with this inarguable proposition: Every justice in *Bush v. Gore's* five-member majority voted in a way that maximized the likelihood that the next justice appointed to the Court would be more similar to him or her in terms of likely votes, especially on the core questions of federalism and equal protection that have occupied the Court's attention for the last decade. Though it is speculative, I think it is safe to say further that every one of the five voted in a way that maximized the likelihood that the candidate for whom he or she voted on election day would prevail. (The same cannot be said, by the way, of the four dissenters, two of whom—Breyer and Souter—voted to remand the case to the Florida Supreme Court, a course that at least compromised Vice President Gore's chances compared to the state Court's order.)

Of course, the mere fact that the conservative presidential candidate benefitted from the Court's intervention and decision is insufficient evidence of the majority's political motivation. But the manifest inadequacy of their reasoning, and the inconsistency of that reasoning with the positions taken by the conservative majority in other cases, more than fills the gap.

THE MAJORITY OPINION: IS THAT YOU, BABY, OR JUST A BRILLIANT DISGUISE?

To Marshall came *Marbury*. To Taney came *Dred Scott*. To Warren came *Brown*. And as the twenty-first century opened, to Rehnquist came *Bush v. Gore*. And as on those prior occasions, a Court defined itself unmistakably and unalterably for history. In this instance, the political agenda driving the Court, and the willingness of its conservative majority to forsake intellectual integrity and consistency while pursuing that agenda, left the realm of the debatable for the domain of the sadly indisputable.

The majority's equal protection analysis was manifestly inconsistent with prevailing doctrine, and with strong positions taken by the conservatives in prior cases. Indeed, if the *Bush v. Gore* reasoning actually becomes the controlling law, the Court will have changed equal protection law more completely than it has since it overruled "separate but equal" in *Brown v. Board of Education*. These inconsistencies exist on at least three levels: the remaking of "fundamental rights" jurisprudence, the peculiar definition of "inequality" the majority adopted, and the startling adoption of disparate impact theory.

Fundamental Rights

Crucial to the majority's analysis was the assertion that the proposed recount would infringe a "fundamental right." The Court virtually took for granted the proposition that an individual's right to vote in the presidential election is fundamental, but two problems mar its assumption. First, the right to vote for President is not fundamental in any way that term has been understood before. Second, even if the right to cast a presidential ballot is fundamental, the Court was not protecting that right. It was protecting the odd "right" *not to vote.*

According to the *per curiam* opinion:

> When the state legislature vests the right to vote for President in its peo-
> ple, the right to vote the legislature has prescribed is fundamental; and
> one source of its fundamental nature lies in the equal weight accorded to
> each vote and the equal dignity owed to each voter.[6]

This reasoning is classic in its circularity. In traditional equal protection
reasoning, the Court asks the question of whether a right is "fundamental" in order to determine whether it will assess the government's explanation for the infringement of the right under the merciless strict
scrutiny test; that is, whether it will demand a justification that constitutes a "compelling government interest," and whether the government
will be put to the task of demonstrating it has chosen the most narrow
means available to further that interest.[7]

Consider that sequence: First the Court must determine whether the
right is fundamental, and then it assesses the justification for the inequality. That means that the initial fundamental right inquiry must be
independent of the question of the equality or inequality with which it
has been treated. But that was not how the Court did things in *Bush v.
Gore*. There, the basis for a finding that the right was fundamental was
the inequality itself, rather than a textual or doctrinal commitment establishing that the right to vote for President is fundamental.

One might reasonably ask: So what? Is there any real dispute that the
right to vote for President is fundamental? In fact, there is such a dispute.
As the Court itself acknowledged, voters have no inherent constitutional
right to vote for President. Rather, the state legislatures have the power
to decide how their states' electors will be chosen.[8] There is no instance
of the Court recognizing a right as "fundamental" where the Constitution itself subjects the continued existence of the "right" to the unfettered discretion of the government. To the contrary. Before *Bush*, one
might usefully have defined a "fundamental right" as one whose existence is *not* subject to the unfettered discretion of the government.

The Court's originalists, in particular, have treated with disdain any
claim that a right is "fundamental" when it rests on so slender a thread
as the whim of a legislature. Consider a claimed "right" Justice Scalia
deemed not to be fundamental: the right of a putative biological father

to establish legal paternity of a child born to a woman married to another man.[9] California law created a presumption of legitimacy for any child born to a married woman living with her husband. It made that presumption irrefutable by anyone other than the husband or the wife, leaving the claimed biological father without any right to establish paternity. In his 1989 plurality opinion in *Michael H. v. Gerald D.*, Scalia took a dim view of Michael H.'s purported fundamental right:

> [T]he legal issue in the present case reduces to whether the relationship between persons in the situation of Michael and Victoria [the child] has traditionally been treated as a protected family unit under the historic practices of our society, or whether on any other basis it has been accorded special protection. We think it is impossible to find that it has. In fact, quite to the contrary, our traditions have protected the marital family (Gerald, Carole, and the child they acknowledge to be theirs) against the sort of claim Michael asserts.[10]

No precedent, and certainly no precedent endorsed by the constitutional conservatives, defines a "fundamental right" to include something the Constitution itself authorizes the government to give or withhold at its pleasure.

Another case illustrates the originalists' pre-*Bush* disdain for such "rights." In 1996, Justice Thomas (writing for himself, Justice Scalia, and Chief Justice Rehnquist) wrote a dissenting opinion in *M.L.B. v. S.L.J.*, a case in which the Court overturned a Mississippi statute requiring a woman whose parental rights had been terminated to pay "record preparation fees" of over $2,000 before taking an appeal.[11] The Court held that this requirement violated the mother's rights under the Equal Protection and Due Process Clauses of the Fourteenth Amendment, but the dissenters would have none of it. They argued that the claimed right to have the state pay for a transcript—even in cases where the fundamental right to avoid permanent termination of parental rights is at stake—is ephemeral, because the state did not have to provide an appeal in the first place. As a result, Thomas explained, there could be no cognizable disparate impact claim challenging a "rule that prevents a person from taking an appeal that is available only because the State chooses to provide it."[12]

The language could be adapted easily to the election case. The "right" to vote for President is available only "because the State chooses to provide it." In *Bush v. Gore*, that did not prevent the Court from defining the right as fundamental; the majority said simply that if the state chooses to permit its voters to select presidential electors, the right is fundamental and must be administered in a way consistent with the Equal Protection Clause. But in the parental rights case, the conservatives considered the contingent nature of the right fatal to precisely the sort of equal protection claim they accepted in *Bush v. Gore*.

Of course, the Court might have meant to say that the discretion vested in state legislatures to adopt the method for selecting electors, once unfettered and hence not plausibly "fundamental," is now fettered by the Equal Protection Clause. But again, that cannot be simply assumed for purposes of deeming the right "fundamental." No case in the Court's history defines a right, for purposes of equal protection analysis, in terms of the very inequality alleged to constitute the violation. If there were, any inequality would, by definition, make every right "fundamental" and require strict scrutiny of every distinction drawn by government.

The Court then compounded its error by never even addressing the possible justifications for the state court's approach. Once it determined that the state court had infringed the fundamental right to have one's ballot treated similarly to all other ballots, the next step *should* have been to apply strict scrutiny (i.e., ask whether the state's action was narrowly tailored to further a compelling governmental interest). Instead, the Court moved directly and without explanation from finding a fundamental right to finding a violation of that right simply because of the risk of unequal treatment.

One of the most striking things about the Court's approach was its failure to consider any justifications for the standard the Florida Supreme Court had utilized. Had it done so, it would have confronted justifications for the purportedly impermissible generality that were both obvious and patently adequate under any standard. First, and most crucially, the order was intended to further the voting rights of Florida voters by using every method available to identify those ballots meeting the requirements for a lawful ballot. As things stood on December 11, tens of thousands of ballots had never been examined by a human being to determine what indicia, if any, they contained of the voters' intent. It is beyond dispute that some ballots which went unexamined would have been included (and under Florida law should have been included) had the Court not intervened. That would have vindicated the right to vote of the citizens who cast those ballots. That, it seems, constitutes an inarguably compelling state interest, especially to a Court that was in the process of rendering that very right "fundamental."

The general standard set forth by the Florida Supreme Court in conducting the manual examination of ballots was also amply justified, had the Court bothered to address justifications. The Court itself had made the first one abundantly clear in its earlier decision. That opinion dealt with the Florida Supreme Court's decision to extend the deadline for certification of the state's vote totals. The opinion on remand impressed upon the Florida Supreme Court the importance of not "rewriting" the Florida Election Code after the November 7 election had already been conducted.[13] This priority was linked to Florida's ability to take advantage of the "safe harbor" provision assuring the validity of its electors; federal law required that the electors be selected pursuant to state law in place prior to the election. In light of this reminder, it is hardly surprising that the Florida Supreme Court would hew closely to the language of the Election Code in setting the standard:

> In tabulating the ballots and in making a determination of what is a "legal" vote, the standard to be employed is that established by the Legislature in our Election Code which is that the vote shall be counted as "legal" if there is "clear indication of the intent of the voter." Section 101.5614(5), Florida Statutes (2000).[14]

Can there be any doubt that if the Florida Supreme Court had gone beyond the text of the statute and crafted a more specific standard, the majority would have faulted it for rewriting the statute and changing the law after election day? This Catch-22 was in place before *Bush v. Gore* was even briefed and argued.

The relatively general standard was further justified by a related aspect of the statutory scheme: the Legislature's evident determination to give discretion to local election officials to carry out the election laws. The law vests in local canvassing boards, for example, the authority to decide whether to conduct a manual recount. To the extent the Florida Supreme Court gave the local boards relatively broad discretion to carry out this mandate, it was reflecting this legislative judgment. These justifications (along with another: the need to begin and complete the count as quickly as possible as the calendar pages turned) might not have risen to the level of a compelling interest to justify infringing a genuine fundamental right, but we will never know because the conservative majority failed or refused to address them, a damning omission for a Court marked by its federalism-inspired willingness to credit and defer to states' justifications for their conduct.

An Inequality Most Strange

Let us assume, however, that the right to vote in a presidential election is "fundamental." In fact, I agree that it is—but then, I think the Court was wrong in *Michael H.* And let us also assume that any justifications for the choice made by the state court would have been found wanting. But even those assumptions don't rescue the Court's peculiar fundamental rights analysis, because it in no way protected the right to vote. Instead, the equality it stood for was in the right not to vote.

The petitioner in the case, of course, was George W. Bush. But Bush was being treated neither more nor less favorably than Gore, at least once the Florida Supreme Court ordered the entire state to be included in the recount of undervotes. At most, he was a (very) interested bystander, with a (very) large stake in how the ballots were treated. The people whose right to equal treatment was alleged to be at stake were a particular group of those who had cast ballots in Florida.

Equal protection doctrine is in many ways like algebra. Both have at their core the equal sign ($=$), and their complexities reduce largely to figuring out how to deduce what goes on each side of the equation. When a mathematician solves an algebraic equation, the point may be to determine the value of the unknown variable(s):

$$3x + 7 = 25$$

Or the point may be something else, as it would be if the formula were:

$$3x + 7 (= \text{ or } \neq) 25$$
$$\text{where } x = 5.$$

In that instance, the purpose would be to determine which sign is appropriate; of course, the "does not equal" sign would be correct. In a nutshell, this is what the courts do in equal protection cases: They determine whether the individuals or groups on either side of the equation have been treated equally. For example:

African-Americans denied the franchise $\neq$ white enfranchisement

Of course, most contemporary equal protection cases raise complex issues surrounding the explanations governments proffer for alleged unequal treatment, but it is impossible to even get to those issues without first identifying who or what is on each side of the equation. In short, x cannot be compared to y unless we know who x and y are.

Bush did not allege, nor did the Court find, this equation:

Bush $\neq$ Gore

Instead, Bush argued that the previously uncounted ballots would be treated unequally if the count went forward. In more basic terms, the equation was:

Some uncounted ballots $\neq$ Other uncounted ballots

On either side of the equation are uncounted ballots. Whose, specifically? Well, according to the *per curiam* opinion, identical ballots would be subjected to differential standards in the exercise of the ballot counters' discretion in applying the general, "clear intent of the voter" test provided in Florida law.[15] In other words, the equation would be something like:

Dimpled chad in Dade County $\neq$ Dimpled chad in Martin County
(Counted as a legal vote)   (Not counted as a legal vote)

That seems simple enough. The voter in Martin County, whose ballot remains uncounted, is being treated differently than the voter in Dade

County, even though their ballots are equally clear and should either both be counted or both be omitted from the count.

The "right" the Court identified, in other words, was the voter's right to have her ballot *remain uncounted* because of the risk that some other voter's uncounted ballot might be examined and given a greater chance of being deemed a valid vote. The Court deemed this treatment "arbitrary." The Court did not protect any sort of "fundamental right to vote," as it purported to do. It protected the "right" of the voters whose ballots had already been disregarded *not to vote*—but at least to do so "equally."

Now, I don't mean to trivialize the importance of equal treatment of voters' ballots. The principle that each vote is entitled to equal weight is, as the Court intimated, a cornerstone of modern voting rights jurisprudence.[16] Think about *Reynolds v. Sims*,[17] the Supreme Court's landmark case involving legislative districting. There, existing district lines for the Alabama Legislature included a Senate district with a population of 600,000 citizens, and another with a population of around 15,000. That system presented obvious, actual inequality in the weight accorded votes for state government. Nothing similar was remotely involved in *Bush v. Gore*, and until then nothing like the potential, hypothetical possibility of vote-counting standards that might differ when applied has ever been seen as a violation of the equal protection principle.

Moreover, algebra is fun, and anyone can play. What about this equation:

$$\text{Ballot in Lake County} \neq \text{Identical ballot in Orange County}$$
$$\text{(Not manually counted)} \qquad \text{(Manually counted)}$$

Just as unequal as the other equation, right? Just as much a violation of the Equal Protection Clause? In this case, though, we'd be talking not about the Florida Supreme Court's aborted recount, but about the *status quo to that point, and reflected in the certified vote totals that ultimately produced the Bush victory in Florida.* In Lake County, officials discarded as "overvotes" ballots in which:

an oval next to [Gore's] name was filled in with a pencil and the voter mistakenly filled in another oval next to a spot reserved for write-in candidates, writing in Gore's name or running mate Joe Lieberman's there as well.[18]

Although there were parallel ballots indicating a preference for Bush, including them would have produced a net gain of 130 votes for Gore in Lake County.

While nothing is inherently wrong with discarding such ballots on the basis of voter error, there is something wrong with doing so only in Lake County. Ballots containing the exact same "voter error" were counted in the certified totals in at least two counties, Orange and Seminole.[19] Such actual inequality of treatment (a step more serious than the mere risk of inequality identified by the majority) cannot be constitutionally permissible if the Court meant what it said in *Bush v. Gore*.

In addition, canvassing boards in some counties made the decision to manually recount ballots, even though their ballots were identical in every respect to those in other counties in which canvassing boards chose not to do so. This choice was governed by a standard no less arbitrary and unequal across the state than the one condemned by the Supreme Court when it came to a proposal to count all of them.

What is still more astonishing is that over 1.5 million ballots were never even recounted by machine, in direct violation of Florida law. According to the *Miami Herald*, 18 counties "never recounted the ballots at all. They simply checked their original results."[20] Perhaps the worst inequality involved neither whether nor how to recount ballots, but how those ballots were cast in the first place. It is clear that different voting systems produced widely disparate results in making the right to vote a reality.[21]

In all of these ways, the vote totals that the Court rendered final, and which placed George W. Bush in the White House, were rife with precisely the same sort of equal protection "violation" inherent in the Florida Supreme Court's order. And yet these inequalities, of constitutional dimension, were of no concern to the majority.

It is difficult to discern a constitutional difference between an arbitrary difference in voting equipment, an arbitrary refusal to conduct mandatory recounts, an arbitrarily vague standard in deciding whether to manually recount ballots, and an arbitrarily vague standard used in actually recounting ballots.[22] Indeed, for this reason, Professor Sunstein sees the potential that *Bush v. Gore's* reasoning will be extended to cover other aspects of our voting process, and perhaps the constitutionally mandated improvements will be a long-term, positive side effect.[23] Nevertheless, all we know is that the Court cared about the perceived flaws in the recount order and not the much greater inequalities in the rest of the process, and that the Court went out of its way to emphasize that its ruling was intended to be unique to the particular case.[24] For now, it seems the Court deems recount procedures constitutionally distinct. So which is more plausible: that the majority really believed that recount procedures are subject to a different constitutional rule because they are distinguishable from voting machines, ballot designs, and the like, or that they are subject to a different constitutional rule because the majority crafted that rule to reach a desired outcome?

One of the many ironies of the Supreme Court's decision is that it left the voters treated *less equally than they would have been under the recount order.* Here is how the hypothetical Martin County voter would have benefitted had the recount gone forward:

Like every other "undervote" ballot statewide, her ballot would have been counted by hand. As it stands, some ballots on which a machine found no vote were counted by hand. Others were not, depending solely on the county where the voter lived. The state Supreme Court's order would have equalized this different treatment.

In distinguishing a non-vote from a valid vote, the state Supreme Court's order would have established a standard—the clear intent of the voter—that had not been applied in the evaluation of undervotes in those counties where a manual count had taken place. The state Supreme Court's order would have put in place a single official, state trial judge Terry Lewis, as a "funnel" through which the actions and standards of county officials throughout the state would have been filtered, assuring at least some standardization.

By identifying valid votes among the undervotes, a manual recount would have reduced the impact of the disparity in the rates at which different voting systems produced undervotes. The punch-card system was vastly more likely to produce a "no-vote" ballot than the optical scanning system.[25]

Consider: The Supreme Court majority was concerned about potential unequal treatment that would occur as the uncounted ballots were pulled from the pile and examined. But it was unconcerned about the unequal treatment that had left them in that pile in the first place. Under any analysis, if the Florida Supreme Court's order constituted a violation of the Equal Protection Clause, then so too does the current (and now final) vote count. If anything, the state Supreme Court's order would have provided a partial remedy for the more egregious violation reflected in the final outcome.

Disparate Impact, or Where Has All the Doctrine Gone?

It gets worse. Not only was the Court protecting a bizarre right to "not vote equally." Not only was it protecting that right in a way that worsened the violation. Its standard for what constituted equal treatment was unprecedented. The fact is that the Florida Supreme Court ordered the ballots to be examined under a uniform standard: They would count as votes if the voter's clear intent to select a particular candidate could be discerned. The problem, according to the Court, did not consist of a nonuniform standard, but in the overly general character of that standard.

Where the Florida Supreme Court erred, in other words, was in proposing a facially neutral, equal rule whose application the U.S. Supreme Court determined might result in unequal treatment of the ballots. Such an equal protection "violation" is utterly without precedent in the cases, for a simple reason: It is the very definition of "disparate impact," a theory of discrimination the Court has held, with the emphatic concurrence of the conservatives, does not state a Fourteenth Amendment violation. Until *Bush v. Gore* this proposition, first established in 1976 in *Washington v. Davis*,[26] was considered as settled as any in the law of equal protection. And this position has enjoyed the strong support of the conservative wing of the Court.

In *Lewis v. Casey*, Justice Thomas wrote a concurring opinion in which he relied heavily on *Davis* as a basis for arguing that the Court either should not follow, or should significantly limit, one of its important precedents regarding prisoners' rights.[27] Thomas regarded the case as resting on a disparate impact theory, about which he said:

> The *Davis* Court was motivated in no small part by the potentially radical implications of [a disparate impact requirement].... [W]e rejected in

Davis the disparate-impact approach in part because of the recognition that "[a] rule that a statute designed to serve neutral ends is nevertheless invalid, absent compelling justification, if in practice it benefits or burdens one race more than another would be far reaching and would raise serious questions about, and perhaps invalidate, a whole range of tax, welfare, public service, regulatory, and licensing statutes that may be more burdensome to the poor and to the average black than to the more affluent white."[28]

Evidently, those "radical implications" became less troublesome to Justice Thomas sometime between 1996, when the Court considered *Lewis*, and 2000, when it adopted a disparate impact model in *Bush v. Gore*.

Justice Thomas's antagonism to disparate impact pre-dated his tenure on the Court. During his time as Chair of the Equal Employment Opportunity Commission, Thomas undertook a systematic transformation of the Commission's litigation focus, moving to bring a substantially greater number of "one-on-one" cases (individual, discrete claims of specific acts of discrimination against a particular employee or applicant). This entailed a simultaneous de-emphasis on systemic, class-wide cases that had been the hallmark of the Commission's docket under the prior Chair, Eleanor Holmes Norton. While there were certainly policy arguments to be made on both sides of this debate over enforcement strategies,[29] one of the key grounds for the shift during the Thomas years was a negative view of the disparate impact theory upon which many of the systemic cases were based.[30] Between 1983 and 1989, the Commission did not file even one adverse impact case.[31]

Justice Scalia's views of disparate impact are no less clear, and no less hostile. In 1996, as I noted earlier, he (along with Chief Justice Rehnquist) joined Justice Thomas's dissent in *M.L.B. v. S.L.J.*, where the Court overturned a Mississippi statute requiring a woman whose parental rights had been terminated to pay "record preparation fees" of over $2,000 before taking an appeal.[32] Besides taking issue with the Court's fundamental rights analysis, the dissenters also criticized the Court for apparently using disparate impact reasoning:

> Since *Davis*, we have regularly required more of an equal protection claimant than a showing that state action has a harsher effect on him or

her than on others. . . . Our frequent pronouncements that the Four-teenth Amendment is not violated by disparate impact have spanned challenges to statutes alleged to affect disproportionately members of one race, . . . members of one sex, . . . and poor persons seeking to exercise protected rights.[33]

And yet, these long-time antagonists to disparate impact said not a word about its use in *Bush v. Gore*.

Of course, the inequalities manifested in the certified vote totals could not have survived application of the new, *Bush v. Gore* disparate impact test. Nor could countless aspects of our electoral system (e.g., the use of different voting systems in different jurisdictions), if the Court really meant it. And the majority, aware that the implications of disparate impact theory were no less "radical" than those Justice Thomas had warned of in *Lewis v. Casey*, moved to limit those implications, writing, "The question before the Court is not whether local entities, in the exercise of their expertise, may develop different systems for implementing elections."[34]

Beware of any court, or lawyer, who answers a challenging hypothetical with, "That's not this case." When a lawyer does it, a skeptical judge often responds, "I know that's not this case. Answer it anyway." We should be equally skeptical of the Court: *Of course* the adoption and use of disparate voting systems was not the question before the Court. The way the votes actually had been cast and counted did, however, produce much greater inequality than the infirm recount order could possibly have brought about. By brushing that inequality to one side, the majority demonstrated that its concern was not unequal treatment, but only unequal treatment that might produce results unfavorable to the Bush candidacy.

One final point regarding the equal protection rationale of the majority opinion. Early in 2001, reports concerning press-sponsored examinations of the ballots in Florida, conducted after the Supreme Court's decision and not completed until after Bush was sworn into office, suggested that he probably would have prevailed even had the Court not halted the recount. As expected, the margin between the candidates varied depending on what standard was used for a valid ballot. Ironically, Bush did best under the very permissive standard Gore's camp advocated all along, amassing a 1,665-vote margin.[35]

Or did he? According to the Miami Herald, that figure did not include the media consortium's review of the ballots in Broward, Palm Beach, and part of Miami-Dade County, because, "The Florida court's order exempted [those areas] where canvassing boards had already reviewed ballots."[36] That made sense. Since one goal of the review was to determine what would have happened had the recount gone forward *as ordered by the Florida Supreme Court*, excluding the already canvassed ballots in Broward, Palm Beach, and Miami-Dade was the logical step.

But what if we are interested in a different question: What would have happened in a recount conducted under the equal protection standard established by the Supreme Court in *Bush v. Gore*? The majority opinion seems to require that ballots be reviewed under a consistent, relatively specific standard across counties, or at least that steps be in place (clear standards in particular) to minimize the risk of arbitrary application of the standard. The media review seems to have met this threshold; the ballots were reviewed under numerous tests (fully detached chad, partially detached chad, dimple, etc.) and results reported for each test. But one part of the count remained inconsistent: the ballots that had been counted not by the media reviewers, but by the canvassing boards in the three counties. That inconsistency would have constituted a serious problem under *Bush v. Gore*.

Fortunately, the media reviewed the canvassed ballots, although it did not include them in the widely reported tally showing a 1,665-vote Bush victory. So what would have been the result if the excluded counties had been reviewed under the same permissive standard which produced a 1,665-vote Bush victory? The answer, according to the *Miami Herald*, is that Gore would have won by 393 votes.[37] That swing, from a Bush margin of over 1,600 votes to a Gore margin of nearly 400 votes, means that the canvassing boards must have been using a different, more restrictive standard than the permissive one, different to the tune of 2,058 votes.

To put the point another way, the inclusion of the canvassed ballots in the vote count certified by the Florida Secretary of State reflected an actual difference in treatment rather than a speculative risk of one. While the widely reported Bush victory might have been the outcome had the recount gone forward and a permissive standard been used everywhere to count previously uncanvassed ballots, it would have been an unconstitutional outcome because of the radically different treatment that had been given to the previously canvassed ballots. The best evidence is that a permissive standard, applied uniformly *everywhere*, would have produced a Gore win.

THE CONCURRENCE: FEDERALISM?
WHAT FEDERALISM?

The concurring opinion written by Chief Justice Rehnquist and joined by Justices Scalia and Thomas (that is, the stance taken by the Court's most conservative members) adds yet another layer of evidence pointing to the political motives behind the decision. Rehnquist faced a formidable task: He needed to show not only that the state Supreme Court's interpretation of Florida statutory law was wrong, but that it was sufficiently egregious to create a federal constitutional issue. His performance was astonishingly unconvincing, his case patently flimsy.

Start with first principles. Most of the time, the interpretation of the state Supreme Court is final, binding even on the federal Supreme Court.[38] Of course, the state law as interpreted may then suffer the indignity of being found to violate the Constitution (as happened in *Bush v. Gore*), but in making that decision the Supreme Court takes the state law as the state courts left it.

But in some rare instances, the Constitution itself alters this state of affairs. According to the Chief Justice, the state courts' interpretation of election law as applied to elections for the presidency is one such instance. This is because the Constitution confers the power to designate the method for choosing electors not on the state generally, but on the state legislature specifically.[39] It is thus a question of federal constitutional import, and not a "mere" state law matter, if the state courts depart significantly from the manner directed by the legislature when they interpret and apply the law.

So far, so good. A rogue state court masking its usurpation of the legislature's authority in this area in the guise of an implausible "interpretation" cannot cloak itself in the sovereign autonomy of the states. But the word "usurpation" suggests the limits of the U.S. Supreme Court's role in cases like this. The interpretation offered by the state court must cross the line separating the arguable, even the dubious, from the implausible and the outlandish. Otherwise, the Court's examination would be indistinguishable from ordinary review of decisions from a lower court. Run-of-the-mill disagreement with the state Supreme Court is manifestly insufficient.

Chief Justice Rehnquist's concurrence offered nothing close to a convincing argument that the Florida Supreme Court misread state law so grossly that it usurped the Legislature's authority. Though the procedural details were discussed in the media in excruciating detail in November and December of 2000, it is helpful to revisit the events leading up to the Court's ruling.

Florida law calls for an automatic recount of ballots in any election decided by less than one-half of one percent of the votes, as was the case with the initial presidential election results in 2000. During this initial, mandatory machine recount, then-Governor Bush's lead narrowed from approximately 1,800 votes to less than 500.

The outcome of the presidential election, in which over 100 million Americans voted, rested on a margin of less than 500 votes. Not surprisingly, and especially in light of serious questions that began to arise about ballot design, voter confusion, and alleged voting irregularities, the next step was a request for manual recounts. Florida law permits candidates to seek manual recounts on a county-by-county basis, and Vice President Gore asked for them in four predominantly Democratic counties: Miami-Dade, Broward, Palm Beach, and Volusia.[40] It was at this point that the controversy mushroomed to include court fights, recount challenges, public protests, and dueling media campaigns.

After it became clear that the recounts undertaken in the counties at issue would not be completed by the deadline set forth in Florida law for county canvassing boards to certify their results and forward them to the Florida Secretary of State, some of the counties involved went to court seeking an extension. Ultimately, the Florida Supreme Court ruled that the Secretary of State was compelled to accept late returns, so long as they were filed by 5:00 P.M. on Sunday, November 26, 2000. The Court also extended an earlier stay preventing the Secretary of State from certifying election results until that date.[41]

It was this decision that spurred the U.S. Supreme Court to get involved the first time around, when it remanded the case and signaled unmistakably serious doubts about the state court's reasoning.[42] Crucially, however, that decision was ultimately irrelevant when *Bush v. Gore* made its way to the Supreme Court. By that time, the certification had been made and the election challenge had entered what we all learned was the next phase under Florida law: the "contest" phase. For this reason, the merits of the Rehnquist opinion in critiquing the Florida Supreme Court's reasoning cannot be judged on the basis of whether it was right or wrong when it decided the issues in the initial go-round.

Once the election was finally certified, at the deadline set by the Florida Supreme Court and with Bush still in front, Gore contested the certified results in state court. Florida law provides that a contestant must demonstrate "[r]eceipt of a number of illegal votes or rejection of a number of legal votes sufficient to change or place in doubt the results of the election."[43] Gore raised several points in attempting to make this showing:[44]

Approximately 9,000 ballots in Miami-Dade County reflected no vote for President, more than enough to place the outcome in doubt.

The Secretary of State had refused to include approximately 200 net legal votes which had been identified by the Palm Beach Canvassing Board, on the ground that the Board did not complete the count until after the certification deadline.

The Secretary of State had refused to include 168 net legal votes for Gore which had been identified by the Miami-Dade Canvassing Board, on the ground that they were the result of a less-than-full manual recount of the county's ballots.

The Florida Supreme Court accepted each of these claims. It ordered the inclusion of the Miami-Dade and Palm Beach ballots, resulting in a net gain of nearly 400 votes for Gore. More importantly (since 400 votes were not enough to make up the difference), the court agreed that the 9,000 "undervotes" in Miami-Dade should have been counted. However, it stunned many observers by ordering that undervotes should be manually examined statewide in any county where such an examination had not already taken place, saying:

While we recognize that time is desperately short, we cannot in good faith ignore both the appellant's right to relief as to their claims concerning the uncounted votes in Miami-Dade County nor can we ignore the correctness of the assertions that any analysis and ultimate remedy should be made on a statewide basis.[45]

Rehnquist, Scalia, and Thomas found this order, and the interpretation of Florida law on which it was based, to be so wrong as to constitute a usurpation of the Legislature's constitutional authority. So what was wrong with it?

First, the court had failed to reckon with the importance of finality. Under a federal statute, the slate of electors certified by a state is entitled to presumptive validity from challenge when Congress meets to count the electoral votes—if the electors are chosen "under laws enacted prior to election day, and if the selection process is completed six days prior to the meeting of the electoral college."[46] According to Chief Justice Rehnquist, the interpretation given to Florida law by the state court had to be wrong because the recount it ordered "jeopardizes the 'legislative wish' to take advantage of [this] safe harbor...."[47]

There is only one problem with this reasoning: It presupposed a "legislative wish" appearing nowhere in the Florida statute. The majority opinion in *Bush v. Gore* explained where it came from: "The Supreme Court of Florida has said that the legislature intended the State's electors to 'participat[e] fully in the federal electoral process,' as provided in 3 U.S.C. § 50."[48] In other words, it was attributed to the state legislature by the very Florida Supreme Court the concurring Justices regarded as a rogue usurper of legislative prerogatives. It appears that the conservatives were willing to treat the Florida Supreme Court as the authoritative source of state law interpretation—so long as they liked what that court said.

This selective deference is all the more remarkable because it got the matter exactly backwards. The Florida Supreme Court attributed two basic goals to the state Legislature: to reach accurate results by mechanisms that protect every voter's right to have his or her vote counted, and to reach a result in a way sufficiently speedy to take advantage of the "safe harbor" provision. The concurrence relied heavily on the second of these two, to the extent that it trumped the first. But it is by far the shakier of the two. Even a cursory reading of Florida election law shows a deep legislative concern with accuracy. The statute includes multiple layers of review, beginning with a mandatory machine recount in especially close elections, running through a right to seek hand recounts in particular counties and the right even after certification to contest the certified result. By contrast, there is no indication the Legislature was even aware of the federal "safe harbor" provision, much less that this was a consideration when the legislature enacted the state election law.

Far more important than the conservatives' selective and dubious acceptance of the Florida court's ascription of legislative purpose, though, was their discussion of the substance of the state ruling. The Florida Supreme Court's interpretation of the contest provisions in the state law was not just defensible; it was far more reasonable than the strained reading of the law in Chief Justice Rehnquist's opinion.

To begin with, it is important to emphasize what the Rehnquist trio did not argue. They did not challenge the Florida Supreme Court's core holding that the trial court judgment was wrong as a matter of law. Indeed, it was virtually inarguable that the trial court applied the wrong legal standard in evaluating the merits of Vice President Gore's contest. The then-ubiquitous Jude N. Sanders Sauls held that in an election contest:

> It is not enough to show a reasonable possibility that election results could have been altered by such irregularities, or inaccuracies, rather, a reasonable probability that the results of the election would have been changed must be shown.[49]

As the Florida Supreme Court noted, this test is not the one set forth in the statute. All that is necessary under section 102.168(c) is for the contestant to establish that enough legal votes were rejected "to change or *place in doubt* the result of the election."[50] Thus, Gore did not need to show a "reasonable probability" the outcome would have changed; he needed only to place the outcome into doubt. In light of this obvious error on the part of the circuit judge, it would be impossible to claim that the Florida Supreme Court erred in reversing his decision.

Instead, the concurrence was reduced to claims that were arguable at best, and simply untenable at worst. For example, the Chief Justice went on at some length in claiming that "the [Florida Supreme C]ourt's interpretation of 'legal vote,' and hence its decision to order a contest-period recount, plainly departed from the legislative scheme."[51] According to the concurrence, the Florida Court had mandated the "counting of improperly marked ballots," and improperly marked ballots cannot reasonably be thought to count as "legal votes." That reasoning presents numerous problems.

First, the Florida Supreme Court was requiring *examination of the ballots* for a determination of whether they were, in fact, "properly marked." Of course the Florida system did not require that "improperly marked ballots" be counted in the sense that they would "count" in the final tally. But it makes all the sense in the world, and it is most consistent with the statutory framework, to say that they should be "counted"—meaning examined to determine whether they were "properly marked" and hence should be included in the final tally.

After all, the only basis upon which Rehnquist could assert that the challenged ballots were "improperly marked" was that the counting machines had not registered a valid vote. Virtually none of the ballots at issue had actually been examined by a human being. So far as the Chief Justice knew—so far as any of us knew—some or even many of these ballots might have been correctly completed in every respect. If the machine's rejection of a ballot were sufficient evidence of its invalidity, then there would be no need for a manual recount provision at all. Such a provision presupposes that some ballots may (and sometimes must) be examined because they represent "legal votes" even though the machine did not count them. For this reason, Chief Justice Rehnquist's reasoning was inconsistent with the statutory scheme and circular in assuming the conclusion that the ballots at issue did not include "legal votes."

Second, any scheme that nullifies "improperly" marked ballots must contain a standard for what constitutes an improperly marked ballot. The contest provision of Florida's election law does not itself set forth a definition of a "legal" vote. The task of defining one is thus a quintessentially judicial job; indeed, we could do worse than to define "statutory interpretation" as the task a court performs when the language of a statute does not provide a clear definition of relevant terms. The Florida Supreme Court chose a perfectly reasonable, and common, way to define the term: It looked to another provision of the same statute. In section 101.5614, the Legislature provided that "no vote shall be ignored 'if there is a clear indication of the intent of the voter' on the ballot, unless it is 'impossible to determine the elector's choice. . . .'"[52] Using this language, the state court determined reasonably enough that a vote is "legal" (which is to say, *properly* marked) if the clear intent of the voter is not impossible to determine.

In answer to this, the concurrence called section 101.5614 "entirely irrelevant," apparently because it was not part of the law dealing with the contest phase.[53] Unfortunately for Chief Justice Rehnquist's credibility, this response followed several paragraphs of analysis in which he relied on other subsections of section 101 to show that the statute provides for instructions to voters. Presumably, these provisions (equally not part of the law on election contests) should have been no more relevant than section 101.5614. If anything, the significance of statutory language mandating that instructions be provided would seem of distinctly less relevance.

Finally, the Chief Justice confused two distinct aspects of the statutory scheme. He criticized the Florida Supreme Court for misinterpreting the term "an error in the vote tabulation" and for failing to defer to the Secretary of State's interpretation of that term.[54] But that is the standard that governs the county canvassing board's decision whether to conduct a manual recount, and it applies at the pre-certification (or the "protest") stage. An election contest, such as the one actually before the Court in *Bush v. Gore*, comes post-certification and is governed by a separate standard. Rehnquist dismissed this point in a footnote, finding it

> inconceivable that what constitutes a vote that must be counted under the "error in the vote tabulation" language of the protest phase is different from what constitutes a vote that must be counted under the "legal votes" language of the contest phase.[55]

But it is not inconceivable at all. To the contrary; what is inconceivable is that the standards for the two stages would be identical, since that would make a circuit court contest entirely duplicative of any judicial review of decisions (e.g., whether to conduct a manual recount; the standard to use in recounting) made during the protest phase. At the very least, the Florida Supreme Court's analysis is a plausible attempt to interpret the statute to make the contest phase provided for by the Florida Legislature meaningful and to avoid rendering an important portion of the statute mere surplusage.

But even if the "error in the vote tabulation" language was relevant, the concurrence was not persuasive even in showing that the Florida Supreme Court was wrong about that term. Here is what Chief Justice Rehnquist said about it:

> No reasonable person would call it "an error in vote tabulation" . . . when electronic or electromechanical equipment performs precisely in the manner designed, and fails to count those ballots that are not marked in the manner [the] voting instructions explicitly and prominently specify.[56]

This argument suffers from the same flaw I have already discussed: It assumes knowledge about the unexamined ballots (why they did not register a vote for President), determination of which was the whole point of the contest.

Even more fundamentally, this argument was a gigantic non-sequitur. The term "error in the vote tabulation" was contained in section 102.166(5), which set the standard for what had to be shown to trigger a county canvassing board's obligation to take corrective action (including, but not limited to, a manual recount).[57] Issues relating to the decision(s) to conduct recounts, and whether they had to be included in the certification by the Secretary of State, were the subject of the first appeal. The question in *Bush v. Gore* was not what constituted a vote tabulation error, and hence what could have triggered a manual recount by a county canvassing board. The question was whether Gore could show that "legal votes" had been rejected in sufficient numbers to "place in doubt the result of the election."[58] Section 102.168(3)(c) does not require those ballots to have been "rejected" because of an "error in the vote tabulation." Hence, even if the Florida Supreme Court was wrong to construe that term broadly, it should not have mattered.

Chief Justice Rehnquist's use of the "error in the vote tabulation" argument suffers from yet another flaw—and irony. He had placed enormous emphasis on the Florida legislature's wish to take advantage of the "safe harbor" provision. A key priority, the Chief Justice explained:

If we are to respect the legislature's Article II powers, therefore, we must ensure that state-court actions do not frustrate the legislative desire to attain the "safe harbor" provided by [federal law].[59]

When he said that, he was referring to the likelihood that the court-ordered recount would carry the election past the December 12 deadline. But there was another threat to the electors' place in the safe harbor: They had to be chosen by a means in place before election day. So the natural question occurs: was the interpretation Chief Justice Rehnquist put forward in place before the election, or would it have amounted to a forbidden post-election rewriting of the election law?

In support of his position, the Chief Justice relied heavily on the opinion of Katherine Harris, the controversial Florida Secretary of State to whom, he said, the Florida Supreme Court should have deferred. She had issued an opinion giving a limited construction to the term "an error in vote tabulation," an opinion which had the immediate effect when issued of delaying the start of the manual recount in Palm Beach County. That opinion, however, was as much a "new" statement of Florida law as anything contained in the Florida Supreme Court's opinions. As such, it should have represented as much of a challenge to the safety of Florida's electors. Evidently, only in some respects was the Florida Legislature's wish to avail itself of the federal safe harbor paramount.

The reality is that the standard contained in the contest statute was itself general. Indeed, in using the term "legal vote," section 102.168(3)(c) was even more general than the definition the Florida Supreme Court engrafted onto it from section 102.166(5). In effect, because no more specific standard was established prior to November 2000, the U.S. Supreme Court's ruling means that no recount was constitutionally permissible. Follow the chain:

First. Usurpation of a state legislature's authority to prescribe the method by which electors shall be chosen violates Article II.

Second. Because of the Florida Legislature's intent to avail itself of the "safe harbor" provision in federal law, an interpretation that either carries the selection process past the safe harbor deadline or that amounts to a change in applicable election

law after election day would usurp the Legislature's authority and violate Article II.

Third.　Because the pre-existing standard for conducting recounts
in the contest phase is insufficiently precise to satisfy the
Equal Protection Clause, only a post-election day revision
could create a recount regime consistent with the Fourteenth Amendment.

Fourth.　Any revision that would satisfy the Fourteenth Amendment
would constitute the sort of alteration that would violate
Article II.

Fifth.　No recount in the presidential race in Florida could be
conducted.

But if this is the necessary implication of the concurrence's reasoning,
then we come back to the point that plagued the majority opinion: The
existing, certified totals were tainted by the exact flaw revealed by the
analysis. Recounts had already been conducted, using the "clear intent of
the voter" standard which, according to the concurring Justices, could be
applied only by rewriting the statute.

In fact, though, neither the recounts that had already been conducted
nor the one set to be conducted when the Supreme Court intervened violated anything resembling a fair interpretation of Florida law. Yet more
certain is that the state court's interpretation of its own state law, even if
wrong, was nowhere near the level of outrageous, virtually willful error
the Court has required in the rare past cases when it has refused to accept a state court interpretation of state law. As Professor Michael Klarman has shown, these cases "seem[] to requir[e] evidence of bad faith by
the state courts in their interpretation of state law."[60] In one of those
cases, *NAACP v. Alabama*,[61] the Court reversed an Alabama Supreme
Court ruling when it "was able to identify no fewer than a half dozen
prior Alabama Supreme Court decisions that had rejected precisely the
procedural distinction relied upon by that court," and also found that
the state Supreme Court had actually "directed the NAACP's lawyers to
seek appellate review via the very procedural route . . . that the state justices later determined to constitute a procedural default."[62]

The absence of any remotely similar shenanigans by the Florida
Supreme Court brings into focus the last, and perhaps most telling, as-

pect of the debacle that was *Bush v. Gore*. The principle that state court interpretations of state law are binding on the federal courts is one of the most well and firmly established tenets of federalism. It is directly linked to the status of the states as separate sovereigns, supreme within their own spheres, limited only by the requirements of the federal Constitution and valid federal laws enacted thereunder. A Justice dedicated to federalism for the sake of the constitutional value it represents would locate this principle at federalism's very core.

The supreme authority of state courts as arbiters of state law is no recent development, nor is it a trifle in the architecture of federalism. It is part of federalism's foundation, a central attribute of the states' retained sovereignty. The interference with state sovereignty the Federalism Five carried out in *Bush v. Gore* dwarfs the "infringements" of state sovereignty with which they were so concerned in the cases I discussed in Chapter 4: the intrusion into state sovereign immunity at issue in *Alden*, the supposed commandeering of state officials they blocked in *Printz*, or the congressional overreaching they halted in *Kimel* and *Morrison*. For a deeply committed federalist, only the most egregious, willful state court error, one which represented an even greater threat to the state's sovereign (and/or national constitutional) interests, could justify a step such as Rehnquist, Scalia, and Thomas took in *Bush v. Gore*. They did not remotely make the case for their position. Instead, they demonstrated that theirs is a federalism of convenience: When they don't happen to like what the federal government is doing in substance, they deem it an unwarranted intrusion into state autonomy and strike it down. But when they themselves, as a part of the federal government, didn't like what a state government was doing, the principles of non-intrusion and respect for state sovereignty vanished as if they never existed.

I was nearly done with the manuscript of this book when the Court decided *Bush v. Gore*. My thesis was that the Supreme Court's originalists have been inconsistent about applying their method, abandoning it when the stakes were high enough and their personal or political interests were not in concert with the original understanding of the relevant constitutional text. I cannot imagine that many writers have been as disappointed to be proved right as I was on December 11.

But that is an important point: *Bush v. Gore* is simply the latest example of the conservative majority's inconstancy. It is also the most important example and the one most devastating to the Court's legitimacy. But still, it is just the latest in a long line of constitutional decisions that are indefensible on the merits and comprehensible only through the prism of the political ideology of the justices. Rather than standing alone as evidence of the politicization of the Court by its most conservative wing, it is the smoking gun an investigator finds only at the end of the trail of other clues, the one that cinches the case.

CHAPTER SIX

A BRIDGE OVER
TROUBLED WATERS?

Whether it be the original Constitution or many of its amendments, we have seen the ongoing work of "originalists" hardly worthy of the label. Originalists who forget to even discuss the original understanding when adherence to it might undermine the legitimacy of their very method; originalists who slip between dogged textual originalism and looser structural originalism when political ideology demands it of them; originalists who forget to consider (or undermine) the impact of subsequent constitutional amendments on the original framework; originalists whose positions have more in common with Jesse Helms than James Madison (and virtually nothing in common with Alexander Hamilton).

In light of this performance, we can only ask: What originalism? The "originalist" justices are, no doubt, loudly and proudly originalist when it comes to abortion rights, the death penalty, and perhaps the Commerce Clause. But they are silently (though no less emphatically) non-originalist when it comes to the Takings Clause, the Equal Protection Clause, the Search and Seizure Clause, and in many respects various provisions related to the recent federalism cases. What do the originalist and non-originalist positions have in common? Just this: All happen to be important causes of the political right.

So what is going on here? For one thing, I might be holding originalism to an unfairly rigorous standard, asking for evidence that it actually constrains the discretion of its judicial practitioners. After all, Justice Scalia himself has admitted that originalism is not an "inoculation" against arbitrary decision-making; he makes only the more modest claim that it, unlike other methods, does not "cater to" a judge's wish to roam free in the vast expanse of her own predilections.[1]

In this chapter, I will raise three difficulties with this defense. First, I will argue that the burden of proof should be on the originalists to demonstrate the truth of their claim. Originalism carries with it significant costs, which we should bear only if the gains are genuine.

Second, the inherent relativism of Scalia's position, presenting originalism as no great shakes but at least better than the alternatives, invites comparison: Is originalism at least more constraining than other methods? The answer is no: Non-originalist judges find themselves constrained to reach unpalatable conclusions as often as originalist judges. When this is combined with the numerous cases of the modern originalists ignoring the original understanding, it becomes evident that originalists cannot bear their burden of proving to us that originalism produces even Justice Scalia's relative improvement.

Finally, the modest benefits Scalia claims do not meet the challenge of the counter-majoritarian difficulty. If originalism is merely the best of all the bad choices, the question of how we are to justify the authority of nine unelected judges overturning the will of democratically elected, representative bodies remains unanswered. Recall the *Bridge on the River Kwai*: It is as if the prisoners, compelled to build a bridge useful to the Japanese military, built a rope and wood foot bridge and pronounced their task complete. The counter-majoritarian challenge requires the originalists to build a far sturdier bridge than simply one that does not "cater to" judicial arbitrariness.

Before addressing these three specific points, one observation is in order. While I am willing to take Scalia at his word when, in his more modest moments, he makes relatively limited claims on behalf of originalism, the fact is that he and other originalists often make much more sweeping assertions about the certainty of results it produces. In a less modest moment, Scalia wrote:

> There is plenty of room for disagreement as to what original meaning was, and even more as to how that original meaning applies to the situation before the court. But the originalist at least knows what he is looking for: the original meaning of the text. *Often—indeed, I dare say usually— that is easy to discern and simple to apply.*[2]

In a similar vein, Professor Glenn Reynolds aptly described the standard Robert Bork sets for an interpretive method, which Bork claims originalism satisfies: "courts' actions must be constrained by a theory, one that is capable of predicting results."[3] But the claim staked by Justice Scalia, which is that his approach merely avoids catering to judicial mischief, is hardly one that "is capable of predicting results." Originalism could benefit from a plainer explanation of the benefits its adherents are promising.

SO WHAT ARE WE GETTING FOR OUR MONEY . . . ?

Whatever benefits originalists promise, we had better be awfully certain they deliver the goods. In light of the evidence we have already canvassed, there must be great doubt over the validity even of Justice Scalia's relatively muted claim of originalist constraint. In resolving that doubt, the burden of persuasion should be placed on the originalists to demonstrate both that judicial constraint is achieved, and that it ultimately would be a good thing. This is because their promised benefit comes with a hefty price tag.

The very constraining effect trumpeted by originalists testifies in a general way to these costs. The framers of constitutional text in 1789 or 1868 could not have anticipated much of the modern world. The choices they made, the priorities they set, would not be the same ones *they* would make today. Nor are they the ones we would choose if *we* were starting from scratch today.

But since we're not starting from scratch, and since it is not easy to amend the document, originalism ties us to choices from which our society no longer benefits (at least in the aggregate) but with which we are, it must be said, stuck. In economic terms, originalism deprives us of one tool by which we could maximize societal utilities.

The Second Amendment provides an excellent example of this problem. Let us take as proven the argument some scholars have made that its text, as originally understood by the framers, established a broad right inhering in individual citizens to own and keep weapons free from federal regulation.[4] It is plain that in many key respects, modern conditions do not resemble those of the late eighteenth century, in ways directly relevant to an assessment of the costs and benefits associated with the Second Amendment:

> The framers were fresh off the experience of a revolution against oppressive government, a revolution in which armed individuals formed a continental army to stand against the forces of King George;

> The framers were establishing a new, virtually unprecedented form of central government, experimenting with a dual (state/federal) sovereignty, with the hope but no assurance that its many balances of power would prevent tyranny;

> The framers lived in a world in which "arms" meant bayonets, muskets, and (at worst) cannons;

> The framers lived in a less urbanized world, in which violent crime perpetrated by people more heavily armed than law enforcement officials was not the everyday reality it has become today.

More than 200 years after passage of the Second Amendment, the balance of costs and benefits has changed remarkably—and in every way tilts against the "everyone armed to his heart's content" choice the framers (perhaps) made. In contrast to the lesson of the founders' times, which was the need for an armed citizens' revolution in the cause of liberty, our experience speaks to the need for a strong standing national armed force as a bulwark against tyranny, at least if World War II's lessons continue to have meaning. What seemed untested and risky in 1789 now has endured for well over 200 years, and seems to have been a successful (if still imperfect) experiment in republican rule. And the relatively minor carnage an "armed" individual could wreak in 1789 has given way to the infinitely greater danger posed by individuals possessing modern weaponry (semi-automatic handguns, TNT, and chemical and biological weapons, among others) in the more sobering age of Timothy McVeigh, Randy Weaver, and David Koresh.[5]

To bind us to the framers' choices in this respect means living with dangers they could not have foreseen in an attempt to meet threats much less relevant to our lives. When circumstances change, new needs arise, threats recede only to be replaced by others—these are the times when interpretive flexibility pays a dividend, and originalism carries a high price tag.

If the Second Amendment is not provocative enough, think about the makeup of the U.S. Senate. The Constitution guarantees every state, regardless of its size, equal representation in the Senate.[6] This arrangement was the product of political compromise (about which I shall have much to say later), and it reflected the founders' view that, regardless of population, the states were equal as sovereigns as they joined the federal union. But it also would not have been lost on the framers that when it came to population, the states were not all that far apart. In 1790, the most populous state (Virginia) had only 12 times the population of the smallest, Delaware.

Today, however, the population spread has widened enormously. California currently has nearly 70 times the population of Wyoming.[7] The disproportionate influence in national decision-making the Senate gives to relatively small states now includes the power to frustrate the wishes of a substantially larger proportion of the population. It is one thing for 10 people to be able to deny what is best for 50; it is quite another for 10 people to deny what is best for 50,000.

This is only an illustration; interpretive method is not going to alter the conclusion one reaches in reading the constitutional rules regarding the makeup of the Senate (although it might, as I discuss in the concluding chapter, affect the Court's treatment of the Senate and its conduct). Originalism may not help, but as to the structure of the Senate it does no harm. It is not hypothetical, however, to point out that the gravest constitutional crises in our history have invariably been closely linked to, if not caused by, originalist readings of the Constitution, readings that arguably left the nation faithful to the past but unable to cope with the present.

The first, and still the most awful, surrounded the issue of slavery. The Court's performance in the first 75 years of our nationhood on legal issues arising out of the slave economy was nearly a model of originalist rectitude. The framers expected slavery to be accommodated, and the Court did its part, most infamously in *Dred Scott v. Sandford*. In *Dred Scott*, the Court searched dutifully for evidence of the status of

African-Americans "when the Constitution of the United States was framed and adopted."[8] That search resulted in the most awful passage contained in the *United States Reports*:

> They had for more than a century before been regarded as beings of an inferior order, and altogether unfit to associate with the white race, either in social or political relations; and so far inferior, that they had no rights which the white man was bound to respect; and that the negro might justly and lawfully be reduced to slavery for his benefit.[9]

While Justice Scalia and others have painted *Dred Scott* as the progenitor of substantive due process,[10] Christopher Eisgruber[11] and Cass Sunstein have demolished that fiction. As Sunstein put it, "*Dred Scott* was very much and very self-consciously an 'originalist' opinion—that is, it purported to draw nearly all of its support from the views of the framers. . . ."[12] On the key issue of whether Dred Scott was a citizen (who could therefore invoke the federal courts' diversity jurisdiction to sue his purported owner), Taney said of the late eighteenth century:

> On the contrary, [African-Americans] were at that time considered as a subordinate and inferior class of beings, who had been subjugated by the dominant race, and whether emancipated or not, yet remained subject to their authority, and had no rights or privileges but such as those who held the power and the Government might choose to grant them.[13]

And what was the Court to make of this history? Taney's answer was "a credo to warm the hearts of originalists":[14]

> If any of [the Constitution's] provisions are deemed unjust, there is a mode prescribed in the instrument itself by which it may be amended; but while it remains unaltered, it must be construed now as it was understood at the time of its adoption. . . . [I]t speaks not only in the same words, but the same meaning and intent with which it spoke when it came from the hands of its framers. . . . Any other rule of construction would abrogate the judicial character of this court, and make it the mere reflex of the popular opinion or passion of the day.[15]

Taney stayed true to the framers' initial compromises over slavery, which enshrined and thus granted constitutional legitimacy to the institution. In so doing, he stripped his generation of the flexibility to meet new national circumstances, including the westward expansion and slavery's place in it and the impact of the cotton gin on the conventional wisdom that slavery would wither on the vine of its own unprofitability.[16] Taney's efforts placed the Court high on the list of factors contributing to the inevitability of the Civil War.[17]

Similarly, the Court's rigid originalism incited the constitutional confrontation of 1936–37, which culminated in Franklin Roosevelt's "court-packing" plan as his means of overcoming the Court's pattern of invalidating the New Deal legislation upon which his administration was built. While the Court of the 1930s has been seen as the font of substantive due process—"Lochnerism" run amok—rather than of originalism, in the most important respect leading to the crisis, its position was very much originalist: the limited scope of the federal government's authority under the Commerce Clause. No less an originalist than Clarence Thomas has called for a return to the pre-1937 Court's view that the "substantial effects" of an activity on commerce do not trigger Congress's regulatory authority.[18]

On the other side of the coin, the Court has averted constitutional crises when it has transcended originalism and interpreted the grand, broad phrases of the Constitution as having a meaning for and of the time. Chief Justice Marshall's most crucial assertions of the national government's broad authority ring with bold pronouncements of the need to interpret the Constitution so that the government has means at its disposal to exercise its powers in order to meet the demands placed on it. *McCulloch v. Maryland* exemplifies this approach:

> [A] government, entrusted with such ample powers, on the due execution of which the happiness and prosperity of the nation so vitally depends, must also be entrusted with ample means for their execution.[19]

The newly growing nation, Marshall pointed out in archetypal recognition-based prose, depended on the government's ability to carry out its role in the national economy through the operations of a national bank:

Throughout this vast republic, from the St. Croix to the Gulf of Mexico, from the Atlantic to the Pacific, revenue is to be collected and expended, armies are to be marched and supported. The exigencies of the nation may require that the treasure raised in the north should be transported to the south. . . . Is that construction of the constitution to be preferred which would render these operations difficult, hazardous, or expensive?[20]

In this century, *Brown v. Board of Education* and *Loving v. Virginia* serve as Exhibits One and Two of the necessity for non-originalist constitutional interpretation. The systematic denial of civil rights in the first half of the twentieth century nearly matched slavery as a threat to constitutional legitimacy. As it had been in 1850 (try to imagine anything like the Fourteenth Amendment being ratified prior to the Civil War), the federalist institutions and limitations built into the Constitution rendered its textual mechanisms for change useless in 1950 on the issues of racial justice. Neither a specific constitutional ban on state antimiscegenation laws nor on segregated schools could have been ratified by three-fourths of the states at the time the Supreme Court decided *Loving* and *Brown*. Only the courts stood able to bring about these constitutional transformations, and then only because the Warren Court assumed the responsibility of interpretive transformation.

The point is simply that the balance of costs and benefits that led the framers to each choice they made has changed, and the more closely we lash ourselves to their choices, the less flexibility we have to readjust that balance. Originalism ties us especially closely. That may be a price we should pay, but this is not self-evidently so. Originalists should bear the burden of persuading the rest of us that their approach truly "delivers the goods" they promise before we sacrifice interpretive flexibility.

CONSTRAINT: A VIRTUE PARTICULAR TO ORIGINALISM?

I accept the claim that originalists, even bad ones, are at least sometimes constrained by their approach to reach results with which they are not comfortable. The most famous case is probably *Texas v. Johnson*,[21] in which Justice Scalia provided the crucial fifth vote to strike down a state

law banning flag burning as a violation of the First Amendment. Less famously, Justice Scalia took the position in *Maryland v. Craig*[22] that
statutes permitting child sex abuse victims to testify without having to
be in the same room as the defendant violate the Confrontation Clause.
Although his vigorous dissent in that case leaves room for doubt
whether he would regard that outcome as unfortunate,[23] let us assume
that, were the Constitution his to write from scratch, Justice Scalia
would include a proviso for closed-circuit testimony by children at the
discretion of trial judges. But, as he said in classic originalist prose:

> I have no need to defend the value of confrontation, because the Court
> has no authority to question it. It is not within our charge to speculate
> that, "where face-to-face confrontation causes significant emotional dis-
> tress in a child witness," confrontation might "in fact disserve the Con-
> frontation Clause's truth-seeking goal." If so, that is a defect in the Con-
> stitution—which should be amended by the procedures provided for
> such an eventuality, but cannot be corrected by judicial pronouncement
> that it is archaic, contrary to "widespread belief," and thus null and void.[24]

Craig might therefore be, like *Johnson*, an occasion where an originalist
left his individual preferences at home as his method says he should.

More recently, the conservatives gave another compelling example of
fidelity to originalist principles in the face of a powerful political incentive. In *United States v. Hubbell*,[25] the Court dealt with the Self-Incrimination Clause in the context of a key participant in the dramatic confrontation between Whitewater Independent Counsel Kenneth Starr
and President Bill Clinton. Former Justice Department official and Clinton friend Webster Hubbell had been indicted by Starr several times, the
final time after Starr was unsatisfied with the information and coopera-
tion Hubbell provided under a prior plea agreement. Seeking to determine whether Hubbell's perceived failure to "give up the goods" had resulted from payoffs from Clinton associates, Starr subpoenaed documents relating to Hubbell's finances. When Hubbell asserted his Fifth
Amendment right against self-incrimination, the Independent Counsel
granted him immunity.

Despite this immunity, Starr used the information contained in the
documents to secure an indictment against Hubbell for "tax-related

crimes and mail and wire fraud."[26] Ordinarily, material contained in documents is not considered "testimonial" and hence is not subject to the constitutional privilege. In some cases, however, the very act of producing the documents has testimonial significance; the production itself effectively states the individual's belief in the existence, validity, and nature of the documents. The Fifth Amendment bars compulsory production when it has such testimonial significance. This is known as the "act-of-production" doctrine.

In *Hubbell*, the Court held that use of the documents would violate the Self-Incrimination Clause because it would have been based at least in part on the testimonial quality of Hubbell's act of production. This was a significant setback for the Independent Counsel's office.

The political destruction of Bill Clinton was a continuing crusade for much of the conservative right in American politics. A political vote by Scalia and Thomas in this instance would have been to side with the Independent Counsel. Nevertheless, Justices Thomas and Scalia concurred with the Court's ruling in *Hubbell*, setting forth an originalist argument that went even further than the majority.

In fact, their performance in *Hubbell* was apolitical at another level as well. Their view questioned the traditional rule that use of documents prepared by an individual is not testimonial unless the act-of-production doctrine applies. The opinion, written by Thomas, suggested that there is "substantial support" for the view that when the Fifth Amendment was first added to the Constitution, "the term 'witness' meant a person who gives or furnishes evidence,"[27] including evidence via the production of documents. If adopted by the Court, this rule would substantially expand suspects' rights during criminal investigations, making police and prosecutorial work that much more difficult.

In other words, the proposed rule would be just the sort of "pro-defendant" criminal procedure "technicality" conservatives have been fuming about for nearly 40 years. It is thus to their credit that Thomas and Scalia called upon the Court to reconsider the act-of-production rule on originalist grounds. Of course, we don't know if either or both men would be displeased by this particular result, so I may be finding methodological constraint where none exists. But in light of the politics of a ruling in favor of Webster Hubbell, and since the general terrain at the intersection of politics and law would deem their position a "liberal" rule, it seems fair to deem this an instance where originalism came before politics or personal preferences for Thomas and Scalia.

Acknowledging the originalist fidelity that seemed to be on display in *Johnson, Craig*, and *Hubbell*, and acknowledging that it shows originalism has at least some constraining effect on judges, originalists are still left with a hole in their position. Their claim is not just that their method is constraining, but that it is *uniquely* constraining. Odd, then, that almost every instance of originalist virtue is also an occasion for *non-originalist* virtue.

Consider the flag-burning issue decided in *Texas v. Johnson*. Justice Scalia was part of a five-member majority in *Johnson*, a majority that included some very prominent non-originalists. Are we to understand that flag burning is somehow anathema only to an originalist? To the contrary; Justice Brennan's vote is evidence that he too was willing to abide unpalatable results in the service of the First Amendment, as he made clear in his opinion for the Court in *Johnson*:

> The way to preserve the flag's special role is not to punish those who feel differently about these matters. It is to persuade them that they are wrong. . . . And, precisely because it is our flag that is involved, one's response to the flag burner may exploit the uniquely persuasive power of the flag itself. We can imagine no more appropriate response to burning a flag than waving one's own, no better way to counter a flag burner's message than by saluting the flag that burns, no surer means of preserving the dignity even of the flag that burned than by—as one witness here did—according its remains a respectful burial. We do not consecrate the flag by punishing its desecration, for in doing so we dilute the freedom that this cherished emblem represents.[28]

While it was not a commitment to originalism that obliged Justice Brennan (not to mention Justices Marshall, Blackmun, and Kennedy) to vote as he did, he plainly refused to make an exception to the First Amendment's rule of freedom of expression for the flag. His stance reflected not support for flag burning, but the constraining effect of Brennan's own methodological imperatives.

Similarly, Justice Scalia's dissent in *Craig* was joined by three other, non-originalist Justices. There is no basis for believing that they were any happier with the prospect of forcing young victims of sexual abuse to face their tormentors. But like Justice Scalia, they were *constrained* by their own views of proper constitutional interpretation to vote as they did.

Nor can the votes of those other Justices be attributed to a rare flash of originalist insight. In *Craig*, it is true, the others joined Justice Scalia's generally originalist dissent. However, Justice Brennan's majority opinion in *Johnson* was entirely consistent with Brennan's approach to constitutional interpretation. He utilized a balancing test, weighing the state's asserted interests against those of the individual in expressing himself by burning the flag, just the sort of approach Justice Scalia tries wherever possible to avoid. Brennan's opinion also moved through the intricacies of the Court's numerous First Amendment tests, depending on whether the speech was "pure" speech or "expressive conduct," whether it was likely to incite a breach of the peace or constituted "fighting words," and whether the state's regulation of the speech was "content-based."

This insight into Justice Brennan's performance in *Johnson* is revealing. Once we acknowledge that he was no great fan of flag burning, and appreciate that his vote was as much the product of constraint as Scalia's, we can also see that the rigorous test-based approach of modern non-originalists like Brennan is the constraining force. The originalists have criticized this test-based aspect of the Court's modern jurisprudence, arguing that it leaves the Court to apply tests with "nothing more than policy intuition[s] to support [them]," rather than interpreting the actual Constitution itself.[29] For non-originalists, however, it is applying these tests that affords the predictability the originalists claim can be found only in jurisprudence bound by the original understanding.[30]

It is, after all, not just constraint the originalists are after; it is relative certainty of meaning. Their concern about potentially arbitrary judges is matched by their worry over the indeterminacy of language; hence the need for the original understanding to provide the meaning for words that might otherwise be open to numerous translations, none more presumptively legitimate than the rest. Justice Brennan's test-based approach was both his source of constraint and his solution to the problem of finding the correct meaning among several or many.

Originalists are simply wrong to suggest that their approach either uniquely constrains judges or anchors interpretation in the stormy seas of indeterminacy. Judges spanning the spectrum have often been compelled to live with results they themselves find abhorrent. Indeed, some of the very cases the originalists point to with pride are also examples of non-originalists being constrained by interpretive fidelity. It's just not fidelity to the approach the originalists prefer. Anchors come in many shapes, and there is no evidence that the particular one preferred by originalists is the best one at keeping the constitutional boat in place.

I'VE GOT A BRIDGE I'D LIKE TO SELL YOU . . .

A real, honest-to-goodness constraining effect is essential to any defense of originalism. The claim made on its behalf is that it bears the load placed upon on it by the counter-majoritarian difficulty, finding sufficient support in the legitimacy of the constitutional framing to hold up against the constant wear of decisions made by unelected judges. Judges must always keep to that bridge, which means they must accept that they will arrive only where it takes them. They may be tempted by other bridges, leading other places, but those spans will collapse into the water below.

But the originalist bridge is not strong enough either. Perhaps Justice Scalia takes comfort in the claim that it is the strongest of all the unsafe spans, but accepting his arguments means leaving constitutional interpretation bereft of a truly safe span: a democratically legitimate basis for judicial review.

For at least the past 40 years, courts and constitutional scholars have been preoccupied with the counter-majoritarian difficulty.[31] They see judicial review as a questionable practice because it imposes the will of unelected, life-tenured judges on the democratically elected institutions and, hence, on the peoples' right to govern ourselves.

Originalists claim to have resolved it. Their claim starts with a crucial premise: Judges may not use their authority to impose their own personal views on the rest of us. Originalists offer their method as the way to prevent them from doing so, because it commits judges to impose something other than their own personal preferences: the views of the founders. The originalists' injunction to the judges is to speak not for themselves but for James Madison and Alexander Hamilton.[32]

Justice Scalia retreats from the difficult task of defending originalism on this basis, claiming the more modest benefit that his method does not "cater to" judges' personal preferences. As I have shown, however, Justice Brennan's test-based approach can persuasively claim the same virtue: It caters not to a judge's personal views but to the outcome dictated by the applicable test.

The truth is that these methods are equally susceptible to manipulation by results-oriented judges. As I argued in the first five chapters, examples abound of "originalist," politically conservative judges (including Justice Scalia) reaching politically conservative, non-originalist results. And, no doubt, an equally strong case could be made that the multi-part tests characteristic of Justice Brennan's jurisprudence can be and have been manipulated by judges to reach results politically palatable to them.

What does this show? Under *either* approach it is possible for judges to find their hearts' desire in the Constitution, and under either approach they frequently have taken advantage of the opportunity. The claim that originalism is (somehow) somewhat more constraining is not borne out by the evidence.

More important, once it is acknowledged that non-originalist methods have some power to compel judges to reach unpalatable results, it becomes clear that they, no less than originalism, avoid "catering to" personal or political whims. In light of this insight, it is apparent that the broader claim Scalia disclaims is the one he *must* make to establish some advantage for originalism. It simply is not enough that originalism does not "cater to" the impulse to cut the Constitution to fit the individual judge's personal fashions. If that is all originalism offers, it is indistinguishable from non-originalism. We are, in short, back where we began, confronting the counter-majoritarian difficulty with no safe bridge beneath our feet.

Permit me one further example. The Court faced the counter-majoritarian difficulty when, in 1998, it decided *Eastern Enterprises v. Apfel*.[33] *Apfel* was a landmark: the first case since the New Deal in which the Court declared a federal economic regulatory statute unconstitutional under the Takings Clause.[34] The Court did this not in a case involving an actual physical expropriation of property by the federal government,[35] but instead where the government had purportedly taken property through regulation. As I discussed earlier, the entire regulatory takings doctrine finds no support in the original understanding. Justices Thomas and Scalia, both of whom joined Justice O'Connor's plurality opinion, thus assumed the counter-majoritarian responsibility of invalidating the will of the people, expressed through Congress, *without the original understanding as a basis for doing so.*

The facts of *Apfel* were complex, but reduced to their essence, they involved the entreaty of Eastern Enterprises, which had been a coal mining company until 1963. At that time, it created a subsidiary, the "Eastern Associated Coal Company," which "assume[d] all of Eastern's liabilities arising out of coal mining and marketing operations in exchange for Eastern's receipt of EACC's stock."[36] From 1965 to 1987, Eastern received over $100 million in dividends from its EACC stock.

On the basis of this transfer of assets, Eastern was able successfully to assert before the Supreme Court that it was not a coal company in 1974. Why did it care? Because it was in 1974 that, for the first time, the health benefit plan between the United Mine Workers and the coal industry formally promised health benefits for retirees.[37] For this reason, it was a "taking" when in 1992 Congress rendered Eastern liable for the benefits due to retirees whom Eastern had employed prior to 1963 (and their widows). When it was a "coal company," Eastern had made no promise to pay those benefits.

This was not only a regulatory taking rather than an actual physical taking, but as Justice Kennedy pointed out in his dissenting opinion:

> The Coal Act imposes a staggering financial burden on the petitioner, Eastern Enterprises, but it regulates the former mine owner without regard to property. It does not operate upon or alter an identified property interest, and it is not applicable to or measured by a property interest. The Coal Act does not appropriate, transfer, or encumber an estate in land (e.g., a lien on a particular piece of property), a valuable interest in an intangible (e.g., intellectual property), or even a bank account or accrued interest. The law simply imposes an obligation to perform an act, the payment of benefits. The statute is indifferent as to how the regulated entity elects to comply or the property it uses to do so. To the extent it affects

property interests, it does so in a manner similar to many laws; but until today, none were thought to constitute takings.[38]

So it was doubtful this was a taking within the framers' understanding of that concept, and it was doubtful the case involved the sort of property interest they envisioned could be "taken." If in these circumstances the originalists could vote to overturn the democratic choice of the Congress, then they have left the counter-majoritarian difficulty no less imposing than they found it.

The case for originalism founders in three ways. As our history bears out, the method carries with it significant costs in terms of interpretive flexibility. Instances wherein the Court adhered doggedly to originalism in the face of social upheaval have stood as some of the Court's, and the nation's, worst moments. In light of this price, originalists must bear the burden of demonstrating countervailing benefits. This they cannot do. The suggestion that we get more in the way of judicial constraint is not borne out by the evidence, which seems to show as many constrained non-originalists as there are originalists, and (worse) too many instances of unconstrained originalists. In sum, originalism fails to meet the challenge posed by the counter-majoritarian difficulty.

CHAPTER SEVEN

ANY MORE SUCH VICTORIES . . .

In the prior chapter, I attempted to show that originalism is a poor solution to the counter-majoritarian difficulty. It does not constrain judges any more than other interpretive approaches do, and what little value it provides comes at a very high price. But even if I am wrong as to all of that (even, that is, if originalism is the vaccine that inoculates judicial review from the counter-majoritarian difficulty), there remains another, insuperable problem. In attempting to address the counter-majoritarian difficulty, originalists have been aiming at the wrong target all along. They (and we) have largely ignored the relationship between judicial review and a more fundamental problem: the anti-democratic origins of the Constitution itself.[1] Those origins are the *real* threat to constitutional legitimacy, and in meeting it originalism is the worst possible approach. An originalist "triumph" over the counter-majoritarian difficulty would be the most Pyrrhic, and costly, of victories.

In making this case, I intend first to advance the proposition in the abstract: A Constitution can be democratically illegitimate to a sufficient extent that judicial review is a less dangerous threat to its legitimacy than one or more of its other aspects (its origins, its allocation of powers, etc.). In addition, I will argue that judicial review might, in the right conditions, actually increase overall legitimacy. Then I will make the case that ours is such a Constitution, and that those conditions exist in the United States.

CAN JUDICIAL REVIEW BE THE LEAST OF A CONSTITUTION'S PROBLEMS?

Alabama enacted a new Constitution in 1901. That document was the product of a state Constitutional Convention, presided over by Mr. John

Knox. Knox set the agenda that would guide the Convention's work in his opening address: "And what is it that we want to do? Why it is within the limits imposed by the Federal Constitution, to establish white supremacy in this State."[2]

Among the actions the Convention took was to delete Article I, Section 2 of the 1875 Constitution, which had provided that "all persons resident in this state . . . are hereby declared citizens of the State of Alabama, possessing equal civil and political rights."[3] Moreover, the Convention repeatedly rejected proposals to include the text of the 1875 equal protection provision.[4] The resulting absence of an equal protection guarantee has not changed in the ensuing century.

This history gained contemporary notoriety in the astonishing case of *Ex Parte Melof*, a case decided by the Alabama Supreme Court in 1999, in which the plaintiffs tried to persuade that court that the state Constitution guaranteed them the right to equal protection of the laws. The author of the majority opinion, Justice Houston, acknowledged that the Constitution was the product of "racist motives,"[5] and he agreed that the Convention that gave it life was a prominent feature of Alabama's "egregious or embarrassing" history.

Can such a Constitution pretend to democratic legitimacy? Perhaps if all Alabamians had participated fully and equally in its adoption we might fairly regard their decision as unfortunate and one to be rectified, but not as a dilemma in democratic legitimacy. But of course the racism of 1901 cannot be validated by participatory democracy, because the Convention that year was the culmination of the systematic removal of African-Americans from every aspect of governmental decision-making, from wielding legislative power to voting[6] to sitting on juries. Adoption of the 1901 Constitution, including its removal of a guarantee of equal protection of the laws, was possible because it was enacted exclusively by racist whites. Its effect was immediate and overwhelming: black voter registration "plummeted from 180,000 in 1900 to 3,000 in 1903. . . ."[7]

I will leave for the next chapter the rest of the *Melof* story. For now, my point is simply that the undemocratic origins of that Constitution, manifested in the motives and actions of the conventioneers, are manifestly a threat to democratic legitimacy. And it does not matter in the slightest whether the Alabama Constitution provides for judicial review;

legitimacy is a function of factors other than the relationship of the judiciary to the rest of the government.

Thus, if judicial review is at one level counter-majoritarian and hence problematic, that is nevertheless only one dimension of the inquiry we must undertake to evaluate its net impact on the democratic legitimacy of our constitutional system. After all, judicial review within any system of government does not stand in isolation; it is more or less democratic depending on factors like the composition of the judiciary (other things being equal, an elective judiciary presents fewer and less thorny problems) and the nature of the remainder of the government. A judiciary, even unelected, with the power of judicial review to overturn the edicts of an otherwise unconstrained tyrant would be a net plus for democratic legitimacy, at least if we are persuaded by James Madison's insights into the value of checks and balances.

Moreover, the way courts exercise the power of judicial review makes a big difference in whether the power can be justified in democratic theory. Originalists, of all people, cannot quarrel with this proposition, since their central premise is that a jurisprudence based on the original understanding is more legitimate than a jurisprudence framed around a "living Constitution." Interpretive method makes a difference.

So does the decision-making process. To the extent we consider open, public decision-making democratically preferable, courts that deliberate in the open, accept public comment and input, and explain the basis for their decisions are superior to closed, secretive tribunals.

But are they, really? Our Supreme Court gets at best a mixed grade on the question of open decision-making. Briefs submitted by parties are public documents, and oral arguments are open to the public. The Justices explain themselves in written opinions. So far, so good. On the other hand, the Court is not as "open to the public" as modern technology and conditions would permit; its proceedings are not televised or broadcast in any way and the courtroom has seats only for a tiny audience of citizens (tiny enough that observers cannot even stay for the full argument of even a single case before they are ushered out to make room for others). At least some of the Justices were infuriated when law professor Peter Irons had the temerity to publish transcripts and sell them together with audio tapes of oral arguments in some of the landmark cases of the past 40 years. The Court does not accept general public comments or lobbying. Most importantly, the Court's deliberations are closed to the public, and no formal record is published or even kept of the post-argument conferences.

Yet we have heard no outcry from constitutional conservatives over the Supreme Court's secretive decision-making process. There has been no call for the Court's decision conferences even to be transcribed, much less broadcast. And for good reason: pure democratic theory notwithstanding, courts as institutions require and traditionally have utilized secretive deliberation—juries and appellate courts retire to make their decisions behind closed doors, and trial judges ordinarily do the same.

What should we make of this? Courts are democracy's paradoxical institution: They are operationally problematic, if not downright antidemocratic, but they are systemically essential. That is, courts function in ways that are unrepresentative and secretive, but without them the rest of the system breaks down. We can think of this mathematically. In the best of all possible worlds, the Constitution would be perfectly legitimate: democratically enacted, respecting individual rights, assuring equality before the law, and providing a mechanism for democratic governance through representative institutions. If such "pure" representative government rates a 100, then the workings of courts move us away from that perfect score—to a 90, perhaps, depending on how the courts operate. But we have to take that "hit" on our perfect score, since without the courts, the best score we could obtain would be a 50—or actually, a lot less than 50. Without courts, criminal laws could not be enforced to permit the civil society and its democratic institutions to operate freely; government officials would not be constrained by an institution with legal authority to limit their conduct. Without courts, or at least some court-like institution performing their functions, it is impossible to imagine how democratic society could exist.

This has implications for interpretive method as well. Even if the originalists are correct that we take a legitimacy "hit" for non-originalist constitutional interpretation, that penalty might still leave us in a position of maximized legitimacy. Non-originalist interpretation might knock us down from a 90 (the best we can get once we have courts at all) to an 80.

An originalist might argue that the penalty is much higher, but I am aware of no originalist who believes the Constitution as it has been non-originally interpreted is not legitimate at all.[8] For all his vigor in dissent, Justice Scalia has yet to claim the Court has opened the door to justifiable armed revolution. Once we agree the penalty for non-originalist interpretation is not 100 percent, then the possibility exists that the penalty is worth paying compared to the alternative.

If there are serious issues surrounding enactment of the Constitution and the substance of its original terms, issues that would result in a legitimacy "score" of 70, and if non-originalist interpretation would reduce or eliminate that penalty, then we should take the deal: Accept the penalty which leaves us at 80 in order to avert the even worse outcome of a more substantial reduction to 70.

Think about Alabama. Its Constitution does not start out with a 100; let us arbitrarily and generously assign it a 70. That score is due to the origins of the Constitution, and the demographics and intent of its framers. We have assumed that judicial review itself (-10), and especially non-originalist interpretation (-10), also move us away from the perfect legitimacy score of 100, and we're stuck with an 80. But if the court providing a non-originalist interpretation removes or ameliorates some of the taint of the origins, the result might be an 80, or a 75; in any event, higher than originalism's depressing 70.

Traditional originalists take and accept the legitimacy of the Constitution they are interpreting as a starting point, and so for them it is natural to see interpretation based on anything other than the original understanding as detracting from that legitimacy. But if we see the situation differently, and posit a Constitution of dubious legitimacy *because of the original understanding*, then the implications of interpretive method for constitutional legitimacy turn upside-down.

IS JUDICIAL REVIEW THE LEAST OF OUR CONSTITUTION'S PROBLEMS?

Ours is not the Alabama Constitution, of course. Nevertheless, the circumstances of its adoption and its substance satisfy the first necessary premise of my argument: There are serious issues surrounding its contemporary legitimacy. This may seem a radical statement, but accepting it requires no more of us than to acknowledge the difference between constitutional aspiration and constitutional reality. The great core principles animating the Constitution are not reflected in every provision, and they are downright contradicted in some provisions. Equality is the constitutional aspiration; the limitations on representativeness and equality built into the Constitution were (and in many ways remain) the constitutional reality. Only at the aspirational level is the Constitution perfectly legitimate; at the section-by-section level at which constitutional decision-making takes place it often is not.

The Constitution of 1789 is not a wellspring of legitimacy, as the originalists suppose it to be. It suffers from two devastating flaws: the racist compromises woven into the document, and the fact that the framers were grossly unrepresentative of the population for whom they established a government. Each of these problems is exacerbated by the barriers to amendment contained in Article V; it is the effect of Article V that renders transformation by interpretation crucial.

As to the first flaw in our constitutional design, history has not judged the Philadelphia Convention kindly on matters of race. Professor Derrick Bell stated the case directly and accurately when he wrote, "[T]he racial grief that persists today . . . originated in the slavery institutionalized in the [Constitution]." And, he rhetorically asked the framers, "Is this . . . an achievement for which you wish to be remembered?"[9]

It is enough to observe that the choice to count slaves as 60 percent of a human being for purposes of apportioning congressional seats accomplished the amazing feat of being offensive both for treating individual human beings as less than a full person and for treating them as if they counted at all when they had no say in electing "their" representatives.[10] At best, this abomination is usually defended only on the basis of cruel necessity, unavoidable if a union was to be formed.

On the other hand, Professor Cass Sunstein has discerned in the Three-Fifths Compromise a heretofore undiscovered virtue: It "create[d] an incentive to free slaves, by giving slave states more political power if they became nonslave states."[11] How odd, then, that not a single slave state perceived this easy path to political influence and abolished slavery. Perhaps they knew that if they freed slaves, there was no reason to believe those slaves would stick around to be counted as Georgians or South Carolinians at the next census. If they left, of course, abolition would reduce rather than enhance the state's political power.[12]

More: By Sunstein's reasoning we must assume that by freeing the slaves, Abraham Lincoln's Emancipation Proclamation was intended to give the confederate states enhanced political influence once they returned to the union! The point is that the Three-Fifths Compromise gave the slave states political power unwarranted by the driving principle of the revolution (government without representation is tyranny) *without* abolishing slavery. If Sunstein is correct that the Constitution did not "reflect any judgment that a slave is just 3/5 of a 'person,'"[13] it is only because it rendered the even more awful judgment that a person could be both a master's property and an important source of her owner's political power.

Then, too, consider Article I, Section 9, which denied to Congress the authority to prohibit the slave trade until 1808. Notwithstanding Professor Sunstein's odd proclamation that this clause "is hardly an endorsement of slavery,"[14] it in fact endowed slavery with unique constitutional protection, limiting Congress's power only in this area among all the myriad types of interstate and international commerce. Granting that the protection expired after two decades, the fact remains that it was given only to slavery.

Finally, the Fugitive Slave Clause, Article I, Section 3, required that free states return escaped slaves to their owners. Sunstein calls this an "extremely limited" clause, because "it does not say anything about the obligations of states to respect slave-owners who voluntarily come, with their slaves, into nonslave states."[15] Acknowledging this "limitation," which undoubtedly limited a slave owner's property rights to some degree (he could bring money or a chattel—but sometimes not a slave—into a neighboring state without worrying about losing his ownership of it), it remains true that the Fugitive Slave Clause left the slave owner with control over his continuing ownership of this "property": he merely had to refrain from bringing the slave into the nonslave state. So long as he did so, the slave's own entry into that state would avail him or her nothing.

Of course, one can see the Civil War and the resulting amendments as "curing" the illegitimacy of this aspect of the founding. And it is true that originalist jurists are not called upon to give life to the slavery clauses of the original Constitution. Nevertheless, the Civil War amendments have proved an imperfect cure for what ails the originalist Constitution. As I have shown, the originalist Fourteenth Amendment permitted (and, if given voice, would permit today) antimiscegenation laws and segregated schools. Non-originalist jurisprudence of the last half-century has been a vital booster shot to permit the "cure" of the 1860s to rid us of the very worst lingering symptoms—state-sanctioned, overt racial separation—of the originalist disease.

Moreover, putting the slavery clauses to one side, the Constitution accommodated slavery in more than the most obvious ways, and most importantly did so in ways still given life by a jurisprudence of original understanding. And, I should add, these aspects of the Constitution are not dealt with adequately even by traditional, non-originalist interpretive methods.

First, while the Three-Fifths Compromise itself has no modern-day application, it was intrinsically linked to another constitutional provision still very much with us. As Professor Bruce Ackerman has recently shown, Article I, § 2 of the Constitution was part and parcel of the founders' compromise with slavery. That section requires that direct taxes (like the seats in the House of Representatives) "shall be apportioned among the several States . . . according to their respective Numbers." Section 9 of the same Article makes the point even clearer, stating, "No Capitation, or other direct, Tax shall be laid, unless in Proportion to the Census. . . ."[16] The effect of these provisions is that anything that constitutes a "direct tax" must be apportioned by population, not by wealth or income or any other criterion. Consider two states of equal population:

	Population	Avg. Income
STATE A	1,000,000	$25,000
STATE B	1,000,000	$50,000

The tax would have to be borne equally by the two states, meaning that the tax burden for each person in State A (as a percentage of income) would be twice as high as the burden in State B. It would, in other words, require that any direct tax be enormously regressive in practice.

And how is this constitutional oddity a legacy of slavery? The southern states' insistence on enhanced representation in Congress based on their slave populations led to an irrefutable response: If the rallying cry of the Revolution had been "no taxation without representation," then the South could not object to being taxed commensurate with their population—the *full* population they were insisting be counted for purposes of apportioning seats in the House of Representatives.[17]

It grows worse. While in the abstract the direct tax/apportionment provisions can be seen as the price the South was compelled to pay for the Three-Fifths Compromise, they actually benefitted the South and its slave-based economy. As Justice William Paterson attested in the early case *Hylton v. United States,*

> The provision was made in favor of the southern states. They possessed a large number of slaves; they had extensive tracts of territory, thinly settled, and not very productive. . . . The southern states, if no provision had been introduced in the Constitution, would have been wholly at the mercy of the other states. Congress, in such case, might tax slaves, at discretion or arbitrarily, and land in every part of the Union after the same rate or measure; so much a head in the first instance, and so much an acre, in the second.[18]

This understanding of the direct tax provision led the Court to a narrow construction, finding the set of taxes subject to its requirements almost null, beyond an actual capitation tax.[19]

The Constitution's many protections of private property must be understood as standing in the shadows cast by a time in which "private property" included human beings. That is not to say that protection of slavery was the driving force behind inclusion of the Contracts Clause, the Takings Clause, and "property" in the Due Process Clause. But the "origins of property rights in the United States are rooted in racial domination,"[20] and as to the Constitution specifically the importance some of the framers attached to the protection of property rights against federal interference was linked to their fear that nonslave states would come to dominate the federal government and use its powers to infringe the institution.[21] The South Carolina delegation made the link explicit: "[T]he security the Southern states want is that their negroes may not be taken from them."[22]

And those fears were, at least to a degree, justified. Robert Cover and others have written extensively about the dilemma of northern judges compelled to assist slave owners. Most often, this took the form of enforcement of the Fugitive Slave Clause, but the more general constitutional protections of private property played a role as well. These judges often expressed their personal anguish over these cases, but insisted that the obligations of their office, and the Constitution's plain terms, left them no choice. If we take them at their word, we must suppose that absent these provisions, slavery would not have enjoyed the reluctant support of the northern judiciary.

The association between property (and hence the Constitution) and racism is not of mere historical concern. Professor Cheryl Harris's influential article, *Whiteness as Property*, explored the ways in which the law has invested racial status as "white" with a wide range of advantages and entitlements, which together can best be understood as the equivalent of vested property rights. As she explained:

> Whiteness as property continues to perpetuate racial subordination . . . and, indeed, is part of the protection that the court extends to whites' settled expectations of continued privilege.[23]

Ironically, the non-originalist, "color-blind" affirmative action jurisprudence crafted by the Court's conservative wing is also a primary example of how the law operates, even today, to make status in the superordinated racial group a form of property.[24]

Does this mean the protections in the Constitution for private property are themselves illegitimate? Of course not. Their place in our tradition of respected rights, crucial to the preservation of liberty and the pursuit of happiness, is secure. And this book is about constitutional interpretation, not about possible constitutional amendments; no reasonable interpretive method could pretend the property protections in the Due Process Clauses, the Contracts Clause, the Just Compensation Clause, etc., do not exist. But respecting that tradition and the limits of reasonable interpretation does not require us to ignore the mixed pedigree of the constitutional property right we respect today, nor the motivations that contributed to their inclusion in the Constitution. To the contrary, our choice of interpretive method should be guided by keen awareness of that history, in ways I will explain in greater detail in the next chapter.

Beyond the clauses protecting private property, the Constitution also accommodated slavery by its very structure. The two most significant accommodations were the very notion of federalism, and its most important expression, the Great Compromise creating a legislative upper house in which every state, large or small, would receive equal representation. We do well to recall that federalism has a more pejorative synonym: "States' rights," the slogan of segregationists across the centuries of American history. Even as ardent a defender of federalism as Justice Thomas admits:

> Federalism has sometimes been used to justify the most terrible tragedies ever inflicted by Americans upon Americans, slavery and segregation. For that reason, the idea of state sovereignty has acquired a negative connotation.[25]

But federalism has not just been *used* for racist ends. It was *devised* largely to empower Southern states to prevent the federal government from interfering with the institution of slavery.[26]

Akhil Amar has taken a decidedly different view of federalism, linking it not with slavery but with protection of individual liberty. The "states'-rights tradition," Amar writes, was based on "the ability of local governments to protect citizens against abuses by central authorities."[27] For the founders, "states' rights and citizens' rights were seen as complementary rather than conflicting."[28]

The problem with this view is what it doesn't say. Certainly, federalism was seen as a key protection for "citizens" against potential abuse by the untested central government the Constitution was creating. But as *Dred Scott* reinforced 60 years later, blacks were not among the "citizens" enjoying that protection. Had their voices been heard at the founding, a very different experience with the virtues of local and state government would have informed the debate, and a quite different balance between state and federal authority drawn. Professor Amar virtually concedes as much, noting with less than accurate understatement that on the question of slavery, "states did not shine." To the contrary, as he more accurately observes, "Slavery was almost exclusively a creature of state law."[29] Because of their exclusion from the deliberative process, only the experience of those who saw local government as a bulwark against oppression—rather than as the oppressor—was heard.

Worse still, blacks were not only not heard; protection of their rights and interests (i.e., abolition of or interference with slavery) was one of the potential acts many of the "citizens" felt constituted the "abuse" about which they were most worried. Even Amar acknowledges:

> Sadly, *states' rights* and *federalism* have often served as code words for racial injustice and disregard for the rights of local minorities—code words for a world-view far closer to Jefferson Davis's than James Madison's.[30]

What Amar ignores is that even Madison's world view, or at least that of his generation, was not that different from Davis's when it came to matters of "racial injustice" and "disregard for the rights of local minorities." To the contrary, southern assertions of the limits of federal authority from the founding of the Constitution all the way to the Civil War always had preservation of slavery at their heart.[31]

Perhaps I am attacking a ghost. One could concede that federalism as it existed at the initial founding was an illegitimate balance because it included slavery as one of the interests entitled to consideration in drawing the balance, but proclaim it a moot point. In two important ways, the Fourteenth Amendment restruck the balance and created a better, legitimized federalism. First, it incorporated the bill of rights so that it applied to the states. Second, its fifth section empowered Congress to enforce the requirements of the Amendment against the states, producing a significantly different balance of power between Washington, D.C. and the state capitals.

As for incorporation, Professor Amar sees it as the signal change of the Civil War era. While he doesn't speak in terms of legitimation, I don't think it overreads him to say he regards it as crucial to creating a democratically legitimate constitutional regime (or at least restoring legitimacy to a regime gone badly wrong). Amar writes:

> As it had for the Anti-Federalists in the 1780s, the Bill [of Rights] encompassed for Republicans in the 1860s an armory of indispensable weapons against a tyranny that people had seen with their own eyes. . . . Just as the

price of peace and union in 1789 was a bill of rights against the center, so the price of peace and (re)union in 1866 was a bill of rights against the periphery.[32]

The difficulty here, though, is that Professor Amar sees incorporation as *limited by* the original Constitution's devotion to federalism. He urges that the Fourteenth Amendment incorporates only those provisions in the antebellum Constitution (including but not limited to the Bill of Rights) which involve a "personal privilege—that is, a private right—of individual citizens, rather than a right of states or the public-at-large."[33] As a cure for the constitutional infection that is federalism, incorporation under this model falls well short because it makes federalism-based protections immune from incorporation.

That is an abstract point, for it is difficult to imagine the circumstance in which the limit to incorporation suggested by Amar would actually leave the states, empowered by federalism, in a position to do the bad things that made federalism an originalist dilemma. What is neither abstract nor difficult to see, though, is that incorporation does not solve the underlying problem. We have already seen that the Fourteenth Amendment was not intended to prevent the states from continuing to enact and implement numerous types of racist policies. They would not have been prevented from doing so by the magic of incorporation, and Amar never suggests otherwise.[34]

One final point on the virtues of incorporation as a salve for the racist wounds of the framing era: the debate over incorporation is about the relationship between the Bill of Rights and the Fourteenth Amendment, and hence between the Bill of Rights and the states. It has no effect on the pre-Bill Constitution; that is, on the structural defects of the constitutional order built in Articles I–V. I will have much more to say about these defects in the ensuing chapter, but it is enough for now to note that the best that can be said of the Fourteenth Amendment and incorporation is that it imposed limits on the previously unconstrained states. But that is the problem: The states had previously been unconstrained, and in the fullness of their power had exercised vast influence in shaping the governing framework which still exists today, relatively unaffected by incorporation. Reducing that power keeps them from doing it again, but it doesn't change what they already did.

For related reasons, Section 5 of the Fourteenth Amendment is an inadequate cure to the federalist disease. It simply empowers Congress to enforce an Amendment which, *as originally understood*, did not apply to laws and practices like segregation of public schools and other facilities and antimiscegenation laws. This is inadequate on two levels: Section 5's reliance on Congress counts on a federalist institution to overcome federalism, a hope which has not borne much fruit since 1868. And even if Congress had been the ideal enforcer of the Fourteenth Amendment, the amendment itself permitted states to egregiously offend contemporary notions of equality.

Worse still, 130 years of interpretation have drained section 5 of much of whatever vitality it had. The history is well rehearsed. In Chapter 4, I discussed the current Court's astonishing campaign, in cases like *City of Boerne, Morrison,* and *Kimel,* to limit Congress's section 5 authority in the name of federalism. As interpreted in *Kimel,* section 5 of the Fourteenth Amendment does not permit Congress to fill in the gaps where inadequate, arbitrary, or even invidious inaction by the states results in private violations of constitutionally protected rights. It does not permit Congress to provide more expansive protections against discriminatory state actions that burden rights than the Supreme Court has said already exist under the Constitution. This is not a provision equipped to overcome the severe challenges inherent in the founders' federalist design and manifested in our historical reality living under that design.

But the evisceration of section 5 began much earlier, in 1883 with the *Civil Rights Cases.* There, the Court held that section 5 did not authorize Congress to pass laws barring private discrimination.[35] Confident that this interpretation left Congress well armed, or unconcerned that it did not, the Court pointed out:

> The wrongful act of an individual, unsupported by [state] authority, is
> simply a private wrong . . . an invasion of the rights of the injured party,
> it is true, whether they affect his person, his property, or his reputation;
> but if not sanctioned in some way by the state, or not done under state
> authority, his rights remain in full force, *and may presumably be vindi-
> cated by resort to the laws of the state for redress.*[36]

The effect of this highly questionable interpretation of the Fourteenth Amendment[37] was that Congress could prevent the states from affirmatively violating the civil rights of newly freed slaves, but could do nothing if the states simply stepped aside and by their inaction allowed private citizens to accomplish precisely the same thing.[38] Which, of course, is what they did—effectively turning over the post-Reconstruction business of restoring white supremacy to the Ku Klux Klan and other "private" organizations whose activities Congress was powerless to regulate under section 5.[39] Despite substantial criticism of this decision,[40] the present Court has shown no inclination to revisit the *Civil Rights Cases* but instead reaffirmed its validity in 2000 in *Morrison*,[41] the case involving the Violence Against Women Act I discussed in detail in Chapter 4.

Even if the Constitution were not laced with echoes of its racist origins, it would still suffer from the profound changes in the make up of the body politic from 1789 to 2000. The portion of the populace privileged to take part in the constitutional deliberations of the late eighteenth century was not representative of the population whom the Constitution governs today. The framers, the Philadelphia conventioneers as well as the ratifiers in the states, were richer, whiter, and maler than "We the People" are.

While I have focused primarily on the racism inherent in the founding, I have not meant to ignore the exclusion of women from political influence. There is an important difference: The constitutional framework established in Philadelphia included numerous provisions designed for the express purpose of protecting the racist institution of slavery, while the Constitution did not include similar provisions aimed specifically at preserving sex and gender-based inequality. Contrary to the race/slavery issues, no one at the Convention negotiated with the protection of sexism as his overt agenda. There is, though, an important similarity: Women were as absent as non-whites, and we are equally unable 220 years later to know how different the constitutional framework might have been had women's voices been heard.

For these reasons, the original Constitution, even as altered via amendments since 1789, rates far less than a perfect 100 when it comes to democratic legitimacy. It has been suggested, however, that the Article V amendment process must be considered in the equation, because it gives succeeding generations the opportunity (even if we have not fully availed ourselves of it) to make once-excluded voices heard.

THE ARTICLE V AMENDMENT PROCESS

The potential for transformation is a critical element in assessing the legitimacy of the Constitution. Professor Cass Sunstein suggests:

> Ultimately obedience [to the Constitution] is justified, if it is, for some amalgam of substantive political reasons: our Constitution is on balance a good one; it has a democratic pedigree, both in its original adoption *and in the possibility of amendment. . . .*[42]

If it has a democratic pedigree. We have already seen that it does not in the first respect mentioned by Sunstein, the original adoption. Nor is the possibility of amendment enough, at least not within the confines of Article V. To the contrary: Article V is not the salvation of the founders' Constitution. It is an important part of the problem.

Article V erects serious barriers to formal amendment. By one method, two-thirds of both Houses of Congress must propose an amendment, sending it on to the states for ratification. By the other, two-thirds of the state legislatures can compel Congress to convene a constitutional Convention to propose amendments. In both instances, the proposed amendments must then be ratified, either by three-fourths of the state legislatures or by Conventions in three-fourths of the states (Congress having the power to select the method). The amendment process, then, involves multiple decision-makers, all of whom must reach a formidable super-majority consensus.

These barriers must, as Kenyon Bunch suggested, be taken seriously.[43] But originalists take Article V seriously by decrying a "living Constitution" interpretive approach as a usurpation of the constitutional design. There is, however, quite another way to take Article V seriously, which is as part of the democratically problematic origins of the Constitution. The terms of Article V demonstrate how enmeshed it was with the racism inherent in the document and the unrepresentativeness of the framers. Article V made the Constitution unamendable in two respects, one temporary and one permanent. The temporary restriction (in effect until 1808) applied to "the first and fourth Clauses in the Ninth Section of the first Article." The "first Clause" referred to, of course, was the prohibition on legislation regulating the importation of slaves, while the "fourth Clause" was the direct tax provision I discussed earlier. Not only did the Constitution bow to the interests of the slave trade; it gave those compromises special constitutional status outside the reach of Article V. Under Article V, not only could Congress not prohibit the importation of slaves; the nation could not amend the Constitution to remove this restriction.

The second aspect of Article V requiring our attention is the prohibition (this one still in effect) on any amendment depriving a State, "without its Consent, . . . of its equal Suffrage in the Senate." Delaware and Wyoming have a voice equal to that of California and New York, a departure from pure democratic principle that would seem odd if we weren't so accustomed to it. The Senate's make up resulted from one of the most important compromises reached at the Philadelphia Convention, a compromise usually portrayed as one between large and small states. But that is a thin and misleading version of events, as no less an authority than James Madison let on. Madison understood that the differences the compromise attempted to bridge were not truly ones of size:

> [T]he states were divided into different interests not by their difference of size, but by other circumstances; the most material of which resulted partly from climate, but principally from the effects of their having or not having slaves. These two causes concurred in forming the great division of interest in the U. States. It did not lie between the large & small States: it lay between the Northern & Southern, and if any defensive power were necessary, it ought to be mutually given to these two interests.[44]

If the Great Compromise was not directly about slavery, then the indirection was slight indeed.

With these oft-overlooked aspects of Article V in mind, it takes on a different appearance and its true purpose emerges. It was designed to protect against the possibility of amendments that might interfere with the framers' own handiwork, amendments that might compromise their interests and priorities. And the greatest protection of all was afforded to two of the principal ways in which the Constitution accommodated slavery.

Article V should, in other words, be seen as the framers' insurance policy against the possibility that then-excluded groups, including women, slaves, and free blacks, could one day change the government structure the founders had erected without regard to the needs, views, or priorities of the members of those groups. As Bruce Ackerman suggested, it is difficult to respond:

> [T]o today's black or female American who wants to know why she should give any respect at all to old-time politicians who thought they could speak for "the People" without even making an effort to consult people like her.[45]

Ackerman's reply, that "these old-timers provided a constitutional language and institutions through which later generations of women and blacks have won fuller citizenship,"[46] has much force, but it is unavailable to an originalist. The transformational potential upon which Ackerman rests his support for the Constitution is based on his argument that it is amendable outside the textual, Article V process. Were the process of constitutional transformation as completely limited by Article V as an originalist approach demands, the progress cited by Ackerman would never have been achieved.

The Article V problem can be seen in another light. I have been somewhat critical of Professor Sunstein in this chapter; let me now balance the scales a bit and engage in the sincerest form of scholarly flattery by imitating his discussion of the "endowment effect" in law and public policy.[47] Private preferences, he suggests, are not shaped in a vacuum. Instead, they are "often in part a function of whether the government or the law has allocated it to them in the first instance."[48]

In Sunstein's view, this means that traditional liberal neutrality between private preferences is an illusion; if those private preferences are themselves often "an artifact of law,"[49] then the government is not in any meaningful sense "neutral." It instead has helped create preferences rather than merely maximize their satisfaction. This insight has even deeper implications than Sunstein discusses, however.

The Constitution itself represents our most profound initial allocation of rights, obligations, and opportunities. The "endowment effect" suggests that, like any other allocation, the constitutional allocation has shaped our preferences. In fact, when the endowment comes via constitutional law, modern neutrality is even more pernicious because it is that much more difficult for the body politic to overcome the built-in barriers. That is, apparent neutrality not only *helps* the pre-existing choices by failing to recognize how they might be overvalued, it sometimes fully prohibits the alteration.

To illustrate: If government allocations of rights and resources by statute have created a strong majoritarian preference for retention of Social Security benefits, Sunstein suggests we will overvalue those benefits, demanding more to forego them than we would pay to obtain them. Had the initial allocation not included these benefits, we would not enact them; since the initial allocation did include them, we will not reduce them. The difference the allocation makes when it is made in a statute is whether we will or will not continue to do something. When it comes to constitutional law, though, the difference is about whether we can or can not do something. The Constitution not only shapes personal preferences. It shapes political possibility.

Article V redoubles the endowment effect. The effect is already magnified by the simple reality that we not only give greater value to what we have (Sunstein's insight), but we give greater value still to instances where the endowment is in the Constitution. But even in those rare instances where we come to value our endowment more neutrally, so that we are willing to give it up for something like the price we would have paid to obtain it in the first place, Article V of the Constitution makes it extraordinarily difficult for us to do so. The result? The valuations placed on rights and on allocations of power by the founders remain in place long after they have ceased to make sense, and even if the allocations were suspect from the beginning.

GENUINE TRANSFORMATION VIA JUDICIAL INTERPRETATION

Article III courts, especially the Supreme Court, are our constitutional safety valve. The pressures for change brought about by a changing culture, a changing people, are simply greater than Article V can accommodate. Many of the constitutional changes that have been most critical in preserving the union and maintaining the constitutional structure have come outside the regular Article V process. The Civil War, of course, brought about a fundamental change in the relationship between the states and the federal government. The judicial "change in time" in 1937 radically expanded the regulatory authority of the federal government at a time when economic and political conditions seemed to require a muscular central government.

The latter of these transformative events is most critical to this project. The late 1930s and 1940s began an era in which the Supreme Court substantially (if not radically) reshaped our constitutional structure, *without the benefit of a single constitutional amendment* related to the major changes of the period. The "switch in time" was followed quickly by the Court's vigorous debate over incorporation. Although the issue had arisen before,[50] and the Court had even (in 1932) held one protection in the Bill of Rights applicable to the states,[51] it was not until the famous exchange between the "total incorporation" view of Justice Black and the "selective incorporation" stance of Justice Frankfurter in *Adamson v. California*[52] that the Court truly began the process of subjecting the states to the requirements of the Bill of Rights. While the selective incorporation approach ultimately carried the day, by the 1990s the Court had employed it to render most of the guarantees of the Bill of Rights applicable to the states,[53] though not in a way identical in every detail to their direct application to the federal government.

Thus, while on the surface the Court has followed the same approach to incorporation it laid out as early as 1908 in *Twining*, it has overturned the result in that case as well as others dating before 1940. The consistency in label masks a deep difference in the constitutional meaning and significance the Court has attached to the Fourteenth Amendment's mandate that the states afford all persons due process of the law. Yet neither the text of that provision nor the history of its adoption have changed. This was, at the end of the day, constitutional transformation via judicial interpretation.

More famously, perhaps, the same process occurred in the Court's interpretation of the Equal Protection Clause during the same era. The Thurgood Marshall–led NAACP campaign against "separate but equal" did not begin in 1954, but much earlier, with foundation-building cases like *Missouri ex rel. Gaines v. Canada*[54] in 1938 and *Sweatt v. Painter.*[55] In these cases and others, the Court applied the standing interpretation of the Equal Protection Clause established in *Plessy v. Ferguson,*[56] permitting "separate but equal" facilities on the basis of race. But in reality, the Court was doing very much the same thing it was simultaneously doing with selective incorporation: Adhering to the label but transforming the meaning. In this case, though, the ultimate outcome transformed both label *and* meaning, as the Court finally overturned separate but equal in *Brown v. Board of Education.*[57] Again, as it was with incorporation, this was a process of transformation not by amendment but by interpretation.

I have already argued at length that the judicial re-imagining of the Equal Protection Clause was a thoroughly non-originalist process, even though the modern-day originalists have latched on to it without a word of explanation. I do not propose to launch into a similar extended exploration of the originalist status of selective incorporation in its post-1940, more robust form. My point here is not whether the originalists have been consistent when they apply Bill of Rights guarantees to the states. Rather, my point is that the Constitution as we know it, and which twenty-first-century Americans regard as an essential part of the constitutional framework, has been constructed in vital respects by judicial transformation rather than by Article V amendment. More: Without out the judicial reshaping of the last 60 years, our constitutional system—with states far freer to ignore the Bill of Rights and to discriminate on the basis of race—would not be regarded as a legitimate framework for governance.

An important goal of interpretation, then, must be to enhance the legitimacy of the Constitution. Professor Sunstein's alternative idea, that "interpretive principles should attempt to reduce judicial discretion,"[58] is exactly wrong, because judicial discretion has been essential to the process of constitutional transformation, more essential than even the formal Article V amendment process. Worse still, Sunstein would sacrifice the interpretive potential that can rescue the Constitution from its origins by urging that "courts should be cautious in giving broad meaning to open-ended phrases whenever such a meaning would require courts to undertake large-scale social reform on their own."[59] It may well be that there are values served by such a "caution-based" interpretive approach, and I have no objection to it as a second-order priority guiding interpretation. But the Court's first and overriding interpretive mission should be legitimation. Only when that is maximized should we turn our attention to the less critical threat posed by the non-democratic aspects of judicial review.

There exist two threats to democratic legitimacy: the actions of contemporary, but unelected, judges interpreting the Constitution flexibly to strike down decisions by the elective branches of the government, and the racist and non-representative, but originalist and enduring, character of the Constitution itself. Even if originalism successfully saved us from the former threat, it would leave us facing the latter menace. That is a bargain we should speedily reject.

CHAPTER EIGHT

LEGITIMATION

My life has been a tapestry
of rich and royal hue.
An everlasting vision of an ever-changing view.[1]

Once we realize that originalism is an ineffective solution to the wrong problem, and that it is the worst possible solution to the real problem, the natural remaining question is what to do about the Constitution's "legitimacy gap." Or, perhaps more pointedly, can the Supreme Court's interpretation of the Constitution help overcome the troubling origins that continue to taint many of its provisions?

I believe it can, through an approach to interpretation I call legitimation. A legitimizing Supreme Court would examine constitutional provisions at issue in cases, searching carefully for the taint of the original sins permeating too much of our Constitution. Where it finds the taint, the Court should interpret the provision not in accord with the original understanding of its framers; that would be the worst possible interpretation. Instead, within the range of plausible interpretive choices, the Court should read the provision in a way consistent with the core principles essential to constitutional legitimacy: respect for individual rights, equality before the law, and democratic governance through republican institutions.

Perhaps the simplest way to explain the interpretive strategy I envision is to outline a set of "rules" for a legitimizing judge.[2]

RULES FOR CONSTITUTIONAL LEGITIMATION

First. Because concerns over legitimacy exist with respect to many portions of the Constitution besides the practice of judicial review, a court must examine the democratic legitimacy of the constitutional provision before it.

Let us return to the Alabama Constitution of 1901, and the Alabama Supreme Court's engagement with it in 1999, when that Court decided *Ex Parte Melof*.[3] The Convention that drafted the Constitution pursued the goal of establishing white supremacy. It self-consciously removed the prior Constitution's guarantee of equal protection of the laws. Nearly a century later, *Ex Parte Melof* came along. The particulars of the plaintiffs' claims (they challenged Alabama's system of taxing retirement benefits) are unimportant. What is important is that their claims against the state depended on the existence of a state constitutional guarantee of equal protection.

Their problem (as I explained in the previous chapter) was that in 1901 a state constitutional convention, driven by the stated purpose of establishing white supremacy in the state, replaced the Reconstruction Constitution, with its explicit guarantee of equal protection, and in the new Constitution consciously refused to include such a provision. What would an originalist do with an argument that Alabama had violated an individual's right to equal protection of the laws under the state Constitution? Well, the plaintiffs would have some reasonable arguments. For instance, a good lawyer might argue that the language had been unnecessary even in 1875, because language other than Article I, section 2 of that Constitution provided equal protection of the laws. If those provisions were retained in 1901, the removal of that one section would be irrelevant.

The Alabama Supreme Court, however, speedily rejected that argument. It examined the 1875 adoption of the equal protection language (as well as its 1868 precursor), arguing persuasively that the historical record demonstrates that the language was considered crucial; without it, the Constitution would not have guaranteed equal protection of the laws.[4] The Court also noted the Convention had repeatedly rejected proposals to include the text of the 1875 equal protection provision.[5] This was a conscious decision, not an oversight.

An originalist would thus reject the state law equal protection claim as one the Alabama legal system does not exist to adjudicate. It is not one a judge can re-cognize because it was not seen first by the eyes of the 1901 constitutional framers.[6] And that is precisely what the Alabama Supreme Court held: There is no guarantee of equal protection of the laws under the Alabama Constitution.

The Court's analysis was lawyerly, careful, and a model of originalist deference. But it was also plainly wrong. And why? Ironically, for the very reason originalists proclaim—democratic legitimacy. As Justice Houston, the author both of the majority opinion and his own separate concurring opinion, grandly opined:

> I have attempted to keep the Court from corrupting not only the Constitution, but itself as well. We pour corruption on both sacred entities by failing to resist the urge to drink from the chalice of illegitimate, but available power. . . .
>
> [T]he people [expect] that we, as judges, will interpret our Constitutions and their amendments as they are written, in order to effectuate the will of the people. To go any further would be to usurp the powers of the people, and we should not do that simply because we can get away with it. . . .
>
> Might does not make right. We should not, simply because we can, shift the power to amend the Constitution from the hands of the people into the hands of nine Supreme Court Justices.[7]

Justice Houston's comments could not be better suited to demonstrating the underlying emptiness of originalism. He accorded *sacred* status to the very Constitution which he acknowledged was the product of "racist motives,"[8] and which he agreed was a prominent feature of Alabama's "egregious or embarrassing" history. Sacred. He worried over "usurpation" of the peoples' authority, with no evident concern over the usurpation committed by the 1901 convention. Might, he told us, does not make right. On what other basis can the 1901 Constitution pretend to democratic legitimacy?

The question in *Melof* was whether the Alabama Constitution provides a guarantee of equality. It is impossible to take seriously the claim that it is more democratic that this question be answered for contemporary Alabama by the racist, exclusively white-produced 1901 Alabama Constitution than by the current justices of the Alabama Supreme Court. Such a claim might be many things: the lesser of evils, an unfortunate by-product of a preferred interpretive method, even (some would say) an outcome to be celebrated. But it is not democratic.

My first point, then: A court must consider the democratic legitimacy of a provision (or, as in *Melof*, the deletion of a provision) before embarking on the task of interpreting that provision. The result of that inquiry should make a difference in the interpretive approach the court adopts.

Second. A legitimizing court must engage in serious originalism, of a kind which shows respect for the full historical record. This means examining not just the original understanding of the founders, but their motives as well.

I come not to bury originalism, but to rescue it from the narrowness of its judicial practitioners. Justices Thomas and Scalia engage in a historical inquiry that fails to respect the fullness of the history they examine. Their elision of the "whys" of history follows naturally from their acceptance of the legitimacy of the originalist vision. If we follow their path and disregard the challenge to legitimacy inherent in our constitutional history, then we need only ask what the understanding was; it is presumptively (if not conclusively) legitimate. But if we recognize as part of the purpose of judicial review to minimize history's challenge to democratic legitimacy, then addressing the "why" of things becomes essential.

The Alabama Supreme Court's discussion in *Melof* rendered the real history of the adoption of the 1901 Constitution irrelevant. Justice Houston acknowledged the context in his concurrence, calling "well-documented" Justice Cook's "account of the racially biased forces that were present at the Constitutional Convention of 1901," referring to Alabama's "egregious or embarrassing" history," and admitting, "It is true . . . that racist motives were behind the action of the 1901 Constitutional Convention eliminating the equal-protection clause from our Constitution."[9] But did any of this count when it came time to interpret the Constitution? Not for the majority it didn't.

Originalists identify a concern with democratic legitimacy as the primary reason for their focus on the founders' understanding of the Constitution. But then they ignore the single aspect of the historical record that is often most relevant to democratic legitimacy. Judicial review costs us some legitimacy points. Perhaps non-originalist judicial review costs us even more. But it does not come close to matching the towering costs associated with adherence to the original understanding of the 1901 Alabama Constitution.

A fuller originalism would take account of the entire history and examine the entire context surrounding the constitutional provision at issue. We mistake means for ends when we admonish judges to adhere to the original understanding of a provision in the name of legitimacy, when history teaches us that the provision itself is tainted by anti-democratic origins, purposes, or effects. In this sense, legitimation is actually a fuller, richer originalism because it is informed by the complete history.[10] Legitimation can be seen as non-originalist in the sense that it permits, even calls upon, judges to interpret constitutional language in ways not necessarily consistent with the framers' interpretation. But at another level, it is originalism taken seriously because it honors parts of the original understanding that Justices Houston, Scalia, and Thomas ignore.

The truth is that not all constitutional provisions are created equal, and not all the founders' motives (nor all the founders) are equally worthy of deference. Originalism, as practiced by Justices Thomas and Scalia, ignores this. They ask of history only what the framers understood to be the meaning of what they did, not why they did it. Justice Houston's performance in *Melof* is an extreme example, but the lesson it has to offer applies to the federal Constitution as well.

The crucial difference between originalism's limited historical inquiry and what I propose can be seen by examining the Fourteenth Amendment. Originalists would look at what the framers understood the Equal Protection Clause to mean, and be forced to concede that it was the Radical Republicans' compromise with racism. The sponsors of the Fourteenth Amendment aspired to language that would have provided a greater measure of equality, with substantially more precision.[11] Fear of political backlash over the "horrible parade" of interracial schools and mixed marriages, however, compelled them to push the relatively vague language we find in the Constitution today. Since that is what the framers understood the Fourteenth Amendment to mean, Justices Thomas and Scalia (if they were consistent about their methods) would be forced by this history to permit segregated schools, and antimiscegenation laws.

By making the "Why?" question relevant, however, legitimation finds the historical basis for a genuine guarantee of equal protection, contrary to the understanding of the framers. A legitimizing court would point to the framers' appreciation of the text as sanctioning racism, and the exclusion of those victimized by racism from the debate. In light of this inherently anti-democratic state of affairs, the counter-majoritarian difficulty with "activist" judicial review becomes the lesser threat to democratic legitimacy.

This approach is "backward-looking," in Professor Dorf's phrase, in that it asks whether a constitutional provision is a tainted "product of a [past] political compromise." But he is wrong to suggest that the approach therefore "works against the demands of justice."[12] Any approach that *exclusively* looked backwards would suffer from this flaw. But rendering constitutional interpretations that take account of the past does not prevent the Court from filling out its analysis by also looking at the present and ahead to the future. Failing to take account of the past creates a grave risk of injustice. The demands of justice can sometimes be heard only as echoes.

THIRD. *A legitimizing court must, within the range of plausible interpretive choices, read constitutional language to eliminate or ameliorate any threat to legitimacy posed by the constitutional text. In interpreting a constitutional provision, a court should examine the provision's consistency with the core constitutional values of individual rights, equality before the law, and democratic governance through republican institutions, and should interpret the provision so as to maximize its consistency with those values.*

It is important to stress what I am not proposing. I do not suggest the Supreme Court assume Article V-like authority actually to amend the Constitution or delete language when the Court is convinced that particular provisions are tainted by their origins or are anti-democratic in operation. But in any case worth the conversation, the Court confronts a range of interpretive choices. This is particularly true in the case of constitutional language like "equal protection of the laws," where clarity gives way to ambiguity, specificity to grandiloquence. As to many provisions, the worst choice in that range of interpretive choices is the one the originalists offer: Adopt the substance of the disquieting framing.

I believe the Court should strive for interpretive coherence: consistency of the specific provision at issue in the case with the core principles of the document, as we have come to understand those principles today. Those core principles provide the judicial anchor originalists hope to find in the original understanding, thus providing the constraint on personal discretion necessary to meet the counter-majoritarian difficulty. At the same time, this approach avoids the terrible price *traditional* originalism would exact in tying us to results familiar to and desired by the framers, but now grossly inconsistent with the modern constitutional landscape.

Of course, our constitutional conservatives avoid paying some of that price as well, simply by forgetting about the original understanding when the price gets too high, when antimiscegenation laws would have to be upheld or the democratic decision to enact affirmative action programs permitted to stand. In their own way, Thomas and Scalia prove by their sins against originalism that it is not a feasible strategy for constitutional interpretation. They practice sleight-of-hand, not interpretation.

Far better than this, we can identify at the heart of our constitutional order a set of principles, aspirations for which we aim and standards to which we expect our government to conform. Among these I would identify individual freedom, equality under the law, and democratic governance through republican institutions.

The first of these principles finds its clearest expression in the Bill of Rights, of course. The framing generation rejected the claim that the inherent limits on the power of the federal government would be sufficient to protect individual freedom,[13] and instead insisted on the inclusion of a Bill of Rights to tend to the task.

Beyond the specific protections in Amendments I–VIII, and beyond even the message communicated by the importance the enacting states attached to them, there is also the Ninth Amendment: "The enumeration in the Constitution, of certain rights, shall not be construed to deny or disparage others retained by the people."[14] The ambiguity of this famous "inkblot" recently led Justice Scalia to state both that he could identify a fundamental right it encompasses, *and that he would not in his capacity as constitutional interlocutor enforce that right!* In *Troxel v. State of Washington,*[15] he dissented from the decision striking down a "grand-parents visitation" statute as a violation of a parent's constitutional right to direct the upbringing of his or her children. According to Justice Scalia, "that right is . . . among the 'othe[r] [rights] retained by the people' which the Ninth Amendment says the Constitution's enumeration of rights 'shall not be construed to deny or disparage.'"[16] Nevertheless, he asserted in *Troxel*:

> [T]he Constitution's refusal to "deny or disparage" other rights is far re-moved from affirming any one of them, and even farther removed from authorizing judges to identify what they might be, and to enforce the judges' list against laws duly enacted by the people.[17]

That view is plainly wrong. Its effect is that those "rights" are, in reality, "denied" because the only authority that might enforce them would be declining to do so. The Ninth Amendment calls them "rights" for a rea-son, but they become nullities under Justice Scalia's argument.

But placing that disagreement to one side, my point is that the Ninth Amendment can have this meaning, at least: It indicates that there is a general constitutional commitment to individual freedom, a commit-ment that extends beyond the specific enumerated rights. Even if courts cannot identify and enforce the specific (but unnamed) rights to which the Ninth Amendment refers, as Justice Scalia believes, surely judges can be faithful to the general commitment when they interpret the provi-sions they are able and/or willing to enforce.

Similarly, the Constitution's commitment to equality before the law is reflected not only in the (imperfect) Equal Protection Clause, but also in the protections during criminal justice proceedings afforded all persons, equally, in the Bill of Rights (especially in the Sixth Amendment man-date of a trial by a jury of one's peers, a heritage that sounds in equality if any does); in the prohibition on "Titles of Nobility";[18] in the ban on bills of attainder;[19] and in the Fifteenth and Nineteenth Amendments' protection of the right of all citizens to vote.

In deriving this core principle of equality before the law, we are forced to confront the same compromises and inequalities that create the con-

stitutional legitimacy gap in the first place. It is here that rejecting originalism is most important, for we could not find a guiding equality principle in the originalist Constitution, even as amended by the imperfect
Fourteenth Amendment. The provisions I listed in the prior paragraph
would point us in the direction of equality, but too much of the rest of
the document went squarely the other way, leaving us with a constitutional stalemate rather than a guiding principle. But our shared constitutional understanding when it comes to equality has shifted since 1789
and 1868. Perhaps "constitutive" understanding would be a better term
here, because I mean "constitutional" in the sense of what "constitutes"
us as a self-governing people. The equality constituted in the first founding does not speak for us today, and neither does the notion of equality
constituted in the 1868 founding, with its overlay of white and male supremacy taken for granted and its acceptance of white-enforced racial
separation.

The contemporary principle of equality is as thoroughly constitutional as the notion of individual freedom, even though it is not the
equality principle that the framers of those other eras had in mind. That
is not to claim a consensus on the full meaning of the Equal Protection
Clause, of course. Such a claim would be foolish in light of our passionate legal and political disputes about race-conscious government action
in areas such as affirmative action and voting rights.

But those are, to my mind, arguments over means rather than the
principle itself. That is not to trivialize them; disputes over means can be
important, even critical, as they surely are in this instance. The issues involved in trying to make the equality principle a lived reality are among
the most crucial we face. More fundamentally, the very fact that we wrestle with such deep disagreements over the application of one of our most
fundamental principles in and of itself limits how effective we can be in
making the principle a living reality. But still, those issues and the disputes over them do not call into question the principle itself. Even as we
carry those debates forward, we can make reference to our commitment
to equality before the law as a guide to interpreting other provisions of
the Constitution.

Finally, the principle of democratic governance through republican
institutions constitutes the framework for the constitutional design. The
framers established institutions for representation of individuals and of

interests, rather than for direct democratic government. This is most obvious, of course, when it comes to the legislative branch of the federal government, whose two houses represent the interests of individuals (the House of Representatives) and the sovereign states (the Senate).[20] But the principle finds its place in Article II as well, via the creation of the Electoral College to select the President in lieu of direct election by the voters.

There are two sides to this principle. It is easiest to think in terms of the limits that the government by representation places on direct democratic decision-making, but the opposite is true as well: The command *to represent* limits the discretion of those who serve in the republican institutions. To the extent that those institutions fail or refuse to make decisions in the service of democratic governance, they manifestly do not serve in a way either contemplated by the constitutional design (the original framers, after all, having taken their revolutionary stand over their right to be represented as governing decisions were made) or consistent with our contemporary notions of legitimate governance.

The fight over campaign finance reform illustrates this idea. Surveys show that the vast majority of Americans believe that "special interests" are able to buy influence through campaign contributions to members of Congress and the major political parties. The Public Interest Research Group's Internet Website reflects this view:

> We live in a country where the voices and concerns of the common people are drowned out by the interests of big money campaign donors. Big money controls who can run for office and who can't, who wins and who doesn't, and ultimately what issues are talked about in Congress and what issues are swept under the table. It is inevitable that politicians will respond to the people who determine their fate.[21]

A similar point, made with even more pointed reference to democratic principles, appears elsewhere on the same site:

> The real problem is not that access and influence are granted to active supporters of a campaign or political party, but that the price tag for access is unobtainable to 99 percent of all Americans. In a country based on democratic ideals, the concerns of wealthy individuals and businesses

should not be the only concerns heard by politicians. If money in politics were limited and every citizen could afford to buy access and influence, a true representative democracy might emerge.[22]

Putting to one side the merits of proposals for any particular reforms, the implicit premise of the movement for campaign finance reform is that Congress, as a republican institution, has a representative obligation.

The Court should be guided by these core principles with an eye toward developing interpretive consistency. This is far from a revolutionary idea. The Court has from the beginning been consumed with interpreting the Constitution in a fashion consistent with its nature ("We must never forget that it is a *constitution* we are expounding"[23]), its overall structure and its historical roots ("[A]s the Constitution's structure, and its history, . . . make clear, the States' immunity from suit is a fundamental aspect of the sovereignty which the States enjoyed before the ratification of the Constitution, and which they retain today"[24]).

The very idea of interpretive consistency presumes we have something in mind with which the interpretation is supposed to be consistent. If someone presents you with a blue fabric and asks if it is consistent with "Duke blue," you must know what shade of blue is used by Duke University (a rich, dark blue). It may be very important to that person to avoid wearing "Carolina blue" (a lighter shade, sky blue), given the intense rivalry between Duke and the University of North Carolina. Interpreting "blue" for consistency requires some knowledge of blue (and the social construction of certain shades of blue) before you embark on interpreting the blue at issue.

So we come to the question: Where do judges get their foreknowledge of "the Constitution" when trying to interpret a provision—give it meaning—*consistent with* the Constitution? After all, if the judge is interpreting the Constitution, and has not prejudged the matter, she is not supposed to know in advance what the Constitution means.

But of course, she does know what the Constitution means in advance. I don't mean she's prejudged the case; we at least hope the Justices open their minds to the question before them as they approach each case, and even if they don't, their closed-mindedness is not my point. It's not that they know what the particular provision at issue means as applied to the particular set of facts; if that were known in advance it is unlikely the Supreme Court, which considers only the hard cases, would be considering the matter. But the Constitution generally, that they know. It has been given shape and substance and texture by over 200 years of practice, and even at the outset it arose from a political and social context that allowed the early Justices to begin each case with an important kind of foreknowledge about what the Constitution means.

The Court has been using just such a consistency-based approach to constitutional interpretation for its entire history, and by originalists and non-originalists alike. It appeared prominently in *Martin v. Hunter's Lessee*, in which the Court held that the structure of the Constitution demonstrates its (the Court's) appellate authority over judgments of state courts. Justice Story's opinion compared the proposed jurisdiction with other aspects of the Constitution (e.g., "the tenth section of the first article [which] contains a long list of disabilities and prohibitions imposed upon the states"[25]), and found that it fit comfortably into the relationship between the national and state sovereigns.

Even more famously, the Court's foundational decision in *McCulloch v. Maryland*[26] rested Congress's power to incorporate the Bank of the United States not on any explicit authorization in Article I, section 8 (which does not exist), but on "a fair construction of the whole instrument."[27] A national government given the power to lay and collect taxes, to raise and support armies, must also possess the means to exercise those powers for the benefit of the people, including the discretion to determine those means best suited to accomplish the ends entrusted to Congress in the Constitution.

For non-originalists, the same approach has found more contemporary expression in the search for "penumbras" and "emanations" emerging from the background shadows and interstices of the Constitution, in the gloaming of which the Court found the right to privacy. From this insight has followed specific limits on state authority to regulate the sale and use of contraceptives, the availability of abortions, and the perusal of obscene material in the privacy of one's own home.[28]

For originalists, emanations from the general notion of federalism have informed an accelerating campaign of limiting the federal government's powers vis-à-vis the states, even where the specific limitations can be found nowhere in the express language of the Constitution nor in the expressed contemplations of any of the framers. In 1999, the five-member majority (which included Justices Scalia and Thomas) acknowledged in *Alden v. Maine*[29] that the Court has "looked to 'history and experience and *the established order of things*,' . . . rather than '[a]dhering to the mere letter' of the Eleventh Amendment . . . in determining the scope of the States' constitutional immunity from suit."[30] Even more tellingly, Chief Justice Rehnquist wrote that "the scope of the States' immunity from suit is demarcated not by the text of the Amendment alone but by *fundamental postulates implicit in the constitutional design*."[31] One is hard-pressed to fathom the difference between the "privacy penumbras" the originalists loathe and the "implicit postulates" of federalism they champion.[32] But no matter; even if we assume that the non-textualism of *Alden* is justified as an originalist refusal to "engage in . . . ahistorical literalism,"[33] the key point is that in the pursuit of "historical non-literalism" the constitutional conservatives validate the notion of interpretation via assessment of the Constitution's general design.

Justices from John Marshall to William O. Douglas to Clarence Thomas interpret specific provisions through the filter of their perception of the general animating principles of the Constitution. For Marshall, that meant a more robust national government than had existed under the failed Articles of Confederation; for Douglas, a deep commitment to individual autonomy and privacy; for Thomas, a federalist balance that reserves important areas of independence for the states. Legitimation takes the license employed by a vast range of Justices and turns it to the service of dealing with the troubling origins of the Constitution, a project I submit is far more compelling than protecting state courts from being forced to adjudicate federal claims, and at least as compelling as ensuring our access to condoms.

We can come at the issue of interpretive consistency from another direction as well. Originalists (and probably a good many non-originalists) will protest that this might be all well and good if there were some source, itself democratically legitimized, judges could look to in assessing whether a particular provision is anti-democratic and hence inconsistent with core constitutional principles, thus triggering a legitimizing interpretation. Rather than superimposing the Constitution's will on the government, Thomas might contend, legitimation would impose a judge's will on the Constitution. The concept of judicial review is justified by the notion that judges are empowered by Article III to determine the meaning of the Constitution, a notion we have accepted (with varying levels of enthusiasm) since *Marbury v. Madison.* It is this power that justifies measuring the validity of a statute. What empowers them, however, to pass judgment *on the Constitution itself?*

The problem of the 1901 Alabama Constitution illustrates this dilemma. In 1985, the U. S. Supreme Court invalidated section 182 of that Constitution, pointing to the prevailing racist purpose of the Convention, its place as "part of a movement that swept the post-Reconstruction South to disenfranchise blacks,"[34] and the ongoing racially disproportionate effects of the provision.

But the Supreme Court had a measuring stick against which to judge section 182: the requirements of the federal Constitution. One might suppose the Court could not have declared the provision a violation of the *Alabama* Constitution, since it was a part of that very Constitution. And, to complete the circle, when it comes to the federal Constitution, there is no "higher" or external measuring stick, making it impossible for the Court to judge the "constitutionality" of a provision of the federal Constitution.

Well, of course. It would be easy to dismiss the argument that the Supreme Court possesses the power to hold provisions of the federal Constitution . . . unconstitutional. But that is not what I am suggesting. What I suggest instead is that the Court rely on certain core constitutional principles both to identify the problematic provisions and to guide interpretation of them.

Professor Vicki Jackson recently suggested something resembling this idea, proposing to distinguish between constitutional provisions that reflect constitutional principles and those that are the result of political compromise, and treat the latter as "something to be contained, so as not to obstruct the larger 'principle' of equal representation. . . ."[35] I part company with Jackson, however, in that I would not further distinguish, as she does, between matters of compromise that were, whatever their problematic origins, "central to the union." It is on the basis of this distinction that Professor Jackson places state sovereign immunity on one side of the interpretive line (it should be narrowly construed as a compromise "at the periphery of those constitutional features that most importantly constitute the federal union"), but the Senate on the other.[36]

This distinction has the virtue of a kind of pragmatic recognition of what the Supreme Court is and is not likely to do: It is not, for example, going to venture forth anytime soon and tinker with the rules for electing Senators. But it is ultimately unsatisfying, because it bows to rather than tackles the underlying reasons why some of those early compromises were "central to the union."

Indeed, the Senate itself is a powerful example of this. Throughout most of the twentieth century, a minority of the members of the U. S. Senate blocked votes on civil rights legislation. They did this by bottling up bills in committees chaired by staunch segregationists from the South, or by filibustering debate on the floor.[37] In 1957, for example, Senator Strom Thurmond broke the record for the longest filibuster, speaking continuously for more than 24 hours,[38] as part of an effort that eventually forced sponsors to water down the Civil Rights Act of 1957 so much that it had almost no impact and is, rightly, hardly even remembered today.[39]

Such conduct by the Senate constituted a major challenge to the democratic legitimacy of that institution. As I have already argued, the Senate itself is an unmistakable manifestation of the original sin propounded in 1789. Obviously, though, it would be well outside the scope of a legitimate interpretive effort for the Supreme Court to declare the Senate unconstitutional, and then either to abolish it (!) or to order a population-based transformation of its roster. However, it is not too much to ask that the Court recognize the anti-democratic implications of the composition of the Senate, acknowledge its roots as (in part) an accommodation of slavery, and examine challenges to the Senate's conduct accordingly.

Imagine that a suit had been filed to break the 1957 filibuster. While it is pretty clear the courts would have refused to entertain the *Filibuster Case*, deeming it an interference with the internal operations of a co-equal branch of government,[40] I believe they should not only have heard the claim, but should have ruled in favor of the hypothetical plaintiffs, ordering a floor vote without any need to invoke cloture.[41] The tactics of the segregationists were unconstitutional as applied to civil rights proposals. The filibuster grants extraordinary power to a small minority of members in a body already designed to give extraordinary power to a small minority of the people.

This assertion may seem startling. After all, Article I, section 5 of the Constitution provides, "Each House may determine the Rules of its Proceedings. . . ." In light of this text, it seems at first glance difficult to claim that an anti-filibuster ruling would fall within the range of plausible interpretive choices. But the Constitution contains language outside Article I, section 5 that is very relevant to the question.

The Court could have begun with Article I, section 3 of the Constitution, which states, "The Senate of the United States shall be composed of two Senators from each State, chosen by the Legislature thereof, for six Years; and each Senator shall have one Vote."[42] The filibuster has the effect of stripping some Senators (the majority) of their right to "one Vote" by giving greater weight to each vote of the filibustering minority.

The Court could further have looked to the provisions of the Constitution which create super-majority requirements for Senate action, including the Impeachment Clause,[43] the Override Clause,[44] and the Treaty Clause.[45] It could have reasoned that the framers knew how to create anti-democratic, super-majority requirements when they wanted them as barriers to Senate action, and they did not do so when it comes to ordinary legislation. The filibuster thus constitutes an attempt by the Senate itself to amend the Constitution, arguably a violation of Article V, as well.

Of course, any such suit would have to reckon with the Constitution's grant of authority to each House to "determine the Rules of its Proceedings. . . ." This authority is not unlimited, however. The Senate could not prescribe a rule that Jerry Springer would preside at presidential impeachment trials (even if his presence might, in some cases, seem entirely fitting), nor that a simple majority of Senators could convict the President and oust him from office. Nor could it pass a "rule of proceeding" that no African-American Senators will be permitted to serve as committee chairs. Each of these "rules of proceedings" would be contrary to specific constitutional mandates. Once the door is open to some judicial oversight of Senate rules, the filibuster is no more sacrosanct than any other rule.

If it seems startling to suggest that the Supreme Court could declare the Senate's filibuster rule unconstitutional when it is used to prevent consideration of civil rights legislation, consider the legitimacy of the Senate under the Court's own decision in *Hunter v. Underwood*, the case where the Court struck down section 182 of the infamous 1901 Alabama Constitution. According to the Court, the section ran afoul of the Equal Protection Clause because it was motivated in part by racist motives and continued to have a disproportionate effect in disenfranchising African-Americans. I have already shown that creation of the Senate was motivated (again, in part) by the racist motive of preserving enslavement of blacks. And its structure continues to have a significantly disproportionate effect on the influence of African-Americans.

The ten least populous states[46] had a combined population in 1998 of just over 8 million people. Of these, only 249,175, or 3.1 percent, were black—a drastically lower proportion than the national figure of 12.7 percent. The ten most populous states[47] had a combined population of over 146 million people, of whom 19,443,154 (13.3 percent) were black. Yet the people of the bottom ten had the same number of Senators (20) representing them as the citizens of the top ten. If, however, the 100 Senate seats were apportioned by population, the top ten states would receive 54 Senators rather than 20,[48] and the bottom ten, disproportionately white states would receive only three Senators.

Population distribution between large and small states is not the only way the Senate disfavors African-Americans. State-wide elections by their nature dilute the impact of minority groups. No state has a majority black population (Mississippi has the highest percentage, at around 36 percent). Black majority districts can and frequently do elect African-American members to the House of Representatives, but election of black Senators is extremely rare; there has never been anything close to 13 percent black Senate membership.

By the reckoning of *Hunter v. Underwood*, then, the Senate is (or ought to be) on decidedly shaky ground. Yet I am not arguing for a constitutional decree requiring reapportionment of the Senate, but only a recognition of its problematic roots and its tension with the core constitutional principles of equality before the law and democratic decision-making by representative institutions. That tension strains the constitutional fabric to the point of tearing when a disproportionately small number (34 of 100) of the representatives of the disproportionately represented minority of the people can block democratic decision-making on matters affecting the equality of citizens before the law.

Adopting a constitutional rule barring filibusters when the Senate considers civil rights legislation is most consistent with the core constitutional principles I have outlined. Such filibusters compromise the goal of achieving equality under the law, and they are inconsistent with the responsibility of republican institutions to govern in a representative fashion.

A similar case can be made for judicial oversight of the filibuster in an area of more contemporary controversy, campaign finance reform. I suggested earlier in this chapter that the issues underlying the debate over the way in which we finance federal elections implicate the constitutional value of democratic government through republican institutions. The current dominant place of monied interests threatens the representative quality of those institutions. When it comes to campaign finance reform aimed at meeting that threat, the undemocratic character of the Senate and the power of a minority to block a vote on legislation are an intolerable departure from the representative obligation. Use of the filibuster in this area is no more constitutionally permissible than it is when employed to block civil rights legislation.

Lest it seem that the U. S. Senate is the only target in my sights, let me suggest another area of constitutional interpretation as to which these rules of legitimation make a difference. I noted earlier that the constitutional preoccupation with protection of property rights is, like the Senate, linked historically to the southern agenda of protecting slavery. *Dred Scott* is potent evidence of the constitutional connection between respect for property rights and protection of the institution of slavery.

This fact also has relevance for a legitimizing court. The Due Process Clause precludes deprivations of life, liberty, and property without due process of law. Much to Justice Scalia's consternation, this apparently procedural provision has been given substantive content, which the Court abandoned in 1937 as to property but has continued to recognize when it comes to life and liberty ever since.

The Court accomplished this, in part, through application of Justice Stone's famous fourth footnote in *United States v. Carolene Products*.[49] The case would otherwise be an unremarkable and probably little-remembered step in the Court's abandonment of *Lochner* (it was, after all, decided in 1938, a year after the "switch in time"), but footnote four set forth types of cases in which "[t]here may be a narrower scope for operation of the presumption of constitutionality," cases in which a "more searching judicial inquiry"[50] is called for. In other words, a group of cases in which the Court might continue to subject some legislation to the same discredited rough handling that had produced the confrontation between the executive and judicial branches in the first place.

Ever since then, vociferous advocates of property rights have decried the "second-class" treatment they have received at the hands of the Court.[51] But the distinction finds support in the constitutional baggage carried by property. Far from being solicitous of property rights, courts should carefully scrutinize property-contingent constitutional claims.

For that reason, legitimation might have resonance in the area of regulatory takings. As I discussed in Chapter 3, the originalists have accepted and extended the non-originalist notion that the Takings Clause applies to situations where government does not physically take an individual's property, but instead reduces its value by enacting and enforcing a regulation (often but not always an environmental regulation). In other words, led by Justice Scalia the Court has been more solicitous of property rights than the framers of the Fifth Amendment.

Legitimation would pull the Court in precisely the opposite direction. The problematic origins of the constitutional security given to property rights should trigger a search for a *plausible* interpretation of the Takings Clause that minimizes its inconsistency with the core constitutional values of equality before the law, individual liberty, and democratic governance through republican institutions. The *Pennsylvania Coal/Lucas* rule deeming "regulatory takings" compensable is inconsistent with at least two of those values: equality before the law and democratic governance.

The regulatory takings doctrine fosters inequality because it elevates property owners' interest in the value of their property (distinct from the concept of ownership itself) above other, competing public interests. Citizens who benefit from the regulation are compelled to find another way to achieve the public policy purposes underlying it, and such an alternative may be either unavailable or far less effective.

As a result, the regulatory takings doctrine elevates the private over the public interest. The Court protected the property owner in *Lucas* from the loss of the development value of his parcels, approximately $1,000,000. It did this by characterizing that loss as a "total" deprivation, and then analogizing a total loss to an actual physical taking. But the characterization itself missed the mark; the regulation was not a "total" deprivation of ownership rights anything like that involved in a physical taking. The Court's later decision in *College Savings Bank* illustrates this. In explaining why the statutory "right to be free from a business competitor's false advertising" is not a property right, the Court pointed out that this "right" did not carry with it the right to exclude others, which the Court characterized as a "hallmark of a protected property interest."[52] If the "right to exclude others" is such a fundamental stick in the bundle of property rights, then it follows that a regulatory taking is not the same thing as an actual physical taking, for only the latter deprives the owner of the right to exclude others. The Court's analogy collapses.

Instead, the deprivation worked by a regulatory taking is only partial, and hence better analogized to the types of interests that compete in the political marketplace all the time, and are supposed to compete on equal footing. After *Lucas*, however, the partial deprivation of a property owner's right (so long as it is a "total" deprivation of the one particular stick represented by economic development rights) trumps the common public interest in (for example) preserving the coastal beaches of South Carolina. This is inconsistent with the ideal of equality before the law.

For related reasons, the regulatory takings doctrine also constitutes a tremendous interference with democratic governance. Madison saw the republican institutions as interest-balancers. They are performing precisely this function when they weigh property owners' interest in the value of what they own against other public interests like preventing environmental degradation and beach erosion.

Of course, the same arguments could be made against the compensation requirement itself, even when applied to an actual physical taking of property. But it would take an implausible reading of the Fifth Amendment to deny property owners their right to compensation when their property is actually taken by the government. When property is physically taken away, ownership itself is at stake, and if that interest does not require compensation then the Takings Clause itself is a nullity. Thus, even if that right is out of step with identifiable constitutional values (I don't happen to think that it is), we are stuck with it. But when we step beyond government interference with actual ownership, to so-called "regulatory takings"? It is hardly implausible to read the Takings Clause as being irrelevant to those cases; indeed, the Supreme Court itself did so for the first 145 years of our constitutional history.

Finally, what about the 1901 Alabama Constitution? How would legitimation have prevented the outrageous conclusion the state Supreme Court reached in *Melof*, that the state Constitution provides no guarantee of equal protection of the laws? First, the Court would have taken the history of the 1901 enactment seriously, recognizing that it could not concede the Constitution was a product of racist motives, a reflection of Alabama's egregious history, and at the same time accord that Constitution "sacred" status. This was a case not of taint, but of a Constitution that was corrupt to its core and in a way directly relevant to the issue before the Court.

Second, the Court would have moved easily to the related conclusion that the 1901 convention itself was a violation of the core values of democratic governance through republican institutions and equality before the law. Alabama's African-American citizens, having already been disenfranchised in the quarter-century of intimidation, violence, and lynchings that followed the end of Reconstruction, had no voice in the convention. The convention lacked any claim to legitimacy; it was a usurpation of the 1875 Constitution.

It was in the existence of the 1875 Constitution that a legitimizing Court could have met its responsibility to arrive at a plausible interpretation of the 1901 Constitution that would have removed or minimized the challenge. Absent a full and equal opportunity for the entire Alabama polity to participate in the process in 1901, the convention lacked authority to repeal those provisions of the earlier Constitution which guaranteed precisely that full and equal opportunity to participate.

If that seems implausible, remember that the 1901 convention was called and conducted under the provisions of the 1875 Constitution. Let us assume, for example, that section 23 of the existing Constitution provided that a convention could not be called without the assent of at least one member of the state legislature from each county. Further, assume that the proponents lacked a sponsor from one or more counties. A state court at the time would have had the authority to block the convention from proceeding as a violation of section 23.

Fast-forward a century. If the convention had gone ahead unchallenged, what could a court almost a century later do about it? The answer is that the court should ask whether the rump convention had done anything that undermined the very provision it was violating, and whether that alteration is relevant to the case before the court. Presumably, a hypothetical rule like a "county veto" over a convention would be intended to empower counties to preserve prerogatives guaranteed under the existing Constitution. If the court in 2001 found that the convention in 1901 had left counties with the same independence and power they'd enjoyed in 1875, then its role would be at an end, and the fact of the violation of section 23 would be of historic interest only.

But if the 1901 Constitution limited counties' authority (for example) to issue bonds, and the case before the court raised a claim that a county had exceeded its bond cap, then a different question presents itself. In that instance, the court should bring forward the 1875 rule governing bonds and incorporate it into the 1901 Constitution, superceding the contrary rule. Any other outcome gives effect to an action that was, at the time, unconstitutional.

This reasoning applies to the absence of an Equal Protection Clause in the Alabama Constitution. The convention itself was a blatant violation of the Equal Protection Clause that had been in the 1875 Constitution, and the relationship between that violation and the elision of the Clause itself could hardly be more direct. In those circumstances, the restoration of the Equal Protection Clause is a plausible remedial step, and it should have been given legal effect in *Ex Parte Melof.*

I began with an observation about the dual character of "recognition" in constitutional interpretation. Even if their pretense to originalism were more than that, the constitutional conservatives would be practicing recognition, a narrow and ultimately unsatisfying form of originalism. They ask what the framers of the constitutional text understood their work to mean, but fail to examine the purpose the framers had in mind.

And if we look just a bit beyond the surface, we see an even more troubling reality. The so-called "originalists," while claiming to eschew recognition in the Blackmun sense, have in fact authored a clear and compelling pattern of politically conservative, non-originalist decisions. They constantly take into account (they *recognize*) the political and policy implications of the cases before them. Sometimes they even do so explicitly, as Justice Thomas did in the Kansas City school desegregation case, *Missouri v. Jenkins*. Other times, implausible reasoning and obvious inconsistency with their own past positions make the implication that they did it overwhelming. So it was in the era's defining case, *Bush v. Gore*.

There remains yet a more disturbing possibility: Originalism was interpretation's last, best hope. What if the originalists are right that the only way to find anything approaching a fixed meaning in the Constitution besides the whim of its interpreters of the day is to adhere to the original understanding? That certainly is the position taken by Professor Walter Benn Michaels, who argues not that we *should* interpret the Constitution based on the original understanding, but that only adherence to the original understanding can even be called "interpretation."[53] If that last hope has failed because the originalists have demonstrated they cannot honor their commitment to the founders' intended meaning, then what is left of determinacy, of the validity of interpretation itself? Does the Constitution have a discernible meaning, or is the entire enterprise merely politics in disguise?

From a very different perspective, Professor Robin West has urged progressives to consider the option of constitutional skepticism: rather than criticize the Court for interpretations of the Constitution that either block or at least do not advance progressive outcomes, we should consider the possibility that such interpretations are right and the Constitution itself is the problem.[54] Professor West wonders why:

> constitutional scholars are peculiarly reluctant to see either the Constitution or a particular constitutional guarantee as being at odds with our political or moral ideals, goals, or commitments.[55]

Those who favor abortion rights also see them as constitutionally protected; those who believe pornography should be regulatable because of its harmful effects on women argue that (properly interpreted) the First Amendment permits such regulation. For Professor West, this reluctance masks a truth that verges on despair: "[O]ur Constitution is fundamentally and irreversibly at odds with progressive egalitarianism, and that because of that it is a seriously flawed document."[56]

There is an important link between West and Michaels. For many of the reasons I have discussed, West is right that the Constitution is "a seriously flawed document." Most of its flaws, however, can be traced back to the aspects of its origins that tear at the foundations of its democratic legitimacy. Interpretation that strengthens that foundation is the answer, rather than the near-despair of constitutional skepticism.

But such an interpretive strategy must first reckon with Professor Michaels' inevitable argument that it would not be "interpretation" at all. If he is right, we face a profound difficulty: The only path to constitutional legitimacy involves not interpreting the Constitution at all, and the only activity that can be called interpretation leaves us with an illegitimate (Professor West says anti-progressive, but the problem is worse than that) Constitution.

We are thus fortunate that Professor Michaels' answer misunderstands the special nature of legal interpretation. While both the Constitution and *A Tale of Two Cities* are texts requiring interpretation, the act of interpretation is fundamentally different in the two cases. We may choose to walk away from *A Tale of Two Cities* at our whim, but we cannot walk away from the Internal Revenue Code so easily. The law makes demands upon us; it claims authority over us. It must therefore have legitimacy.

Certainly, a breakdown in interpretation can undermine legitimacy, but so too can literalist, originalist interpretation (of the Michaels variety) if the document itself lacks legitimacy. Our aim, after all, is not just to interpret the Constitution correctly in the syllogistic sense of that term (it is correct because that's what the framers intended), but to interpret it so that its status as our governing document is legitimate. If, in other words, we have to compromise either the integrity of the interpretation or the legitimacy of the Constitution, the former is the only reasonable choice.

Moreover, the prevailing legal text does change over a period of decades. *A Tale of Two Cities* has exactly the same words today as it did when Dickens wrote it. But what we understand as "constitutional law" has changed. Most obviously as I discussed in Chapter 4, the meaning of an earlier provision can be transformed by the enactment of a later amendment. We cannot interpret the First Amendment solely by reference to the views of its framers. We must also inquire whether any of the later amendments affects its contemporary meaning.

But subsequent amendments are not the end of the story. The legal doctrine of *stare decisis* makes judicial rulings from 1889 and 1989 a part of the text the judges of 2001 must interpret. Those rulings are not mere guides to interpretation of the text, like the Federalist Papers or Justice Story's Commentaries on the Constitution. Rather, they are themselves part of the body of constitutional law.

Like other legal texts, in other words, the Constitution is meant to be interactive. When Dickens wrote a novel, he expected it to be read and interpreted, and to affect his audience. But he did not expect those readers to affect the book itself. If I borrow *A Tale of Two Cities* from the library, it is the same book when I return it. Nothing in my interpretation or interaction with the text affects the experience of the next patron. What she gets out of *A Tale of Two Cities* is between her and Dickens.

In this respect, the framers of the Constitution were not like Dickens. They understood that the judges of future eras would interpret the Constitution influenced by intervening "readers," at least the authoritative intervening readers. Michaels ignores this distinguishing characteristic of law.

My point is this: We can concede Michaels his semantic point without conceding anything of substance. If a non-originalist approach to constitutional decision-making does not constitute "interpretation" *of the Constitution* as he wishes to define the term, fine. It nevertheless remains interpretation of *constitutional law*, a necessarily distinct enterprise. And as I have argued, it is an enterprise whose net effect is to maximize the democratic legitimacy of the Constitution by minimizing the anti-democratic aspects of its origins.

At the last, then, we return to the basic choice I posed in the introduction: Which definition of recognition should guide constitutional interpretation? Should it be re-cognition in a truly (though narrowly) originalist sense, looking only to what the framers understood the text to mean, while simultaneously ignoring contemporary policy implications and refusing to examine the framers' motives? Or should we look more broadly, seeing constitutional interpretation as a call to recognize not just the original understanding, but also the original compromises that taint the Constitution as well as the disturbing ramifications of narrow, originalist interpretation?

An important indication of the answer is this: Even those who have claimed to take the re-cognitive road have proved manifestly incapable of keeping to it. The dismal record of the constitutional conservatives—their repeated "sins" against originalism—is a strong sign that the price of genuine, unadulterated originalism is unbearable and unsustainable. Justice Thomas's world is one not just of back-alley abortions, as Edward Kennedy famously said of Robert Bork, but of antimiscegenation laws, segregated schools, and race-conscious affirmative action; of uncompensated government regulation of property; of substantial tort damages for unreasonable searches; of widened federal authority under section five of the Fourteenth Amendment. But Clarence Thomas cannot live in that world, which should by all rights be Justice Thomas's world.

That in turn means that re-cognition-style originalism has not, and probably can not, deliver the one virtue always claimed on its behalf: its power to constrain. Those who worry over the counter-majoritarian difficulty must look elsewhere for ties that bind the judges. In the meantime, the greater threat to democratic legitimacy commands our attention—and our recognition.

NOTES

Notes to the Preface

1. 388 U.S. 1 (1967). One might quarrel with this characterization of *Loving*, but in my view its only serious rival as the "most important case" the Court considered between October 1965 and June 1967 was *Miranda v. Arizona*, 384 U.S. 436 (1966), and for reasons I shall make clear, Thomas would surely have seen *Loving* as the more significant of the two.

2. *See* Naim v. Naim, 350 U.S. 891 (1955).

3. A copy of the draft dissent appears in Chapter 1.

4. A copy of the draft concurring opinion appears in Chapter 1.

5. One can imagine a lonely Justice Thomas, waiting through the Warren Court years issuing blistering dissents from non-originalist decisions. Finally, in 1972, Thomas would gain a fairly reliable ally in his crusade, when William Rehnquist joins the Court. Then, in 1986, Antonin Scalia would become the first truly constant devotee of Thomas's jurisprudence. The three together would become known as the "Thomas Wing," with Justice Thomas being the unquestioned leader of the group, having spent years sounding a solitary call for a sea change in the Court's approach. Scalia, in fact, would be much criticized as a mere acolyte of Thomas, without a vision or voice of his own. Finally, in 2001, George W. Bush would appoint Justices Edith Jones and Kenneth Starr to replace Justices John Paul Stevens and Sandra Day O'Connor, giving the Thomas Wing a clear majority. When Jones and Starr join Thomas, Rehnquist, and Scalia, Thomas will have gone from lone dissenter to triumphant visionary, and a slew of non-originalist decisions would shortly fall by the wayside. *See, e.g.,* Gideon v. Wainwright, 372 U.S. 335 (1963); New York Times v. Sullivan, 376 U.S. 254 (1964); Heart of Atlanta Motel, Inc. v. United States, 379 U.S. 241 (1964); Katzenbach v. McClung, 379 U.S. 294 (1964); Miranda v. Arizona, 384 U.S. 436 (1966); Griggs v. Duke Power Co., 401 U.S. 424 (1971); Roe v. Wade, 410 U.S. 113 (1973).

Notes to the Introduction

1. Board of County Commissioners v. Umbehr, 518 U.S. 668, 711 (1996) (Scalia, J., dissenting).

2. WEBSTER'S NEW WORLD DICTIONARY 1186 (2d. Coll. Ed. 1982).

3. *See* CHARLES R. CALLEROS, LEGAL METHOD AND WRITING 58–59 (3d ed. 1998) (describing process of applying *stare decisis* as "far from an exact science," requiring judges to evaluate the similarity and relevance of particular factual aspects of prior cases); ANTONIN SCALIA, A MATTER OF INTERPRETATION: FEDERAL COURTS AND THE LAW 7–8 (1997) ("[I]t is critical for the lawyer, or the judge, to establish whether the case at hand falls within a principle that has already been decided. Hence the technique—or the art, or the game—of 'distinguishing' earlier cases").

4. *See* U.S. Constitution, Am. 1 ("Congress shall make no law abridging the freedom of speech. . . .").

5. *See* William Safire, *Malaysian Malaise*, The New York Times, Sept. 20, 1999 (discussing criminal charges filed against reporter).

6. *See Umbehr*, 518 U.S. at 686 ("There can be no dispute that, like rewarding one's allies, the correlative act of refusing to reward one's opponents . . . is an American tradition as old as the Republic. . . . If that long and unbroken tradition of our people does not decide these cases, then what does?").

7. Justice Scalia appears to be developing a thread in his jurisprudence focusing on post-ratification traditions to glean the meaning of constitutional text, at least in instances where the language of the provision is not clear on its face. The predicate of his extensive discussion in *Umbehr* of the ubiquity of political patronage in American life was that tradition is relevant because "[t]he constitutional text is assuredly as susceptible of one meaning as of the other." *Id.* at 688.

8. 489 U.S. 189 (1989).

9. *Id.* at 193.

10. *Id.* at 213.

11. 492 U.S. 490 (1989). In *Webster*, Justice Blackmun predicted that overruling *Roe v. Wade* would produce the result that "every year hundreds of thousands of women, in desperation, would defy the law, and place their health and safety in the unclean and unsympathetic hands of back-alley abortionists, or they would attempt to perform abortions upon themselves, with disastrous results. Every year, many women, especially poor and minority women, would die or suffer debilitating physical trauma, all in the name of enforced morality or religious dictates or lack of compassion, as it may be." *Id.* at 557–58 (Blackmun, J., concurring in part and dissenting in part).

12. 488 U.S. 469, 561–62 (1989) ("I never thought I would live to see the day when the city of Richmond, Virginia, the cradle of the Old Confederacy, sought on its own . . . to lessen the stark impact of persistent discrimination. But Richmond, to its great credit, acted. Yet this Court, the supposed bastion of equality, strikes down Richmond's efforts as though discrimination had never existed or was not demonstrated in this particular litigation. . . .").

13. *See* Miranda v. Arizona, 384 U.S. 436, 445–56 (1966) (describing the real-world situation of varying methods of physical and psychological coercion by which suspects are subjected to "incommunicado interrogation . . . in a police-dom-

inated atmosphere, resulting in self-incriminating statements without full warnings of constitutional rights").

14. *See* Mapp v. Ohio, 367 U.S. 643, 657–58 (1961) (noting that prior rule allowing unconstitutionally seized evidence to be admitted in state but not federal prosecutions meant that "federal officers, being human, were . . . invited to and did, as our cases indicate, step across the street to the State's attorney with their unconstitutionally seized evidence. Prosecution on the basis of that evidence was then had in a state court in utter disregard of the enforceable Fourth Amendment").

15. *See* Gideon v. Wainwright, 372 U.S. 335, 344–45 (1963) (concluding that the right to counsel is "fundamental" because "in our adversary system of criminal justice, any person haled into court, who is too poor to hire a lawyer, cannot be assured a fair trial unless counsel is provided for him").

16. Justice Scalia would probably go further still, giving the short answer that the significance of the provision *even at the time of its adoption* also does not matter. Even if the provision served a cause that is by present-day standards irrational and even evil, a judicial originalist should not permit that unfortunate state of affairs to change the result. There is a long answer as well, which is that it depends on what you mean by "matters." If the provision at issue in the case is clear on its face, then the social and political implications of the text would not matter. For instance, the language in Article V of the Constitution precluding any amendment prior to 1808 which "shall in any manner affect the first and fourth Clauses in the Ninth Section of the first Article" is quite clear. An originalist would ignore its primary significance, which was to maintain the slave trade until at least 1808. On the other hand, the significance attributed to a provision at the time of its adoption might matter if the language is ambiguous, since it would aid in establishing the original understanding of the provision. In short, the significance cannot overcome the original understanding, but it might help discern it.

17. As Justice Scalia himself put the point when discussing the interpretive function judges perform, "I . . . question whether the *attitude* of the common-law judge—the mind-set that asks, 'What is the most desirable resolution of this case, and how can any impediments to the achievement of that result be evaded?'—is appropriate. . . ." SCALIA, A MATTER OF INTERPRETATION, *supra*, at 13. *See also* CASS R. SUNSTEIN, THE PARTIAL CONSTITUTION 131–32 (1993) (describing "role differentiation" argument favoring using the status quo as a "baseline" for constitutional interpretation, based on the conclusion that "the question whether to alter the status quo is to be answered by politically accountable officials").

18. 494 U.S. 872 (1990).

19. *Id.* at 890.

20. Go tell it to the legislature—except that in the particular instance of *Employment Division v. Smith*, critics did exactly that, with abysmal results. Worried about the decision's implications for the free exercise of religion, Congress passed the Religious Freedom Restoration Act, only to see the Court strike the statute down

as an unconstitutional congressional usurpation of the Court's authority. *See* City of Boerne v. Flores, 521 U.S. 507 (1997).

21. Chapters 1 and 2 are adapted from my article, *Colorizing the Constitution of Originalism: Clarence Thomas at the Rubicon*, published in Volume 16 of the Law and Inequality Journal in 1998.

22. 121 S. Ct. 525 (2000).

23. Clinton v. City of New York, 524 U.S. 417, 452–53 (1998) (Kennedy, J., concurring).

24. *See* Glenn Harlan Reynolds, *Sex, Lies and Jurisprudence: Robert Bork, Griswold and the Philosophy of Original Understanding*, 24 Ga. L. Rev. 1045, 1050 (1990) (describing as the "nub" of Judge Robert Bork's originalist approach the idea that "courts' actions must be constrained by a theory, one that is capable of predicting results").

25. SCALIA, A MATTER OF INTERPRETATION, *supra*, at 9.

26. U.S. Constitution, Art. I, § 3.

27. *See* McCulloch v. Maryland, 17 U.S. [4 Wheat.] 316, 407 (1819).

28. *See* AKHIL REED AMAR, THE BILL OF RIGHTS: CREATION AND RECONSTRUCTION 124–25 (1998) (urging a less "clause bound approach" that looks at each provision in isolation because they are "not a jumble of disconnected clauses").

29. Ex Parte Melof, 735 So.2d 1172 (Ala. 1999).

30. *See, e.g.*, Printz v. United States, 521 U.S. 898, 945–54 (1997) (Stevens, J., dissenting) (exhaustively reviewing historical record to demonstrate widespread "commandeering" of state government officials to carry out federal responsibilities in the first years following adoption of the Constitution); U.S. Term Limits, Inc. v. Thornton, 514 U.S. 779 (1995) (majority opinion ruling unconstitutional state-imposed limits on number of terms which members of Congress may serve).

31. *See* Laurence H. Tribe, *Taking Text and Structure Seriously: Reflections on Free-Form Method in Constitutional Interpretation*, 108 Harv. L. Rev. 1221 (1995).

32. See Cass R. Sunstein, *Foreword: Leaving Things Undecided*, 110 Harv. L. Rev. 4 (1996).

Notes to Chapter 1

1. *See* David R. Tribble, "Solution to the Liar's Paradox," at www.flash.net/~dtribble/text/liar.htm (visiting on June 28, 2001) (discussing a similar construction of the same problem, called the "Epimenides Paradox").

2. *See* McIntyre v. Ohio , 514 U.S. 334, 359 (1995) (Thomas, J., concurring in the judgment) ("When interpreting the Free Speech and Press Clauses, we must be guided by their original meaning, for '[t]he Constitution is a written instrument. As such its meaning does not alter. That which it meant when adopted, it means now'") (quoting South Carolina v. United States, 199 U.S. 437, 448 [1905]).

3. *See* Antonin Scalia, *Originalism: The Lesser Evil*, 57 U. Cin. L. Rev. 849, 862 (1989) (observing the problem of the "faint-hearted originalist," who is unable or

unwilling to adhere to the original understanding in the most difficult cases). I take some comfort in the knowledge that, after today, few would accuse me of being "faint-hearted" in my application of originalism.

4. *Bennis v. Michigan*, 516 U.S. 442, 454 (1996) (Thomas, J., concurring).

5. The Court also concludes that the Virginia statute violates the Due Process Clause because it interferes with the fundamental right of marriage. *Loving*, 388 U.S. at 12. I have elsewhere expressed my disagreement with the premise that the Due Process Clause has any such substantive content, United States v. Carlton, 512 U.S. 26, 39 (1994) (Scalia, J., joined by Thomas, J., concurring in the judgment), and will not repeat my position here.

6. On one occasion, I joined an opinion expressing the view that antimiscegenation laws would violate the Equal Protection Clause as it was originally understood. *See* Planned Parenthood v. Casey, 505 U.S. 833, 980 n.1 (1992) (Scalia, J., concurring in the judgment in part and dissenting in part) (arguing that the "tradition" supporting antimiscegenation laws "was contradicted *by a text* — an Equal Protection Clause that explicitly establishes racial equality as a constitutional value"). Obviously, the question raised here was not at issue in *Casey*. Hence, the view expressed in passing in that opinion cannot substitute for careful analysis of the question, and did not resolve it definitively.

7. 163 U.S. 537, 554 (1898) ("In respect of civil rights, common to all citizens, the Constitution of the United States does not, I think, permit any public authority to know the race of those entitled to be protected in the enjoyment of such rights").

8. *See Loving*, 388 U.S. at 11 ("There can be no question but that Virginia's miscegenation statutes rest solely upon distinctions drawn according to race").

9. Professor Andrew Kull makes the extraordinary argument that, not only did the Fourteenth Amendment create a color-blindness norm, but that even the antebellum Constitution reflects, to some extent, a commitment to that principle. ANDREW KULL, THE COLOR-BLIND CONSTITUTION 8–21 (1992). For this proposition, he cites two aspects of the text itself: the rejection of racial language in the Articles of Confederation's Comity Clause, which was then incorporated into the Constitution, and the care the Framers took not to mention slavery in the Constitution. *Id.* at 8–10. In attempting to find support for our nation's long commitment to color-blindness in this fashion, Professor Kull overreaches; no Constitution which facilitates chattel slavery on the basis of race could dare to profess a devotion to color-blindness. I regard as incoherent Kull's notion that "[t]he framers had compromised with slavery but not with racial discrimination." *Id.* at 20. The absence of explicit mention of slavery and race reflects shame, not color-blindness.

10. It goes too far to say of color-blindness, as Professor Stephen Carter does, that "the authors of the Fourteenth Amendment intended nothing of the sort." Stephen L. Carter, *Bork Redux, or How the Tempting of America Led the People to Rise and Battle for Justice*, 69 Tex. L. Rev. 759, 778 (1991). While color-blindness has limited utility, and must give way in the face of clearly expressed contrary intentions in particular areas (such as antimiscegenation laws), it may provide a "default"

principle for use in those cases where no more specific intent can be discerned. As Professor Powell has observed, historical investigation yields no definitive intent on the part of the founders more frequently than would be ideal. *See* H. Jefferson Powell, *Rules for Originalists*, 73 Va. L. Rev. 659, 688 (1987) ("Often the historical researcher, or the constitutional interpreter seeking enlightenment from history, will find himself considering opposing accounts of the founders' thought that seem of roughly the same plausibility"). That said, to enforce upon the states a color-blindness norm in areas where the framers of the Fourteenth Amendment clearly did not intend them to be bound would "require[us] to transcend (or ignore, if one prefers) the framers' intentions. . . ." Michael Klarman, *An Interpretive History of Modern Equal Protection*, 90 Mich. L. Rev. 213, 216 (1991).

11. *See* Robert J. Lipkin, *Beyond Skepticism, Foundationalism and the New Fuzziness: The Role of Wide Reflective Equilibrium in Legal Theory*, 75 Cornell L. Rev. 811, 829 n.67 (1990) (originalism requires focus on the intent of the founders, not general values abstracted from the text); David A.J. Richards, *Originalism Without Foundations*, 65 N.Y.U. L. Rev. 1373, 1380 (1990) (originalists who are "hostile to the interpolation of the interpreter's normative values into the interpretive process" must "show that the result is neutrally derivable from the originalist history").

12. *See* Michael H. and Victoria D. v. Gerald D., 491 U.S. 110, 127–28 n.6 (1989) (opinion of Scalia, J.) (in defining "fundamental rights," Court should "refer to the most specific level at which a relevant tradition protecting, or denying protection to, the asserted right can be defined"); Planned Parenthood v. Casey, 505 U.S. 833, 981 (1992) (Scalia, J., concurring in the judgment in part and dissenting in part).

13. In his attempt to provide an originalist justification for *Brown*, Judge Bork makes a passing attempt at advancing this argument, saying that "the ratifiers probably assumed that [school] segregation was consistent with equality but they were not addressing segregation." Robert H. Bork, The Tempting of America: The Political Seduction of America 82 (1990). In other words, he suggests we can justifiably look to the greater abstraction (equality), because the more specific issue (school segregation) was not addressed. As Professor Berger demonstrates, however, the historical record convincingly does address school segregation, *see* Raoul Berger, *Robert Bork's Contribution to Original Intention*, 84 Nw. U. L. Rev. 1167, 1180–83 (1990), and it even more convincingly addresses miscegenation.

14. *See* Richards, *Originalism Without Foundations, supra*, at 1382 ("[A] contemporary view of equality that condemns the unjust ravages that state-supported racism has worked on racial minorities. . . . does not track the Founders' conception"). An originalist, at least one committed to neutrality in deriving the original understanding, cannot "giv[e] supremacy to a more abstract over a more concrete understanding of the Founders' intent." *Id.*

15. *See* U.S. Term Limits, Inc. v. Thorton, 514 U.S. 779, 866 (Thomas, J., dissenting) (the "postratification period," in which "five States supplemented the constitutional disqualifications in their very first election laws," is evidence that the Qualifications Clause of Article I does not prescribe exclusive qualifications for members

of Congress); McIntyre v. Ohio Elections Comm'n, 514 U.S. 334, 358–67 (Thomas, J., concurring in the judgment) (widespread practice of anonymous pamphleteering at time of Founding indicates Framers viewed it as constitutionally protected free press). *See also* Michael W. McConnell, *Originalism and the Desegregation Decisions*, 81 Va. L. Rev. 947, 955–56 (1995) (noting as evidence that Fourteenth Amendment was not intended to eliminate segregated schools the fact that "the practice of school segregation was widespread in both the Southern and Northern states, as well as the District of Columbia, at the time of the proposal and ratification of the Amendment, and almost certainly enjoyed the support of a majority of the population even at the height of Reconstruction").

16. At least twenty-nine states maintained miscegenation laws after the Civil War. *See* Harvey M. Applebaum, *Miscegenation Statutes: A Constitutional and Social Problem*, 53 Geo. L.J. 49, 50 (1964) ("The popularity of the statutes continued so that during the nineteenth century thirty-eight states had miscegenation statutes at one time or another. The period surrounding the Civil War found nine of these states repealing their statutes") (footnotes omitted).

17. *See* KULL, THE COLOR-BLIND CONSTITUTION, *supra*, at 3–4 (noting rejection of Wendell Phillips and Thaddeus Stevens's attempt to promote a constitutional amendment that "would have prohibited state and federal governments from distinguishing between persons on the basis of race, no more and no less: it would thus have made the Constitution color-blind in so many words"). As Kull notes, Wendell Phillips's proposal in 1863 to make the Constitution color-blind was not well received. "Ordinary political opinion, including much of Republican opinion, . . . found his proposal for a color-blind Constitution extravagant to the point of absurdity." *Id.* at 60. Professor Kull chronicles the radical Republicans' campaign for adoption of a color-blind constitutional provision, until its ultimate rejection in 1866 when the more limited and ambiguous "equal protection of the laws" terminology was sent to the States for ratification. *Id.* at 55–87.

18. Garrett Epps, *Of Constitutional Seances and Color-Blind Ghosts*, 72 N.C. L. Rev. 401, 420–21 (1994); *see also* Berger, *Robert Bork's Contribution, supra*, at 1183 ("Proposals to establish overall equality, to banish *all* discrimination, were rejected time and time again") (emphasis in original).

19. *See* KULL, THE COLOR-BLIND CONSTITUTION, *supra*, at 64 (quoting letter from Phillips to Thaddeus Stevens and speech by Phillips reprinted in his newspaper, the *National Anti-Slavery Standard*).

20. Berger, *Robert Bork's Contribution, supra*, at 1178; *see also* KULL, THE COLOR-BLIND CONSTITUTION, *supra*, at vii ("the evidence I adduce tends strongly to refute" the claim that "the Fourteenth Amendment was intended by its framers to require color blindness").

21. Loving v. Virginia, 388 U.S. 1, 10 (1967).

22. Berger, *Robert Bork's Contribution, supra*, at 1179 (citing ALEXANDER BICKEL, THE LEAST DANGEROUS BRANCH 56 (1962) (arguing that the "moderate leadership" of the post-war Republicans "had in mind a limited and well-defined meaning . . . a

right to equal protection in the literal sense of benefitting from the laws of security of person and property").

23. Richards, *Originalism Without Foundations, supra,* at 1380 (citing RAOUL BERGER, GOVERNMENT BY JUDICIARY 20–36 [1977]) (emphasis added).

24. McConnell, *Originalism and the Desegregation Decisions, supra,* at 1023–25.

25. *Id.* at 992 (discussing notion of "'limited absolute equality'—equality that is limited to certain spheres ('civil rights') but is absolute within those spheres") (citation omitted); *see also* Jeffrey Rosen, *The Color-Blind Court,* 45 Am. U.L. Rev. 791, 792 (1996) ("The Framers of the Fourteenth Amendment said repeatedly that the Amendment was intended to protect civil rights, but not political or social rights"). For this reason, it is possible to reject the "separate but equal" principle of *Plessy* as the meaning of equal protection while nevertheless dissenting in this case. "Equal protection" may not tolerate racial classifications, but it must first be shown that the particular classification falls within the original scope of the Equal Protection Clause. *Cf.* Hudson v. McMillian, 503 U.S. 1, 18 (1992) (Thomas, J., dissenting) (criticizing Court's expansion of scope of Cruel and Unusual Punishment Clause, which Framers intended to apply "only to torturous punishment meted out by statutes or sentencing judges, and not generally to any hardship that might befall a prisoner during incarceration").

26. *See* Klarman, *An Interpretive History, supra,* at 1920; Emily Field Van Tassel, *Antimiscegenation, The Moral Economy of Dependency, and the Debate Over Rights After the Civil War,* 70 Chi-Kent L. Rev. 873, 876 n.10 (1995) ("What is clear is that by the time of Reconstruction, 'social equality' would become virtually synonymous with miscegenation").

27. No one has as yet challenged the categorization of marriage (circa 1868) as a "social right," nor tried to bring it within the sweep of "civil rights," as McConnell attempted to do with education. *See* McConnell, *Originalism and the Desegregation Decisions, supra,* at 1103–05 ("By the turn of the century—and certainly by the time of the *Brown* decision in 1954—there could be little doubt that schools satisfied the criteria even the opponents of the 1875 Act understood for the existence of civil rights"). It may be telling that in his reply to Professor Klarman's critique of his position on school segregation, McConnell was silent in the face of Klarman's claim that his analysis of the schools question would not support the result in this case. Michael W. McConnell, *The Originalist Justification for Brown: A Reply to Professor Klarman,* 81 Va. L. Rev. 1936 (1995).

28. *See* McConnell, *Originalism and the Desegregation Decisions, supra,* at 1016 ("Supporters and opponents of the [1875 Act] agreed that the Fourteenth Amendment had no bearing on 'social rights'").

29. I have previously explained the importance, in discerning the original intent, of focusing on what the framers said about their handiwork. In Missouri v. Jenkins, 515 U.S. 70, 126 (1995) (Thomas, J., concurring) (emphasis added), I pointed out that

the Anti-Federalists criticized the Constitution because it might be read to grant broad equitable powers to the federal courts. In response, the defenders of the Constitution "sold" the new framework of government to the public by espousing a narrower interpretation of the equity power. *When an attack on the Constitution is followed by an open Federalist effort to narrow the provision, the appropriate conclusion is that the drafters and ratifiers of the Constitution approved the more limited construction offered in response.*

30. *See* Steven A. Bank, *Comment, Antimiscegenation Laws and the Dilemma of Symmetry: The Understanding of Equality in the Civil Rights Act of 1875,* 2 U. Chi. L. Sch. Roundtable 303, 305 (1995).

31. *See id.* at 319–23; *see also* McConnell, *Originalism and the Desegregation Decisions, supra,* at 1020 n.351 (discussing pre-ratification assurances that the 1866 Act would not interfere with state antimiscegenation laws).

32. Bank, *Antimiscegenation Laws, supra,* at 319.

33. *See* Laurence H. Tribe, *Taking Text and Structure Seriously, supra,* at 1241 (calling the requirements for amending the Constitution "the most fundamental agreement[] . . . among the people and their government").

34. *Id.* at 1233. Professor Tribe proposes that provisions like Article V "be given as fixed and determinate a reading as possible." *Id.* at 1247. In my view, of course, that is true of *every* part of the Constitution.

35. The alert reader—at least the one who pays attention to these notes—will observe that many of the citations included in the opinion post-date 1967, and thus could not have been included in *Loving.* I am not certain this should even be a concern. This is, after all, a fictional opinion written by a non-member of the Court in a world that did not exist; if Justice Thomas can be carried back to 1967, he can take with him some material to which he might refer. More important, it is helpful to cite the real Thomas saying something about what he believes to avoid unfairly mischaracterizing his views, and it only makes sense to cite *all* scholarly work about the original understanding of the Fourteenth Amendment even if some of it would not have been available to a Supreme Court Justice in 1967.

36. There have been numerous attempts to reconcile originalism with the results in landmark cases such as *Loving* and, especially, *Brown v. Board of Education.* Were any of these efforts successful, it would afford our imaginary Justice Thomas a way out of his dilemma, because he could concur in *Loving* while remaining true to his originalist approach. I explained why the works of Judge Bork, Professor McConnell, and others were unpersuasive in my article, *Colorizing the Constitution of Originalism,* and will not reproduce that analysis here.

37. Adarand Constructors, Inc. v. Pena, 515 U.S. 200, 240 (1995) (Thomas, J., concurring in part and concurring in the judgment).

38. 515 U.S. 200 (1995).

39. *Id.* at 240 (Thomas, J., concurring in part and concurring in the judgment).

40. Missouri v. Jenkins, 515 U.S. 70, 120–21 (1995) (Thomas, J., concurring).

41. *See Jenkins,* 515 U.S. at 121 ("The Constitution does not prevent individuals from choosing to live together, to work together, or to send their children to school together, so long as the State does not interfere with their choices on the basis of race").

42. And, in fact, it is not true: "Virginia prohibits only interracial marriages involving white persons. . . ." *Loving*, 388 U.S. at 11. Thus, the different races are not treated equally under Virginia law.

43. *Loving*, 388 U.S. at 11.

44. Having expressed this much agreement with the majority opinion, I feel compelled to record my concern about language in the Court's opinion that could be read as leaving room for undue departures from the Fourteenth Amendment's bar to governmental uses of racial classifications. The Court speaks not of a complete bar, but instead of "the very heavy burden of justification which the Fourteenth Amendment has traditionally required of state statutes drawn according to race." *Loving*, 388 U.S. at 9. So long as the permissibility of some racial classifications this language implies (those that meet the Court's "heavy burden") is limited to crisis situations in which the classification is closely related to an overriding governmental purpose, and is wholly essential to the achievement of that purpose, I have no quarrel with the Court's careful caveat. The classic hypothetical of a prison race riot, in which the authorities are forced to separate—and hence classify—the prisoners by race in order to restore order out of the crisis would be a situation of the type I have in mind. *See* City of Richmond v. J.A. Croson Company, 488 U.S. 469, 520 (1989) (Scalia, J., concurring) (agreeing that "a social emergency rising to the level of imminent danger to life and limb," such as a "prison race riot," would justify exception to color-blindness principle). Such limited, brief racial classifications to serve a truly compelling governmental purpose would not offend the Fourteenth Amendment. I could not, however, accept any broader view of acceptable racial classifications. If the Court intends to sweep more broadly, there will be time enough to object in a case when it actually applies the test in that fashion.

45. *See* United States v. Carlton, 512 U.S. 26, 39 (1994) (Scalia, J., joined by Thomas, J., concurring in the judgment).

46. *Loving*, 388 U.S. at 12.

47. 575 U.S. 70, 114–138 (1995) (Thomas, J., concurring).

48. *Id.* at 121 (Thomas, J., concurring) ("Regardless of the relative quality of the schools, segregation violated the Constitution because the State classified students based on their race").

49. *See* Cass R. Sunstein, *Foreword: Leaving Things Undecided*, 110 Harv. L. Rev. 4, 92 n.465 (1996) ("The constitutional attack on affirmative action programs by Justices Scalia and Thomas, without any investigation of history on their part, is one of the most disturbing features of their purported originalism"). Justice Thomas did include one oblique citation to Professor McConnell's attempted originalist defense of *Brown*. *Jenkins*, 515 U.S. at 120. Even McConnell, however, did not argue that the Fourteenth Amendment's Framers' intent was that "the government may not make [any] distinctions on the basis of race." His argument was only that, at least by the time of *Brown*, school segregation was no longer one of the distinctions that would have been permitted under the Framers' vision.

50. *Jenkins*, 515 U.S. at 114.

51. *Id.* at 119.

52. *Id.* at 122.

53. *Id. at* 126–31.

54. 514 U.S. 779, 846–49 (1995) (Thomas, J., dissenting).

55. 515 U.S. 819, 852 (1995) (Thomas, J., concurring).

56. *E.g., U.S. Term Limits,* 514 U.S. at 869 and n.11 (discussing original understanding of Qualifications Clause); at 877–905 (same).

57. *Rosenberger,* 515 U.S. at 852–63 (discussing Madison's view of church/state separation, and the early practices of federal involvement with churches after ratification of First Amendment).

Notes to Chapter 2

1. WALT WHITMAN, *Song of Myself, in* LEAVES OF GRASS 25, 76 (1992).

2. Daniel A. Farber and Suzanna Sherry, *Telling Stories Out of School: An Essay on Legal Narratives,* 45 Stan. L. Rev. 807, 827 (1993) (citing David Luban, *Difference Made Legal: The Court and Dr. King,* 87 Mich. L. Rev. 2152, 2155–56 [1989]). Farber and Sherry regard the claim that "the legal system itself filters out" out-siders' stories as "perhaps exaggerated," but they acknowledge that the charge has "some substance." *Id.* They understate; we should see originalism as Professor Culp has, as a mandate for courts to ignore those voices the Framers did not hear. *See* Jerome McCristal Culp, Jr., *Toward a Black Legal Scholarship: Race and Original Understandings,* 1991 Duke L. Rev. 39, 69 ("The most important example of the tendency to remove the black experience and perspective from the law is found in the arguments of those who advocate a return to original intent. To rely on original intent is to hitch our interpretational scheme to a vision that excluded blacks").

3. Most prominent among those groups are women (who for most of our constitutional history lacked the right to vote and were ineligible to serve at the constitutional convention and/or in state legislatures), African-Americans (who were either enslaved or deprived of the right to vote), and the poor (only men with property were eligible to vote). The voices of gay men and lesbians have not been heard as such, because laws and social taboos against same-gender relationships have made it impossible for sexual and gender minorities either to organize or speak out for almost all of American history.

4. *Cf.* CATHERINE MACKINNON, FEMINISM UNMODIFIED: DISCOURSE ON LIFE AND LAW 39 (1987) ("[W]hen you are powerless, you don't just speak differently. A lot, you don't speak. Your speech is not just differently articulated, it is silenced. Eliminated, gone").

5. 503 U.S. 1 (1992).

6. *Id.* at 4.

7. *Id.* at 17 (Thomas, J., dissenting).

8. *Id.* at 18 (Thomas, J., dissenting).

9. *Id.* at 18–20 (Thomas, J., dissenting). *See also* Charles Lawrence III, *Listening*

to the Lessons of Our History, in AFRICAN-AMERICANS AND THE LIVING CONSTITUTION 194, 195–96 (John Hope Franklin and Genna Rae McNeil, eds., 1995) (arguing that Justice Scalia's originalist First Amendment opinion in *R.A. V. v. City of St. Paul, MN*, 505 U.S. 377 (1992), is noteworthy for ignoring the story of the African-American family victimized by cross-burning held to be protected speech).

10. *See supra* Chapter 1.

11. This denial resonates all the more powerfully because Thomas is an African-American man in an interracial marriage. The racist norm against interracial sexual contact is based primarily on the white taboo against black men having access to white women. *See* A. LEON HIGGINBOTHAM, JR., IN THE MATTER OF COLOR: RACE AND THE AMERICAN LEGAL PROCESS: THE COLONIAL PERIOD 40–41 (during colonial period, "[t]he legal process was tolerant of white male illicit 'escapades' involving either white females or black females, but it was . . . brutally harsh on infractions between black males and white females"); Andrew Koppelman, *Why Discrimination Against Lesbians and Gay Men Is Sex Discrimination*, 69 N.Y.U. L. Rev. 197, 224–26 (1995) ("[W]hite men took access to black women for granted, before and after emancipation, while the barest hint (or even the projected fantasy) of a black man's desire for a white woman often sufficed to bring out the lynch mob. . . . The taboo connoted a narrative in which black men represented a dangerous, predatory, uncontrollable sexuality, and white women represented a fragile, asexual purity, the protection of which was the special duty of white men") (citations omitted). This concentration on the preservation of the "purity" of white women continues today. *See* Epps, *Of Constitutional Seances, supra*, at 443 (noting similarities between "American attitudes towards race" and "Indian views on caste," including "a desire to bar men of the subordinated group from access to women of the superior group") (citing Andre Beteille, *Race Caste and Gender*, 25 Man 489, 491–94 [1990]).

12. *See* JANE MAYER and JILL ABRAMSON, STRANGE JUSTICE: THE SELLING OF CLARENCE THOMAS 40–42 (1994) (describing as crucial in Thomas's future opportunities the "superior education" he received at racially segregated Catholic schools).

13. *See id.* at 48 (quoting Thomas saying that, while at Immaculate Conception, "Not a day passed that I was not pricked by prejudice").

14. *Id.* at 119.

15. Similar recognitive interpretation on the issue of all-black education can be found in Thomas's concurring opinion in United States v. Fordice, 505 U.S. 717 (1992). He suggested that black students may achieve excellent academic results in primarily black environments:

> Despite the shameful history of state-enforced segregation, [black colleges] have survived and flourished. Indeed, they have expanded as opportunities for blacks to enter historically white institutions have expanded. Between 1954 and 1980, for example, enrollment at historically black colleges increased from 70,000 to 200,000 students, while degrees awarded increased from

13,000 to 32,000. . . . I think it indisputable that these institutions have suc-
ceeded in part because of their distinctive histories and traditions. . . .
Id. at 748.

16. *See* McConnell, *Originalism and the Desegregation Decisions, supra,* at 947. I
have elsewhere set forth the reasons I believe Professor McConnell's arguments fall
short of the daunting challenge he sets for himself. *See* Samuel Marcosson, *Colorizing the Constitution of Originalism: Clarence Thomas at the Rubicon,*16 Law & Inequality 429, 450–57 (1998) (arguing that attempts to find originalist justifications
for *Brown* and *Loving* rely on equivocal, post-ratification evidence that is contradicted by the understanding of the Fourteenth Amendment advanced during the
ratification process).

17. MAYER and ABRAMSON, STRANGE JUSTICE, *supra,* at 53 (quoting Johnson).

18. SCOTT DOUGLAS GERBER, FIRST PRINCIPLES: THE JURISPRUDENCE OF
CLARENCE THOMAS 12 (1999) (quoting Clare Cushman, "Clarence Thomas," in *The
Supreme Court Justices: Illustrated Biographies, 1789–1995,* 528 (Clare Cushman, ed.)
(2d ed., 1995).

19. *See* MAYER and ABRAMSON, STRANGE JUSTICE, *supra,* at 20–21 (discussing
apparent thinness of Thomas's credentials, and quoting Senator Joe Biden as saying,
"Had Thomas been white, he never would have been nominated").

20. Adarand Constructors, Inc. v. Pena, 515 U.S. 200, 241 (1995) (Thomas, J., concurring in part and concurring in the judgment).

21. Clarence Thomas, "The Modern Civil Rights Movement: Can a Regime of
Individual Rights and the Rule of Law Survive?" Toqueville Forum, Winston-Salem,
NC, 18 April 1988, 1–26, 17 (quoted in GERBER, FIRST PRINCIPLES, *supra,* at 195).

22. 512 U.S. 874, 903 (1994).

23. GERBER, FIRST PRINCIPLES, *supra,* at 196.

24. *See* MAYER and ABRAMSON, STRANGE JUSTICE, *supra,* at 118 ("Thomas was
frequently the subject of attacks by civil rights leaders, many of whom considered
him an Uncle Tom and a traitor to his race for abandoning the broader, more active
role of his predecessors at the EEOC").

25. *Id.* at 119.

26. Clarence A. Thomas, *Civility,* 4 Race & Ethnic Ancestry L.J. 1 (1998).

27. *See* Trina Grillo and Stephanie M. Wildman, *Obscuring the Importance of
Race: The Implication of Making Comparisons Between Racism and Sexism (or Other
-isms),* in CRITICAL RACE THEORY: THE CUTTING EDGE 564, 565 (Richard Delgado,
ed., 1995) ("Whites do not look at the world through this filter of racial awareness,
even though they also comprise a race. This privilege to ignore their race gives
whites a societal advantage . . .").

28. *See* Sumi Cho, *Redeeming Whiteness in the Shadow of Internment: Earl Warren, Brown, and a Theory of Racial Redemption,* 19 Bost. Coll. Third World L.J. 73,
125–35 (1998) (arguing that *Brown* reflected Chief Justice Warren's transformation
and was part of his ultimately deficient attempt at redemption for his role in the
wartime internment).

29. Professor Scott Gerber, who certainly is far more sympathetic to Thomas than am I, shares this assessment. *See* GERBER, FIRST PRINCIPLES, *supra*, at 193 ("Justice Thomas appeals to the *ideal* of equality ... when he decides questions involving race, but to the Framers' *specific* intentions ... when he decides questions involving civil liberties and federalism. ... [He] approaches legal questions pertaining to race *differently* than he approaches legal questions pertaining to other matters") (emphasis in original).

Notes to Chapter 3

1. U.S. Constitution, amend. V.

2. William Michael Treanor, *The Original Understanding of the Takings Clause and the Political Process*, 95 Colum. L. Rev. 782, 782 (1995) (emphasis added).

3. *Id.* at 789–90.

4. *Id.* at 792–93 (speaking of state just compensation requirements, and noting that "antebellum courts ... consistently held that state regulation pursuant to the police power did not give rise to a compensation requirement, regardless of how dramatically that regulation affected the value of property").

5. *See* James Madison, Amendments to the Constitution (June 8, 1789), in 12 THE PAPERS OF JAMES MADISON 197, 201 (Charles F. Hobson et al., eds., 1979) ("No person shall be . . . obliged to *relinquish his property*, where it may be necessary for public use, without a just compensation") (emphasis added); Treanor, *Original Understanding of the Takings Clause, supra*, at 838–40 (analyzing other Madisonian discussions of property rights and the occasions demanding compensation).

6. 123 U.S. 623 (1887).

7. *Id.* at 668. To similar effect, the Court stated in Transportation Company v. Chicago, 99 U.S. 635 (1879), that governmental action "not directly encroaching upon private property" does not require compensation, even though the action might "impair [the property's] use," on the ground that such state actions "are universally held not to be a taking within the meaning of the constitutional provision." *Id.* at 642.

8. 260 U.S. 393 (1922).

9. *Id.* at 415.

10. Dolan v. City of Tigard, 512 U.S. 374, 406–07 (1994) (Stevens, J., dissenting).

11. *Pennsylvania Coal*, 260 U.S. at 414.

12. 505 U.S. 1003 (1992).

13. *Id.* at 1057 (Blackmun, J., dissenting).

14. *Id.* at 1057–58 (quoting Siegel, *Understanding the Nineteenth Century Contract Clause: The Role of the Property-Privilege Distinction and "Takings" Clause Jurisprudence*, 60 S.Cal.L.Rev. 1, 76 [1986]).

15. *Id.* at 1014.

16. *Id.* at 1016.

17. *Lucas*, 505 U.S. at 1028 n.15 ("Justice Blackmun is correct that early constitutional theorists did not believe the Takings Clause embraced regulations of property at all . . . but even he does not suggest (explicitly, at least) that we renounce the Court's contrary conclusion in *Mahon*. Since the text of the Clause can be read to encompass regulatory as well as physical deprivations . . . we decline to do so as well").

18. *See* Treanor, *Original Understanding of the Takings Clause, supra*, at 808 (arguing that *Lucas* "neatly illustrates the irrelevance of the original understanding for modern takings jurisprudence," because even the one Justice who discussed the original understanding "does not actually believe that it should be used to decide the case").

19. *Id.* at 858 ("A traditional originalism yields a reading of the Takings Clause that is clearly unpersuasive to almost everyone today—so even originalists such as . . . Scalia are not originalists when it comes to the Takings Clause").

20. *See* Andrew S. Gold, *Regulatory Takings and the Original Intent: The Direct, Physical Takings Thesis "Goes Too Far,"* 49 Am. U.L. Rev. 181, 184 (1999).

21. *Id.* at 182 (emphasis added).

22. *Id.* at 185.

23. Stenberg v. Carhart, 540 U.S. 914, 954–55 (2000) (Scalia, J., dissenting) (emphasis added).

24. Treanor, *The Original Understanding of the Takings Clause, supra*, at 812.

25. *See* SCALIA, A MATTER OF INTERPRETATION, *supra*, at 139 (arguing that originalism, like other methods of interpretation, "cannot remake the world anew," but must defer to *stare decisis* "in the interest of stability").

26. Laurence H. Tribe, *Comment*, in SCALIA, A MATTER OF INTERPRETATION, *supra*, at 83 (criticizing Justice Scalia's invocation of *stare decisis* because, even if he follows a set of "rules" for applying the doctrine, those rules "certainly are not derived from the 'original meaning' of the text of the Constitution, as Justice Scalia's interpretive methodology would require").

27. 60 U.S. (19 How.) 393 (1856).

28. Christopher L. Eisgruber, *Dred Again: Originalism's Forgotten Past*, 10 Const. Comment. 37, 54 (1993).

29. For example, the regulatory takings movement found expression in President Ronald Reagan's Executive Order 12,630, which directed that "[e]xecutive departments and agencies should review their actions carefully to prevent unnecessary takings and should account in decision-making for those takings that are necessitated by statutory mandate." See Exec. Order No. 12,630, 3 C.F.R. For example, the regulatory takings movement found expression in President Ronald Reagan's Executive Order 12,630, which directed that "[e]xecutive departments and agencies should review their actions carefully to prevent unnecessary takings and should account in decision-making for those takings that are necessitated by statutory mandate." See Exec. Order No. 12,630, 3 C.F.R. §§ 554 (1989). Reagan Administration Solicitor General Charles Fried said of Executive Order 12,630:

Attorney General [Edwin] Meese and his young advisors—many drawn from the ranks of the then fledgling Federalist Societies and often devotees of the extreme libertarian views of Chicago law professor Richard Epstein—had a specific, aggressive, and, it seemed to me, quite radical project in mind: to use the Takings Clause of the Fifth Amendment as a severe brake upon federal and state regulation of business and property. The grand plan was to make government pay compensation as for a taking of property every time its regulations impinged too severely on a property right—limiting the possible uses for a parcel of land or restricting or tying up a business in regulatory red tape. If the government labored under so severe an obligation, there would be, to say the least, much less regulation.

CHARLES FRIED, ORDER AND LAW: ARGUING THE REAGAN REVOLUTION—A FIRST-HAND ACCOUNT 183 (1991).

30. *See* N.L.R.B. v. Jones & Laughlin Steel Corp., 301 U.S. 1 (1937) (finding National Labor Relations Act constitutional based on Justice Roberts' shift in position from earlier cases striking down New Deal legislation).

31. *See* West Coast Hotel Co. v. Parrish, 300 U.S. 379, 402–03 (1937) (Sutherland, J., dissenting) ("[T]he meaning of the Constitution does not change with the ebb and flow of economic events. . . . [T]o say . . . that the words of the Constitution mean today what they did not mean when written—that is, that they do not apply to a situation now to which they would have applied then—is to rob that instrument of the essential element which continues it in force as the people have made it until they, and not their official agents, have made it otherwise").

32. United States v. Lopez, 514 U.S. 549, 561 (1995).

33. Wickard v. Filburn, 317 U.S. 111, 125 (1942) (emphasis added).

34. 529 U.S. 598 (2000).

35. *Id.* at 627 (Thomas, J., concurring).

36. *See* Saul A. Cornell, *The Changing Historical Fortunes of the Anti-Federalists*, 84 Nw. U. L. Rev. 39, 54 (1989) (discussing historical claims that "the profound mistrust of centralized authority . . . animated politicians of the Revolutionary generation").

37. SCALIA, A MATTER OF INTERPRETATION, *supra*, at 43.

38. This is the flaw in the argument advanced by Andrew Gold in trying to supply an originalist argument in defense of the regulatory takings doctrine: He speaks at length about the general importance the framers attached to property rights, as if that platitude is determinative on the specific question of which government actions constitute a "taking" of property. *See* Gold, *Regulatory Takings and Original Intent, supra*, at 195–96 (arguing that "there is significant documentation that suggests the majority of the Framers thought the protection of property was a high priority").

39. Planned Parenthood v. Casey, 112 S. Ct. 2791, 2874 n.1 (1992) (Scalia, J., concurring in the judgment in part and dissenting in part).

40. SCALIA, A MATTER OF INTERPRETATION, *supra,* at 148.

41. *Id.* at 149.

42. Akhil Reed Amar, *Fourth Amendment First Principles*, 107 Harv. L. Rev. 757, 757 (1994).

43. 480 U.S. 321 (1987).

44. David A. Sklansky, *The Fourth Amendment and Common Law*, 100 Colum. L. Rev. 1739, 1751 (2000).

45. 526 U.S. 295 (1999).

46. *Id.* at 299.

47. Sklansky, *The Fourth Amendment, supra,* at 1770.

48. *Id.* at 1774–1813.

49. Amar, *Fourth Amendment First Principles, supra,* at 759.

50. *Id.*

51. U.S. Constitution, Amend. IV (emphasis added).

52. AMAR, THE BILL OF RIGHTS, *supra,* at 69 (emphasis added).

53. U.S. Constitution, Amend. IV ("[N]o Warrants shall issue, but upon probable cause, supported by Oath or affirmation, and particularly describing the place to be searched, and the persons or things to be seized").

54. California v. Acevedo, 500 U.S. 565, 581 (1992) (Scalia, J., concurring in the judgment).

55. *Id.* at 581, 583.

56. City of West Covina v. Perkins, 525 U.S. 234,247 n.2 (1999) (Thomas, J., concurring in the judgment).

57. 525 U.S. 83, 91–98 (1998) (Scalia, J., concurring) (arguing that a person has the right to be free from an unreasonable search or seizure only in her own home).

58. 483 U.S. 635 (1987).

59. *Id.* at 636–37.

60. *See* Anderson v. Creighton, 483 U.S. 635, 660 (1987) (Stevens, J., dissenting) (arguing that majority opinion means that "even though an entry into a private home is constitutionally unreasonable, it will not give rise to monetary liability if a reasonable officer could have believed it was reasonable . . .").

61. Wholly apart from the original understanding, it also seems, in Professor Jeffries' phrase, that "[i]t is indefensible, if not exactly illogical, to support restrictions on money damages without embracing exclusion (or some other remedy [for Fourth Amendment violations])." John C. Jeffries, *Disaggregating Constitutional Torts*, 100 Yale L.J. 259, 283 (2000). As he suggests, "[I]t will not do to bemoan the costs of exclusion unless one is willing to accept the costs of civil liability (or vice-versa)." *Id.*

62. *Anderson*, 483 U.S. at 643 (majority opinion).

63. *Id.* at 638.

64. Amar, *Fourth Amendment First Principles, supra,* at 775; *see also* Thomas Y. Davies, *Recovering the Original Fourth Amendment*, 98 Mich. L. Rev. 547, 661–62 (1999) (arguing that an official's misconduct in exceeding his authority by conducting an unlawful search rendered him liable in trespass).

65. Davies, *Recovering the Original Fourth Amendment, supra,* at 625.

66. Amar, *Fourth Amendment First Principles, supra,* at 761 n.5.

67. 121 S. Ct. 2038 (2001).

68. 500 U.S. 44 (1991).

69. *Id.* at 61 (Scalia, J., dissenting).

70. *Kyllo,* 121 S. Ct. at 2045 ("In the home, our cases show, all details are intimate details, because the entire area is held safe from prying government eyes").

71. Amar, *Fourth Amendment First Principles, supra,* at 797 n.140.

72. Davies, *Recovering the Original Fourth Amendment, supra,* at 578.

73. *Id.* at 601. Of course, this argument (even if persuasive as reflecting the original understanding of the framers) runs into a textualist response: The first portion of the Fourth Amendment explicitly protects the right of people to be secure "against unreasonable searches and seizures."

74. *See, e.g.,* Sklansky, *The Fourth Amendment and Common Law, supra;* Donald Dripps, *Akhil Amar on Criminal Procedure and Constitutional Law: "Here I Go Down That Wrong Road Again,"* 74 N.C. L. Rev. 1559 (1996); Carol S. Steiker, *Second Thoughts About First Principles,* 107 Harv. L. Rev. 820 (1994); Tracy Maclin, *The Central Meaning of the Fourth Amendment,* 35 Wm. & Mary L. Rev. 197 (1993).

Notes to Chapter 4

1. 426 U.S. 833 (1976).

2. U.S. Constitution, Amend. X.

3. Hodel v. Virginia Surface Mining and Reclamation Association, Inc., 452 U.S. 264, 288 (1981).

4. Garcia v. San Antonio Metropolitan Transit Authority, 469 U.S. 528, 546–47 (1985).

5. *Id.* at 550–51 (pointing to the states' role, as states, in electing the President and in the Senate).

6. *Id.* at 580 (Rehnquist, J., dissenting).

7. United States v. Lopez, 514 U.S. 549, 601 n.8 (Thomas, J., concurring) ("Although I might be willing to return to the original understanding, I recognize that many believe that it is too late in the day to undertake a fundamental reexamination of the past 60 years. Considerations of *stare decisis* and reliance interests may convince us that we cannot wipe the slate clean").

8. United States v. Morrison, 529 U.S. 598, 627 (2000) (Thomas, J., concurring).

9. U.S. Constitution, Art. II, § 5 ("No person except a natural born Citizen, or a Citizen of the United States, at the time of the Adoption of this Constitution, shall be eligible to the Office of President; neither shall any Person be eligible to that Office who shall not have attained to the Age of thirty five Years, and been fourteen Years a Resident within the United States").

10. SCALIA, A MATTER OF INTERPRETATION, *supra,* at 141 (quoting Laurence H. Tribe, *Comment,* in *id.* at 86).

11. *See* Printz v. United States, 521 U.S. 898, 937–38 (1997) (Thomas, J., concurring) (observing that even if the federal government has Commerce Clause authority to support regulation of "wholly *intra*state, point-of-sale" transactions, the Second Amendment might place off-limits such transactions involving firearms).

12. *See* Akhil Reed Amar, *The Constitutional Virtues and Vices of the New Deal*, 22 Harv. J. L. & Pub. Pol'y 219, 224 (1998) ("Congress does not enjoy unlimited power, and crime in schools might be a genuinely national problem (a problem everywhere), but not a federal problem (not an interstate problem) because the effects are so localized. . . . I fail to see why we would necessarily need an interstate federal government to get involved; it may not be a truly federal problem even though it might be a national problem").

13. United States v. Morrison, 529 U.S. 598, 660 (2000) (Breyer, J., dissenting). *See also* Amar, *Constitutional Virtues, supra,* at 224 ("We have, in my view, broader congressional power to regulate interstate commerce after 1937, not because of some amendment-equivalent adopted as a result of a constitutional moment, but just because, in the real world, a lot more things are interstate due to improvements in transportation and communication technology. The percentage of our genuine Gross Domestic Product that involves people and things that cross state lines—pollution molecules, wild animals, the internet, and so on—is just much, much bigger than it was prior to 1937").

14. *See Morrison*, 529 U.S. at 610 ("[A] fair reading of *Lopez* shows that the noneconomic, criminal nature of the conduct at issue was central to our decision in that case"). The entire *Lopez* distinction between commercial and non-commercial activity is both unpersuasive and non-originalist. It is unpersuasive for the reason explained in Justice Breyer's dissent in *Morrison*: "[W]hy," he asked, "should we give critical constitutional importance to the economic, or noneconomic, nature of an interstate-commerce-affecting *cause*? If chemical emanations through indirect environmental change cause identical, severe commercial harm outside a State, why should it matter whether local factories or home fireplaces release them?" *Morrison*, 529 U.S. at 657 (Breyer, J., dissenting) (emphasis in original). It is non-originalist because there is no evidence the framers ever entertained such a distinction; if we accept Justice Thomas's position on the question, they didn't expect that either economic or noneconomic activity would be regulable simply because it had an effect on interstate commerce.

15. *See Lopez*, 514 U.S. at 559–60; *Morrison*, 529 U.S. at 613 ("[T]hus far in our Nation's history our cases have upheld Commerce Clause regulation of intrastate activity only where that activity is economic in nature"). That assertion by the majority was demonstrably false; as the dissent pointed out, the Court had said in *Wickard v. Filburn*, 317 U.S. 111, 124 (1942), "if appellee's activity be local and though it may not be regarded as commerce, it may still, *whatever its nature*, be reached by Congress if it exerts a substantial economic effect on interstate commerce. . . ."

16. John E. Nowak, *Federalism and the Civil War Amendments*, 23 Ohio N. L. Rev. 1209, 1211 (1997).

17. Douglas Laycock, *Conceptual Gulfs in* City of Boerne v. Flores, 39 Wm. & Mary L. Rev. 743, 758 (1998).

18. Respectively: United States v. Cruikshank, 92 U.S. 542 (1876); United States v. Harris, 106 U.S. 629 (1883).

19. The Civil Rights Cases, 109 U.S. 3 (1883).

20. *Id.* at 24.

21. *See* Laycock, *Conceptual Gulfs, supra,* at 760 (criticizing the Supreme Court's "counterrevolution" against the Fourteenth Amendment, including its holding in *Cruikshank* that "none of the new amendments empowered the United States to prosecute members of a private military that massacred black citizens in a fight to control a local government").

22. Kimel v. Florida Board of Regents, 528 U.S. 62, 84 (2000) (emphasis added).

23. Adarand Constructors, Inc. v. Pena, 515 U.S. 200, 237 (1996) ("Finally, we wish to dispel the notion that strict scrutiny is 'strict in theory but fatal in fact'") (citation omitted).

24. *Kimel,* 528 U.S. at 86.

25. Board of Trustees of the University of Alabama v. Garrett, 121 S. Ct. 955 (2001).

26. *Id.* at 963–64.

27. South Carolina v. Katzenbach, 383 U.S. 301 (1966); Fitzpatrick v. Bitzer, 427 U.S. 445 (1976).

28. Laycock, *Conceptual Gulfs, supra,* at 765.

29. *Id.*

30. 494 U.S. 872, 882 (1990).

31. City of Boerne v. Flores, 521 U.S. 507, 519 (1997).

32. 5 U.S. (1 Cranch) 137 (1803).

33. Akhil Reed Amar, *Intratextualism,* 112 Harv. L. Rev. 747, 820 (1999).

34. Akhil Reed Amar, *The Constitution Versus the Court: Some Thoughts on Hills on Amar,* 94 Nw. U. L. Rev. 205, 210 (1999) (footnotes omitted).

35. Alden v. Maine, 527 U.S. 706, 712 (1999).

36. *Id.* at 729.

37. Professor Erwin Chemerinsky has argued that *Alden* is inconsistent with the conservative approach to assessing constitutional claims for fundamental individual rights, and that these decisions reveal "a value choice by the conservative Justices to favor state governments over individual rights." Erwin Chemerinsky, *The Hypocrisy of* Alden v. Maine: *Judicial Review, Sovereign Immunity and the Rehnquist Court,* 33 Loy. L.A. L. Rev. 1283, 1285 (2000). This argument is persuasive; indeed, I would guess the conservative Justices would concur and respond that this "value choice" is an expression of the very federalist structure *Alden* vindicates.

38. *Id.* at 1292–95.

39. *Alden,* 527 U.S. at 754–55 (emphasis added).

40. Seminole Tribe v. Florida, 517 U.S. 44 (1996); Florida Prepaid Postsecondary Educ. Expense Bd. v. College Sav. Bank, 527 U.S. 627 (1999).

41. *Printz,* 521 U.S. at 905.

42. 2 U.S. (2 Dall.) 419 (1793).

43. *Printz,* 521 U.S. at 903.

44. No question was raised, that is, except for Justice Thomas, who used the case as an opportunity to reiterate his wish for the Court to reconsider the entire "substantial effects" doctrine. *See id.* at 936–37 (Thomas, J., concurring).

45. *See id.* at 905–18.

46. *Id.* at 918 (citation omitted).

47. 379 U.S. 479 (1965).

48. *Id.*

49. *Printz,* 521 U.S. at 922.

50. *Id.* at 907.

51. 14 U.S. (1 Wheat.) 304 (1816).

52. *Alden,* 527 U.S. at 749.

53. *Id.* (emphasis added).

54. *Id.* at 755 ("In ratifying the Constitution, the States consented to suits brought by other States or by the Federal Government").

55. 440 U.S. 410 (1979). To the contrary, the Court carefully and at some length distinguished *Hall,* saying of its decision there, "Since we determined the Constitution did not reflect an agreement between the States to respect the sovereign immunity of one another, California was free to determine whether it would respect Nevada's sovereignty as a matter of comity." *Alden,* 527 U.S. at 738–39.

56. *See* John T. Cross, *Intellectual Property and the Eleventh Amendment After Seminole Tribe,* 47 DePaul L. Rev. 519, 563 (1998) (arguing that although jurisdiction is currently restricted to federal courts, "with a simple stroke of a pen, Congress could give state courts jurisdiction in patent and copyright cases involving state defendants").

57. Republican Party Platform, Part II, *available at* www.yologop.org/plat5.htm. This part of the platform expressed the party's positions on affirmative action ("Because we believe rights inhere in individuals, not in groups, we will attain our nation's goal of equal rights without quotas or other forms of preferential treatment. . . . We likewise endorse this year's Proposition 209, the California Civil Rights Initiative, to restore to law the original meaning of civil rights"); takings ("We reaffirm the promise of the Fifth Amendment: 'nor shall private property be taken for public use, without just compensation.' This Takings Clause protects the homes and livelihood of Americans against the governmental greed and abuse of power that characterizes the Clinton Administration; we will strictly enforce it"); and the exclusionary rule ("We will reform the Supreme Court's fanciful exclusionary rule, which has allowed a generation of criminals to get off on technicalities"). Each stance dovetailed with the non-originalist work of Justices Thomas and Scalia.

58. *Id.* at Part II ("Principles of the 1996 Republican Platform") ("Because we trust our fellow Americans, rather than centralized government, we believe the people, acting through their State and local elected officials, should have control

over programs like education and welfare—thereby pushing power away from official Washington and returning it to the people in their communities and states").

59. *See* Callins v. Collins, 510 U.S. 1141 (1994) (Scalia, J., concurring in the denial of certiorari) (arguing that the "text and tradition of the Constitution" establish that the death penalty is not cruel and unusual punishment in violation of the Eighth Amendment).

60. SCALIA, A MATTER OF INTERPRETATION, *supra*, at 46 (criticizing judicial adherents of the "Living Constitution" approach, noting that "[n]o fewer than three of the Justices with whom I have served had maintained that the death penalty is unconstitutional, *even though its use is explicitly contemplated in the Constitution*") (emphasis in original).

61. *Id.* at 132 ("No textualist-originalist interpretation that passes the laugh test could, for example, extract from the United States Constitution the . . . prohibition of abortion laws that a majority of the Court has found").

62. Republican Party Platform, *supra,* Part V ("Individual Rights and Personal Safety"), available at www.yologop.org/plat5.htm.

63. *Id.* ("We continue our strong support of capital punishment for those who commit heinous federal crimes; including the kingpins of the narcotics trade").

Notes to Chapter 5

1. 121 S. Ct. 525 (2000) (holding that manual recounts of ballots cast in Florida in the 2000 presidential election under standard looking for the "intent of the voter" violates Equal Protection Clause).

2. *See* BRUCE ACKERMAN, THE CASE AGAINST LAMEDUCK IMPEACHMENT (1999). Professor Ackerman argued that the Twentieth Amendment (which moved the inauguration of a new President, and the opening of a new Congress, to January of the year following an election) meant to strip a lameduck Congress of power, including that of the House to pass valid articles of impeachment for trial by the Senate in the next Congress. He also based his argument on the tradition that a bill passed by one chamber but not the other dies with that Congress and must start all over again in the next one.

3. *See* David E. Kendall, *Constitutional Vandalism*, 30 N.M. L. Rev. 155, 172–73 (2000)("After the [impeachment] vote, it was revealed that certain Republican Judiciary Committee members had invited non-Committee members to view so-called "evidence" in the possession of the majority staff — "evidence" which was not contained in the [Independent Counsel's] Referral, nor referenced in the presentations by [Judiciary Committee Counsel] on October 5, 1998, or December 10, 1998, or set forth in the House Judiciary Committee Report transmitting the four articles to the full House. Apparently, this material contained allegations and rumors . . . which were certainly not part of the evidence ostensibly supporting the four articles of impeachment").

4. 506 U.S. 224 (1992).

5. U.S. Constitution, Art. I, § 3, cl. 6.

6. *Bush v. Gore*, 121 S. Ct. at 529.

7. *See* San Antonio Independent School Dist. v. Rodriguez, 411 U.S. 1 (1973) (holding that education is not a "fundamental right" under equal protection doctrine and hence that inequality in public school funding is subject only to rational basis scrutiny).

8. U.S. Constitution, Art. II, § I, cl. 2.

9. *See* Michael H. v. Gerald D., 491 U.S. 110 (1989).

10. *Id.* at 124.

11. M.L.B. v. S.L.J., 519 U.S. 102 (1996).

12. *Id.* at 137 (Thomas, J., dissenting).

13. *See* Bush v. Palm Beach County Canvassing Board, 121 S. Ct. 471, 474 (2000) ("[A] legislative wish to take advantage of the 'safe harbor' [contained in 3 U.S.C. section 5] would counsel against any construction of the Election Code that Congress might deem to be a change in the law").

14. Gore v. Harris, 772 So.2d. 1243, 1262 (2000), *rev'd. and remanded*, Bush v. Gore, 121 S. Ct. 525 (2000).

15. *Bush v. Gore*, 121 S. Ct. at 530–31.

16. *Id.* at 530 ("Having once granted the right to vote on equal terms, the State may not, by later arbitrary and disparate treatment, value one person's vote over that of another").

17. 377 U.S. 533 (1964) (overturning plan to reapportion Alabama Legislature because it violated the "one-man, one-vote" principle).

18. *Gore Would Have Gained Votes in Lake*, Orlando Sentinel, Dec. 19, 2000 (available at www.orlandosentinel.com) (visited December 19, 2000).

19. *Id.*

20. *Human Factor Was at Core of Vote Fiasco*, The Miami Herald, June 1, 2001, at A1 (available at www.herald.com) (visited June 1, 2001).

21. One little-noticed outrage involved Osceola County Supervisor of Elections Donna Bryant, who refused to print Spanish-language ballots because "of the hassle and expense, and because 'we haven't been ordered to by the U.S. Justice Department.'" *Id.* This decision meant that Hispanic residents of Osceola County (29 percent of the population) were treated differently from their counterparts in seven other counties, such as Miami-Dade, in which bilingual ballots were printed, and in which federal law requires their use if the county's voting-age population consists of over 5 percent people with English-language deficiencies. 42 U.S.C. Section 1973b(f)(3)-(4).

22. *See* Siegel v. LePore, 234 F.3d 1163, 1182 (11th Cir. 2000) (Anderson, Ch.J., concurring specially) (noting that the "logical conclusion" of a challenge to disparate treatment in recounting ballots from county to county would be "the untenable position that the method of casting and counting votes would have to be identical in all states and in every county of each state").

23. *See* Cass R. Sunstein, *Order Without Law*, 58 U. Chi. L. Rev. 757, 758 (2001) (arguing that the Court's equal protection rationale (carries "considerable appeal," including the promise of rectifying "various inequalities with respect to voting and voting technology").

24. *Bush v. Gore*, 121 S. Ct. at 532 ("Our consideration is limited to the present circumstances, for the problem of equal protection in election processes generally presents many complexities").

25. *See* Complaint, at ¶ 46, NAACP v. Harris, No. 01-CIV-120–GOLD (S.D.Fl.) ("In the 2000 presidential election, the percentage of ballots recorded as having no vote (non-votes) in Florida counties using a punch-card system was 3.92 percent, while the error rate under the optical-scan systems in use elsewhere in Florida was only 1.43 percent. Thus, for every 10,000 votes cast, punch-card systems result in 250 more non-votes than optical-scan systems") (quoting *Siegel v. LePore*, 234 F.3d 1163, 1196 [11th Cir., Dec. 6, 2000]).

26. 426 U.S. 229 (1976).

27. 518 U.S. 343, 373–78 (1996) (Thomas, J., concurring) (arguing that *Davis's* rejection of disparate impact called into question the decision in *Bounds v. Smith*, 430 U.S. 817 (1977), which held that states have a constitutional obligation, rooted in the Equal Protection Clause, to provide prison inmates with facilities for their use in preparation of legal papers).

28. *Id.* at 376–77 (Thomas, J., concurring) (quoting *Davis*, 426 U.S. at 248).

29. The relatively class-based approach of the Norton EEOC was based in part on the acknowledgment that the Commission lacked the resources to thoroughly investigate every single charge it received, much less to litigate all those it found to have merit. In prioritizing, the Commission put its resources into those cases where relief would have the broadest impact; that is, into systemic cases. On the other hand, the Thomas EEOC envisioned those cases as the most expensive and time-consuming to litigate, and determined that the "smaller" cases would obtain relief more quickly for the most individuals.

30. *See* David L. Rose, *Twenty-Five Years Later: Where Do We Stand on Equal Employment Opportunity Law Enforcement,* 42 Vand. L. Rev. 1121, 1158 (1989) ("Chairperson Thomas also expressed opposition to the adverse impact interpretation of Title VII and to the use of statistics to prove purposeful discrimination").

31. *Id.* at 1159.

32. M.L.B. v. S.L.J., 519 U.S. 102 (1996).

33. *Id.* at 135–36 (Thomas, J., dissenting) (citations omitted).

34. *Bush v. Gore*, 121 S. Ct. at 532.

35. Martin Mertzer, *Review Shows Ballots Say Bush*, Miami Herald (April 6, 2001) (available at www.miami.com/herald/special/news/flacount/docs/032868.htm) (last visited April 7, 2001).

36. Shari Rudavsky and Beth Reinhard, *Recounts Could Have Given Gore the Edge*, Miami Herald (April 6, 2001) (available at www.miami.com/herald/special/news/flacount/docs/038575.htm) (last visited April 7, 2001).

37. *Id.*

38. *Bush v. Gore*, 121 S.Ct. at 534 (Rehnquist, Ch.J., concurring) ("In most cases, comity and respect for federalism compel us to defer to the decisions of state courts on issues of state law. That practice reflects our understanding that the decisions of state courts are definitive pronouncements of the will of the States as sovereigns").

39. U.S. Constitution, Art. II, § I, cl. 2 ("Each State shall appoint, in such Manner as the Legislature thereof may direct, a Number of Electors . . .").

40. *See* Palm Beach Canvassing Board v. Harris, 772 So.2d 1220, 1225 and n.3 (Fla. 2000) (discussing requests for manual recounts).

41. *Id.* at 1239.

42. Bush v. Palm Beach County Canvassing Board, 121 S. Ct. 471 (2000).

43. Fla. Stat. section 102.168(3)(c).

44. I am highlighting here only the points on which the Florida Supreme Court based its ruling in Gore's favor. Gore raised other issues as well, which the Florida Supreme Court rejected and which were not a point of controversy between the U.S. Supreme Court majority and the state Court.

45. Gore v. Harris, 772 So.2d 1243, 1261 (Fl. 2000).

46. Bush v. Gore, 121 S. Ct. at 534 (Rehnquist, Ch.J., concurring).

47. *Id.* at 538 (Rehnquist, Ch.J., concurring).

48. *Id.* at 533 (majority opinion) (citing two Florida Supreme Court opinions).

49. Gore v. Harris, 772 So.2d at 1244 (quoting trial court).

50. *Id.* at 1255 (emphasis supplied by the Court).

51. Bush v. Gore, 121 S. Ct. at 537 (Rehnquist, Ch.J., concurring).

52. Gore v. Harris, 772 So.2d at 1254 (quoting Fla. Stat. section 101.5614(5)-(6)).

53. The Rehnquist concurrence simply cited Florida Chief Justice Charles Wells's dissent for the proposition that section 101.5614 was irrelevant. Bush v. Gore, 121 S. Ct. at 538 (Rehnquist, Ch.J., concurring). Chief Justice Wells, in turn, criticized the state court majority for utilizing that provision because it applies to replacement of damaged or defective ballots, a circumstance not related to a contest challenge. Gore v. Harris, 772 So.2d at 1267 (Wells, Ch.J., dissenting).

54. Bush v. Gore, 121 S. Ct. at 537–38 (Rehnquist, Ch.J., concurring).

55. *Id.* at 537 n.4 (Rehnquist, Ch.J., concurring).

56. *Id.* at 537 (Rehnquist, Ch.J., concurring).

57. Fla. Stat. section 102.166(5) (authorizing county boards to take one of three corrective measures in the event a recount of sample precincts discloses "an error in the vote tabulation which could affect the outcome of the election").

58. Fla. Stat. section 102.168(3)(c).

59. Bush v. Gore, 121 S. Ct. at 534 (Rehnquist, J., concurring).

60. Michael J. Klarman, Bush v. Gore *Through the Lens of Constitutional History*, at 20, available at http://papers.ssrn.com/sol3/papers.cfm?abstract_id=260104 (last visited April 5, 2001).

61. 357 U.S. 449 (1958).

62. Klarman, *Bush v. Gore, supra*, at 21.

Notes to Chapter 6

1. SCALIA, A MATTER OF INTERPRETATION, *supra*, at 140.

2. *Id.* at 45.

3. *See* Glenn Harlan Reynolds, *Sex, Lies and Jurisprudence: Robert Bork, Griswold and the Philosophy of Original Understanding*, 24 Ga. L. Rev. 1045, 1050 (1990).

4. *See* Akhil Reed Amar, *The Bill of Rights As a Constitution*, 100 Yale L.J. 1131, 1162–73 (1991) (arguing that the Second Amendment was intended to protect against oppression by a potentially "aristocratic central government . . . propped up by a standing army of lackeys and hirelings," in part by keeping citizens armed whom the states could "organize and mobilize . . . into an effective fighting force capable of beating even a large standing army"); Saul Cornell, *Commonplace or Anachronism: The Standard Model, The Second Amendment, and the Problem of History in Contemporary Constitutional Theory*, 16 Const. Comment. 221 (1999) (discussing a "new consensus on the meaning of the Second Amendment," which "asserts that the Second Amendment protects both an individual and a collective right of the people to bear arms").

5. Professor Flaherty poses the same dilemma when discussing the Electoral College and the continuing viability of the justifications it was said to serve. *See* Martin S. Flaherty, *Post-Originalism*, 68 U. Chi. L. Rev. 1089, 1109–10 (2001) (noting that the "antidemocratic effects" of the Electoral College can be defended as "the price to pay for the further ostensible founding value of safeguarding 'states' rights,'" but asking whether this "founding value" has "served such goals as preventing tyranny and promoting self-government—ends, then and now, invoked to justify it").

6. U.S. Constitution, Art. I, § 3, cl. 1.

7. *See* George F. Will, *The Long Year*, The Washington Post, at B7 (January 2, 2000).

8. 60 U.S. (19 How.) 393, 407 (1857).

9. *Id.*

10. SCALIA, A MATTER OF INTERPRETATION, *supra*, at 24 ("The first Supreme Court case to use the Due Process Clause in this fashion was . . . *Dred Scott*, not a desirable parentage") (citation omitted); DAVID CURRIE, THE CONSTITUTION IN THE SUPREME COURT 271 (1985) (calling *Dred Scott* "very possibly the first application of substantive due process in the Supreme Court") (quoted in *Planned Parenthood of Southeastern Pennsylvania v. Casey*, 505 U.S. 833, 998 (1992) [Scalia, J., concurring in the judgment in part and dissenting in part]).

11. Christopher L. Eisgruber, *Dred Again: Originalism's Forgotten Past*, 10 Const. Comment. 37 (1993).

12. Cass R. Sunstein, *The* Dred Scott *Case*, 1 Green Bag 2d 39, 40 (1997).

13. *Dred Scott*, 60 U.S. at 404–05.

14. Eisgruber, *Dred Again, supra*, at 46.

15. *Dred Scott*, 60 U.S. at 426.

16. *See* AMAR, THE BILL OF RIGHTS, *supra*, at 160.

17. Professor Sunstein draws from the *Dred Scott* disaster the lesson that the Court should refrain from any like "effort to resolve, once and for all time, an issue that [is] splitting the nation on political and moral grounds. . . . It should leave Great Questions to politics. This is because the Court may answer those questions incorrectly, and because it may well make things worse even if it answers correctly." Sunstein, *The* Dred Scott *Case, supra,* at 41. This is a remarkably broad lesson to draw from a single case; I suggest a narrower and more reasonable conclusion: When the Court attempts to use originalism to resolve Great Questions, it is likely to answer them incorrectly *and* make things worse in the process. At least, this conclusion is more closely tied to the evidence *Dred Scott* actually provides; it tells us little about how the Court might fare if it went another route instead of abandoning the journey altogether.

18. *See* United States v. Morrison, 529 U.S. 598, 627 (2000) (Thomas, J., concurring); United States v. Lopez, 514 U.S. 549, 584–602 (1995) (Thomas, J., concurring).

19. McCulloch v. Maryland, 17 U.S. (4 Wheat.) 316, 408 (1819).

20. *Id.*

21. 491 U.S. 397 (1989).

22. 497 U.S. 836 (1990).

23. *Id.* at 868 (Scalia, J., dissenting) (arguing that any "'special' reasons that exist for suspending [the full right of traditional confrontation] are perhaps matched by 'special' reasons for being particularly insistent upon it in the case of children's testimony").

24. *Id.* at 869–70 (citations to majority opinion omitted).

25. 530 U.S. 27 (2000).

26. *Id.* at 31.

27. *Id.* at 50 (Thomas, J., concurring).

28. Texas v. Johnson, 491 U.S. 397, 419–20 (1989).

29. Liquormart, Inc. v. Rhode Island, 417 U.S. 484, 517 (1996) (Scalia, J., concurring in part and concurring in the judgment).

30. *See also* Sklansky, *The Fourth Amendment, supra,* at 1808 (criticizing Justice Scalia's "caricature" of non-originalism in landmark Fourth Amendment cases, noting that, "In each of these cases the argument, although not originalist, was hardly free-form").

31. *See* Suzanna Sherry, *Too Clever By Half: The Problem With Novelty in Constitutional Law,* 95 Nw. U. L. Rev. 921, 921 (2001) ("[O]ne might say that reconciling judicial review and democratic institutions is the goal of almost every major constitutional scholar writing today"); Barry Friedman, *The History of the Countermajoritarian Difficulty, Part Four: Law's Politics,* 148 U. Pa. L. Rev. 971, 984 (2000) ("Modern constitutional theorists have struggled to reconcile the practice of judicial review with democratic governance. . . . At least since the early 1960s, when [Alexander] Bickel wrote, and actually much earlier than that, academics have tried to justify what they see as a practice in which unaccountable judges interfere with the will of the people and their representatives") (citations omitted).

32. *See* Minnesota v. Dickerson, 508 U.S. 366, 382 (1993) (Scalia, J., concurring) (characterizing non-originalist precedent as reflecting the "good-policy-is-constitutional-law school of jurisprudence").

33. 524 U.S. 498 (1998).

34. *See* Friedman, *The History of the Countermajoritarian Difficulty, Part Four,* *supra*, at 975 n.17.

35. *See Apfel*, 524 U.S. at 530 (acknowledging that the statute at issue did not effect "a permanent physical occupation of Eastern's property of the kind that we have viewed as a per se taking").

36. *Id.* at 516.

37. This crucial aspect of the case came under withering assault in Justice Stevens' dissenting opinion. Stevens demonstrated that while the promise of lifetime benefits had not been reduced to writing until 1974, prior to that time there was "an implicit understanding on both sides of the bargaining table that the operators would provide the miners with lifetime health benefits. It was this understanding that kept the mines in operation and enabled Eastern to earn handsome profits before it transferred its coal business to a wholly-owned subsidiary in 1965." *Id.* at 551 (Stevens, J., dissenting). It was, at the least, rational for Congress to conclude that companies operating in the 1950s and 1960s had created an expectation among workers that they would provide lifetime health benefits, and thus that it was a sound policy decision to impose liability on them.

38. *Id.* at 540 (Kennedy, J., concurring in the judgment and dissenting in part).

Notes to Chapter 7

1. To a lesser degree, Professor Amar has also criticized the preoccupation with the counter-majoritarian difficulty, although he would relocate our focus on the positive value of decentralization, *see* AMAR, THE BILL OF RIGHTS, *supra*, at 128–29 (discussing "agency problem of government," which is the founders' belief that, when it came to intrusions by the state or federal government, "which government [intruded] often made all the difference"), which I believe has the matter exactly wrong.

2. I Official Proceedings of the Constitutional Convention of the State of Alabama May 21, 1901, to September 3rd, 1901 6–7 (1940) (quoted in *Ex Parte Melof,* 735 So.2d 1172, 1202 (1999) [Cook, J., concurring in the result and dissenting from the rationale]).

3. *Ex Parte Melof,* 735 So.2d 1172, 1181 (Al. 1999).

4. *Id.* at 1182–83.

5. *Id.* at 1190.

6. *See* Michael J. Klarman, *The Plessy Era,* 1998 Sup. Ct. Rev. 303, 350 (noting that in Alabama, as early as 1874, by "a combination of fraud, intimidation, and violence, whites gradually reduced the black vote," including "extraordinary campaigns of intimidation and murder"). Professor Klarman describes the 1901 Convention as a

"disenfranchising convention," locating it within the context of similar constitutional efforts in southern states between 1890 and 1908. *Id.* at 354.

7. *Id.* at 356.

8. Indeed, as Professor Suzanna Sherry has recently pointed out, the apparent non-democratic character of judicial review is not unique in our system of government, and it has been exaggerated. See Sherry, *Too Clever By Half,* supra, at 922–23 (noting that the Senate, the Federal Reserve Board, and the Electoral College all perform counter-majoritarian functions or operate in non-majoritarian ways).

9. DERRICK BELL, AND WE ARE NOT SAVED: THE ELUSIVE QUEST FOR RACIAL JUSTICE 29 (1987).

10. *See also* Max Farrand, ed., *The Records of the Federal Convention of 1787,* at 222 (quoting Robert Morris's penetrating query, "Upon what principle is it that the slaves shall be computed in the representation? Are they men? Then make them citizens and let them vote? Are they property? Why then is no other property included?").

11. Sunstein, The *Dred Scott* Case, *supra,* at 45 n.6.

12. Specifically, 100 slaves would gain a slave state the equivalent of 60 free men for apportionment purposes. If more than 40 of those slaves moved north, the slave state would be worse off than it had been before, even if we don't consider the net *gain* in the northern states' populations from this migration.

13. Sunstein, The *Dred Scott* Case, *supra,* at 45 n.6.

14. *Id.*

15. *Id.*

16. U.S. Constitution, Art. I, § 2, Cl. 3 and § 9, Cl. 4.

17. *See* Bruce Ackerman, *Taxation and the Constitution,* 99 Colum. L. Rev. 1, 7–13 (1999) (discussing history of the adoption of the "direct tax" provisions).

18. Hylton v. United States, 3 U.S. (3 Dall.) 171, 177 (1796) (opinion of Paterson, J.).

19. Ackerman, *Taxation and the Constitution, supra,* at 22–24.

20. Cheryl I. Harris, *Whiteness as Property,* 106 Harv. L. Rev. 1709, 1716 (1993).

21. *See* BELL, AND WE ARE NOT SAVED, *supra,* at 29 (quoting South Carolina delegate to the constitutional convention arguing, "property in slaves should not be exposed to danger under a Govt. instituted for the protection of property").

22. *Id.* at 30 (quoting Max Farrand, ed., *The Records of the Federal Convention of 1787,* vol. 1, p. xvi [1911]).

23. Harris, *Whiteness as Property, supra,* at 1758.

24. *Id.* at 1766–69.

25. Clarence Thomas, *Why Federalism Matters,* 48 Drake L. Rev. 231, 234 (2000).

26. *See* Darlene Clark Hine, *Black Lawyers and the Twentieth-Century Struggle for Constitutional Change,* in THE LIVING CONSTITUTION, *supra,* at 33. Hine argues that "the controversy over state versus federal rights and the contradiction inherent in the coexistence of democracy and . . . slavery, and later, racial inequality were so closely intertwined that it would require two reconstructions—one in the aftermath

of the Civil War and another several generations later—to restore the primacy of federal authority over state power and equality of rights over racial subordination."

27. AMAR, THE BILL OF RIGHTS, *supra,* at 4.

28. *Id.* at 5.

29. *Id.* at 160.

30. *Id.* at 6–7.

31. *See* DAVID P. CURRIE, THE CONSTITUTION IN CONGRESS: THE JEFFERSONI-ANS, 1801–1829 347 (2000) (describing opposition to federal power, even in areas seemingly unrelated to slavery, as motivated by southern perception that the power itself constituted a threat to the institution).

32. AMAR, THE BILL OF RIGHTS, *supra,* at 192.

33. *Id.* at 221.

34. There is one partial exception to this omission. Professor Amar does suggest that the Fourteenth Amendment reshapes the concept of "reasonableness" in Fourth Amendment cases, so that "[a] relatively unintrusive search might not be 'unreasonable' in terms of privacy alone; but if, say, blacks are being singled out without good cause, such a search may well offend reconstructed reasonableness." *Id.* at 268.

35. 109 U.S. 3, 11 (1883) (Congress is empowered only "[t]o adopt appropriate legislation for correcting the effects of such prohibited state law and state acts," because "[i]ndividual invasion of individual rights is not the subject-matter of the amendment").

36. *Id.* at 25–26 (emphasis added).

37. *See* PAUL KAUPER, CIVIL LIBERTIES AND THE CONSTITUTION 128–30 (1962) (noting in reference to a "state action" requirement that "the Constitution does not use the word 'action,' a word which is really misleading because it suggests that a violation of the Fourteenth Amendment can arise only when the state acts in some affirmative way," and because "denial of equal rights may occur either by positive action or by failure of the state to act in an appropriate way in a given situation").

38. *See* The Civil Rights Cases, 109 U.S. 3, 34 (1883) (Harlan, J., dissenting) ("Were the states, against whose solemn protest the institution was destroyed, to be left perfectly free, so far as national interference was concerned, to make or allow discriminations against that race, as such, in the enjoyment of those fundamental rights that inhere in a state of freedom?").

39. *See* John E. Nowak, *The Gang of Five and The Second Coming of the Anti-Reconstruction Supreme Court,* 75 Notre Dame L. Rev. 1091, 1108 (2000) (arguing that the holding in the *Civil Rights Cases* "blocked congressional and executive branch actions designed to protect racial minorities," and contributed to "thousands of lynchings of minority persons that might have been prevented by the federal government").

40. *See* United States v. Guest, 383 U.S. 745, 782–84 (1966) (Brennan, J., concurring in part and dissenting in part) (criticizing the *Civil Rights Cases'* interpretation of Congress's section 5 authority).

41. United States v. Morrison, 529 U.S. 598, 624 (2000) ("We believe that the description of the § 5 power contained in the *Civil Rights Cases* is correct . . .").

42. SUNSTEIN, THE PARTIAL CONSTITUTION, *supra,* at 100 (emphasis added).

43. Kenyon D. Bunch, *The Original Understanding of the Privileges and Immunities Clause: Michael Perry's Justification for Judicial Activism Or Robert Bork's Constitutional Inkblot?*, 10 Seton Hall Const. L.J. 321, 326 (2000) (criticizing scholars who "give only lip service . . . to the significance for the originalist project of the extraordinary majorities necessary to amend the Constitution").

44. Robert A. Rutland, Charles F. Hobson, William E. Rachal, and Frederika Teute, eds., 10 The Papers of James Madison 90 (1977).

45. BRUCE ACKERMAN, WE THE PEOPLE: FOUNDATIONS 316 (1991).

46. *Id.*

47. SUNSTEIN, THE PARTIAL CONSTITUTION, *supra,* at 166–70.

48. *Id.* at 165.

49. *Id.*

50. *See* Twining v. New Jersey, 211 U.S. 78 (1908) (acknowledging that some Bill of Rights protections might be incorporated because "a denial of them would be a denial of due process," but holding that the privilege against self-incrimination is not incorporated), *overruled,* Malloy v. Hogan, 378 U.S. 1 (1964).

51. *See* Powell v. Alabama, 287 U.S. 45 (1932) (denying capital defendants assistance of counsel deprived them of due process).

52. 332 U.S. 46 (1942).

53. In the area of criminal procedure, for example, the only Bill of Rights guarantee not incorporated is the fifth amendment right to a grand jury indictment. *See* Hurtado v. California, 110 U.S. 516 (1884).

54. 305 U.S. 337 (1938) (in the absence of a separate state law school for African-Americans, policy refusing to admit African-Americans to the University of Missouri law school is unconstitutional).

55. 339 U.S. 629 (1950) (holding unconstitutional refusal to admit African-Americans to law school at University of Texas in light of inequality of newly established separate school).

56. 163 U.S. 537 (1896).

57. 347 U.S. 483 (1954).

58. SUNSTEIN, THE PARTIAL CONSTITUTION, *supra,* at 148.

59. *Id.*

Notes to Chapter 8

1. CAROLE KING, *Tapestry, on* TAPESTRY (SNY Records 1971).

2. The format of this chapter is styled after Jefferson Powell's important article, *Rules for Originalists,* 73 Va. L. Rev. 659 (1987).

3. 735 So.2d 1172, 1181 (Al. 1999).

4. *Id.* at 1182.

5. *Id.* at 1182–83.

6. *Ex Parte Melof* also presented one of the oddest expressions of the personal constraint aspect of originalism. The author of the majority opinion, Justice Houston, *also authored a separate special concurrence,* stating, "If I were drafting a constitution, I would make certain that there was an equal protection clause in that constitution; however, there is not one in the Alabama Constitution." 735 So.2d at 1188 (Houston, J., concurring in the result) (quoting Moore v. Mobile Infirmary Ass'n, 592 So.2d 156, 175 [Ala.1991]).

7. *Id.* at 1188–90.

8. *Id.* at 1190.

9. *Id.* at 1188–90.

10. This point is independent of a critique of the quality of the historical analysis employed by the Court's incumbent originalists. Even within the confines of the inquiry in which they do engage, Justices Scalia and Thomas have been criticized for sloppy and sometimes misleading renditions of the original understanding. *See, e.g.,* Michael W. McConnell, *Freedom From Persecution or Protection of the Rights of Conscience?: A Critique of Justice Scalia's Historical Arguments in* City of Boerne v. Flores, 39 Wm. & Mary L. Rev. 819, 833 (1998) (charging Justice Scalia with "selective quotation" in historical argument on the scope of the Free Exercise Clause); Nichol, *Justice Scalia and the* Printz *Case, supra,* 70 U. Colo. L. Rev. at 964–65 (arguing that historical record is "relatively straightforward," and so contrary to Justice Scalia's position that "[o]ne can almost imagine the taunting use [he] would have made of [it]—had he only been on the other side"). My challenge here, however, is not to how well they do what they are doing, but to the limits of what they are doing.

11. *See* Garrett Epps, *Of Constitutional Seances and Color-Blind Ghosts,* 72 N.C. L. Rev. 401, 420–21 (1994) ("Congress repeatedly rejected such a measure [barring governments from using all racial classifications], choosing the far more ambiguous language of the present Fourteenth Amendment . . ."); KULL, THE COLOR-BLIND CONSTITUTION, *supra,* at 64 (quoting Wendell Phillips' description of the Fourteenth Amendment as "an infamous breach of the national pledge to negroes . . . [and] a party trick designed only for electioneering purposes").

12. Michael C. Dorf, *No Federalists Here,* 31 Rutgers L.J. 741, 748 (2000) (criticizing Professor Jackson's proposed treatment of issues of state sovereign immunity).

13. This position was expressed at the Constitutional Convention: "Mr. Pinkney & Mr. Gerry, moved to insert a declaration 'that the liberty of the Press should be inviolably observed—' "Mr. Sherman—It is unnecessary—The power of Congress does not extend to the Press." 2 Farrand, *Records of the Constitutional Convention* 617–18 (1911) (Madison's notes for September 14).

14. U.S. Constitution, Am. IX.

15. 530 U.S. 57 (2000).

16. *Id.* at 91 (Scalia, J., dissenting).

17. *Id.*

18. U.S. Constitution, Art. I, § 9, Cl. 8.

19. U.S. Constitution, Art. I, § 9, Cl. 3.

20. If the Senate itself is not indication enough of the importance of this principle, it is worth noting that the states' equal representation in the Senate is the only provision in the Constitution that cannot be amended. U.S. Constitution, Art. V ("[N]o State, without its consent, shall be deprived of its equal Suffrage in the Senate").

21. *More Reform, Less Compromise,* at www.pirg.org/demos/cfr/hist.htm (visited August 22, 2000).

22. *Redefining the Problem of Big Money in Politics: Soft Money Is Only the Tip of the Iceberg,* at www.pirg.org/demos/cfr/prob.htm (visited August 22, 2000).

23. McCulloch v. Maryland, 17 U.S. (4 Wheat.) 316, 407 (1819) (emphasis added).

24. Alden v. Maine, 527 U.S. 706, 713 (1999).

25. 14 U.S. (1 Wheat.) 304, 343 (1816).

26. 17 U.S. (4 Wheat.) 316 (1819).

27. *Id.* at 406.

28. *See* Griswold v. Connecticut, 381 U.S. 479 (1965) (contraceptives); Roe v. Wade, 410 U.S. 113 (1973) (abortion); Stanley v. Georgia, 394 U.S. 557 (1969) (obscene movies).

29. 527 U.S. 706 (1999).

30. *Id.* at 727 (citations omitted; emphasis added).

31. *Id.* at 729 (emphasis added).

32. *See* Judith Resnik, *Trial as Error, Jurisdiction as Injury: Transforming the Meaning of Article III,* 113 Harv. L. Rev. 924, 1004 (2000) (discussing the federalism jurisprudence as consisting of "prohibitions that reside in the penumbra of the Eleventh Amendment, in the vague text of the Tenth, or in a more general but non-text-specific constitutional structure").

33. *Alden,* 527 U.S. at 730.

34. Hunter v. Underwood, 471 U.S. 222, 229 (1985).

35. Vicki C. Jackson, *Principle and Compromise in Constitutional Adjudication: The Eleventh Amendment and State Sovereign Immunity,* 75 Notre Dame L.J. 953, 994 (2000) (discussing Supreme Court's refusal to accept state arguments against "one person, one vote" rule based on analogy to the constitutional compromise creating the U.S. Senate).

36. *Id.* at 1005 (referring to the status of the Senate as part of the "fundamentals of structure [that] were described and have been adhered to").

37. *See* Gary Orfield, *Congress and Civil Rights,* in THE LIVING CONSTITUTION, *supra,* at 145 (arguing that "no civil rights law [was] enacted for more than three-fourths of a century" from 1875 to 1964, and that Congress was an obstacle primarily because of the ability of Southern Senators to block bills using the filibuster and seniority-based committee chairmanships).

38. TAYLOR BRANCH, PARTING THE WATERS: AMERICA IN THE KING YEARS 1954–63 220 (1988).

39. *See id.* at 220–21 (discussing filibuster blocking the Civil Rights Act of 1957,

and the ensuing amendments that secured passage but rendered the Act ineffective in practice).

40. The Supreme Court indicated its skepticism of just such a challenge in James v. Valtierra, 402 U.S. 137, 142 (1971), upholding a law requiring that certain ordinances be enacted by referendum in classic slippery-slope fashion: "[T]his Court would be required to analyze governmental structures to determine whether a gubernatorial veto provision or a filibuster rule is likely to 'disadvantage' any of the diverse and shifting groups that make up the American people." *See also* Barnes v. Kline, 759 F.2d 21, 47 (D.C. Cir. 1984) (Bork, J., dissenting) (criticizing majority rationale because under it, "the opponents of a filibuster have standing to sue for an injunction directing the filibuster to cease"), *judgment vacated as moot and remanded,* Burke v. Barnes, 479 U.S. 361 (1987).

41. In slightly different circumstances, a court should also have looked favorably on a suit filed by a Senator or group of Senators seeking an injunction ordering the Senate to take up and vote on a civil rights bill that had been bottled up in committee by a segregationist chair.

42. U.S. Constitution, Art. I, § 3, Cl. 1.

43. U.S. Constitution, Art. I, § 3, Cl. 6 ("The Senate shall have the sole Power to try all Impeachments. When sitting for that Purpose, they shall be on Oath or Affirmation. When the President of the United States is tried, the Chief Justice shall preside: And no Person shall be convicted without the Concurrence of two thirds of the Members present").

44. U.S. Constitution, Art. I, § 7, Cl. 2 ("Every Bill which shall have passed the House of Representatives and the Senate, shall, before it become a Law, be presented to the President of the United States; If he approve he shall sign it, but if not he shall return it, with his Objections to that House in which it shall have originated, who shall enter the Objections at large on their Journal, and proceed to reconsider it. If after such Reconsideration two thirds of that House shall agree to pass the Bill, it shall be sent, together with the Objections, to the other House, by which it shall likewise be reconsidered, and if approved by two thirds of that House, it shall become a Law").

45. U.S. Constitution, Art. II, § 2, Cl. 2 ("[The President] shall have Power, by and with the Advice and Consent of the Senate, to make Treaties, provided two thirds of the Senators present concur . . .").

46. In order from most to least populous: New Hampshire, Hawaii, Rhode Island, Montana, Delaware, South Dakota, North Dakota, Alaska, Vermont, and Wyoming. *See* U.S. Department of the Census, Population Estimates for States by race and Hispanic origin: July 1, 1998 (available at http://www.census.gov/population/estimates/state/srh/srhus98.txt) (visited July 17, 2000).

47. In order: California, Texas, New York, Florida, Illinois, Pennsylvania, Ohio, Michigan, New Jersey, and Georgia. *Id.*

48. The combined population of the top ten represents just over 54 percent of the national population. *Id.*

49. 304 U.S. 144 (1938).

50. *Id.* at 153 n.4.

51. *See* Richard A. Epstein, *Toward a Revitalization of the Contract Clause*, 51 U. Chi. L. Rev. 703, 704 (1984) ("The dominant distinction today is between 'preferred freedoms' or 'fundamental rights' on the one hand, and all subordinate rights on the other. Economic liberties and property rights are clearly placed in the subordinate class").

52. *College Savings Bank v. Florida Prepaid Postsecondary Education Expense Board*, 527 U.S. 666, 673 (1999).

53. *See* Walter Benn Michaels, *Response to Perry and Simon*, 58 S. Cal. L. Rev. 673, 673 (1985) ("[A]ny interpretation of the Constitution that really is an interpretation and that really is an interpretation of the Constitution is always and only an interpretation of what the Constitution originally meant").

54. Robin L. West, *Constitutional Scepticism*, 73 B.U. L. Rev. 765 (1992) (arguing that the focus on interpretive method has led us to neglect the questions "whether our Constitution is desirable," and "whether it furthers the 'good life' for the individuals, communities, and subcommunities it governs").

55. *Id.* at 770.

56. *Id.* at 771. West concedes there are notable exceptions to the phenomenon she describes, scholars such as Derrick Bell, Alan Freeman, and Mari Matsuda, who take on the Constitution itself as both non- and anti-progressive.

BIBLIOGRAPHY

Books

Ackerman, Bruce. The Case Against Lameduck Impeachment (1999).

———. We the People: Foundations (1991).

Amar, Akhil Reed. The Bill of Rights: Creation and Reconstruction (1998).

Bell, Derrick. And We Are Not Saved: The Elusive Quest for Racial Justice (1987).

Bork, Robert H. The Tempting of America: The Political Seduction of America (1990).

Branch, Taylor. Parting the Waters: America in the King Years 1954–63 (1988).

Currie, David P. The Constitution in Congress: The Jeffersonians, 1801–1829 (2000).

———. The Constitution in the Supreme Court (1985).

Delgado, Richard, ed. Critical Race Theory: The Cutting Edge (1995).

Farrand, Max, ed. The Records of the Federal Convention of 1782 (1911).

Franklin, John Hope, and McNeil, Genna Rae, eds. African-Americans and the Living Constitution (1995).

Fried, Charles. Order and Law: Arguing the Reagan Revolution—A Firsthand Account (1991).

Gerber, Scott Douglas. First Principles: The Jurisprudence of Clarence Thomas (1999).

Higginbotham, Jr., A. Leon. In the Matter of Color: Race and the American Legal Process: The Colonial Period (1978).

Kauper, Paul. Civil Liberties and the Constitution (1962).

Kull, Andrew. The Color-Blind Constitution (1992).

MacKinnon, Catherine. Feminism Unmodified: Discourse on Life and Law (1987).

Mayer, Jane, and Abramson, Jill. Strange Justice: The Selling of Clarence Thomas (1994).

Rutland, Robert A., Hobson, Charles F., Rachal, William E., and Teute, Frederika, eds. 10 The Papers of James Madison (1977).

Scalia, Antonin. A Matter of Interpretation: Federal Courts and the Law (1997).

Sunstein, Cass R. The Partial Constitution (1993).

Articles

Ackerman, Bruce, *Taxation and the Constitution*, 99 Colum. L. Rev. 1 (1999).

Amar, Akhil Reed, *Intratextualism*, 112 Harv. L. Rev. 747 (1999).

Amar, Akhil Reed, *The Constitution Versus the Court: Some Thoughts on Hills on Amar*, 94 Nw. U. L. Rev. 205 (1999).

———, *The Constitutional Virtues and Vices of the New Deal*, 22 Harv. J. L. & Pub. Pol'y 219 (1998).

———, *Fourth Amendment First Principles*, 107 Harv. L. Rev. 757 (1994).

———, *The Bill of Rights As a Constitution*, 100 Yale L.J. 1131 (1991).

Applebaum, Harvey M., *Miscegenation Statutes: A Constitutional and Social Problem*, 53 Geo. L.J. 49 (1964).

Bank, Steven A., *Comment, Antimiscegenation Laws and the Dilemma of Symmetry: The Understanding of Equality in the Civil Rights Act of 1875*, 2 U. Chi. L. Sch. Roundtable 303 (1995).

Berger, Raoul, *Robert Bork's Contribution to Original Intention*, 84 Nw. U. L. Rev. 1167 (1990).

Bunch, Kenyon D., *The Original Understanding of the Privileges and Immunities Clause: Michael Perry's Justification for Judicial Activism Or Robert Bork's Constitutional Inkblot?* 10 Seton Hall Const. L.J. 321 (2000).

Carter, Stephen L., *Bork Redux, or How the Tempting of America Led the People to Rise and Battle for Justice*, 69 Tex. L. Rev. 759 (1991).

Chemerinsky, Erwin, *The Hypocrisy of* Alden v. Maine: *Judicial Review, Sovereign Immunity and the Rehnquist Court*, 33 Loy. L.A. L. Rev. 1283 (2000).

Cho, Sumi, *Redeeming Whiteness in the Shadow of Internment: Earl Warren, Brown, and a Theory of Racial Redemption*, 19 Bost. Coll. Third World L.J. 73 (1998).

Cornell, Saul, *Commonplace or Anachronism: The Standard Model, The Second Amendment, and the Problem of History in Contemporary Constitutional Theory*, 16 Const. Comment. 221 (1999).

———, *The Changing Historical Fortunes of the Anti-Federalists*, 84 Nw. U. L. Rev. 39 (1989).

Cross, John T., *Intellectual Property and the Eleventh Amendment After Seminole Tribe*, 47 DePaul L. Rev. 519 (1998).

Culp, Jr., Jerome McCristal, *Toward a Black Legal Scholarship: Race and Original Understandings*, 1991 Duke L. Rev. 39.

Davies, Thomas Y., *Recovering the Original Fourth Amendment*, 98 Mich. L. Rev. 547 (1999).

Dorf, Michael C., *No Federalists Here*, 31 Rutgers L.J. 741 (2000).

Dripps, Donald, *Akhil Amar on Criminal Procedure and Constitutional Law: "Here I Go Down That Wrong Road Again,"* 74 N.C. L. Rev. 1559 (1996).

Eisgruber, Christopher L., *Dred Again: Originalism's Forgotten Past*, 10 Const. Comment. 37 (1993).

Epps, Garrett, *Of Constitutional Seances and Color-Blind Ghosts*, 72 N.C. L. Rev. 401 (1994).

Epstein, Richard A., *Toward a Revitalization of the Contract Clause*, 51 U. Chi. L. Rev. 703 (1984).

Farber, Daniel A., and Sherry, Suzanna, *Telling Stories Out of School: An Essay on Legal Narratives*, 45 Stan. L. Rev. 807 (1993).

Flaherty, Martin S., *Post-Originalism*, 68 U. Chi. L. Rev. 1089 (2001).

Friedman, Barry, *The History of the Countermajoritarian Difficulty, Part Four: Law's Politics*, 148 U. Pa. L. Rev. 971 (2000).

Gold, Andrew S., *Regulatory Takings and the Original Intent: The Direct, Physical Takings Thesis "Goes Too Far,"* 49 Am. U.L. Rev. 181 (1999).

Harris, Cheryl I., *Whiteness as Property*, 106 Harv. L. Rev. 1709 (1993).

Jackson, Vicki C., *Principle and Compromise in Constitutional Adjudication: The Eleventh Amendment and State Sovereign Immunity*, 75 Notre Dame L.J. 953 (2000).

Jeffries, John C., *Disaggregating Constitutional Torts*, 100 Yale L.J. 259 (2000).

Kendall, David E., *Constitutional Vandalism*, 30 N.M. L. Rev. 155 (2000).

Klarman, Michael J., *The Plessy Era*, 1998 Sup. Ct. Rev. 303.

———, *An Interpretive History of Modern Equal Protection*, 90 Mich. L. Rev. 213 (1991).

Koppelman, Andrew, *Why Discrimination Against Lesbians and Gay Men Is Sex Discrimination*, 69 N.Y.U. L. Rev. 197 (1995).

Laycock, Douglas, *Conceptual Gulfs in* City of Boerne v. Flores, 39 Wm. & Mary L. Rev. 743 (1998).

Lipkin, Robert J., *Beyond Skepticism, Foundationalism and the New Fuzziness: The Role of Wide Reflective Equilibrium in Legal Theory*, 75 Cornell L. Rev. 811 (1990).

Maclin, Tracy, *The Central Meaning of the Fourth Amendment*, 35 Wm. & Mary L. Rev. 197 (1993).

Marcosson, Samuel A., *Colorizing the Constitution of Originalism: Clarence Thomas at the Rubicon*, 16 Law & Inequality 429 (1998).

McConnell, Michael W., *Freedom From Persecution or Protection of the Rights of Conscience?: A Critique of Justice Scalia's Historical Arguments in* City of Boerne v. Flores, 39 Wm. & Mary L. Rev. 819 (1998).

———, *The Originalist Justification for Brown: A Reply to Professor Klarman*, 81 Va. L. Rev. 1936 (1995).

———, *Originalism and the Desegregation Decisions*, 81 Va. L. Rev. 947 (1995).

Michaels, Walter Benn, *Response to Perry and Simon*, 58 S. Cal. L. Rev. 673 (1985).

Nichol, Gene R., *Justice Scalia and the* Printz *Case: The Trials of an Occasional Originalist*, 70 U. Colo. L. Rev. 953 (1999).

Nowak, John E., *The Gang of Five and The Second Coming of the Anti-Reconstruction Supreme Court*, 75 Notre Dame L. Rev. 1091 (2000).

———, *Federalism and the Civil War Amendments*, 23 Ohio N. L. Rev. 1209 (1997).

Powell, H. Jefferson, *Rules for Originalists*, 73 Va. L. Rev. 659 (1987).

Resnik, Judith, *Trial as Error, Jurisdiction as Injury: Transforming the Meaning of Article III*, 113 Harv. L. Rev. 924 (2000).

Reynolds, Glenn Harlan, *Sex, Lies and Jurisprudence: Robert Bork, Griswold and the Philosophy of Original Understanding*, 24 Ga. L. Rev. 1045 (1990).

Richards, David A.J., *Originalism Without Foundations*, 65 N.Y.U. L. Rev. 1373 (1990).

Rosen, Jeffrey, *The Color-Blind Court*, 45 Am. U.L. Rev. 791 (1996).

Scalia, Antonin, *Originalism: The Lesser Evil*, 57 U. Cin. L. Rev. 849 (1989).

Sherry, Suzanna, *Too Clever By Half: The Problem With Novelty in Constitutional Law*, 95 Nw. U. L. Rev. 921 (2001).

Sklansky, David A., *The Fourth Amendment and Common Law*, 100 Colum. L. Rev. 1739 (2000).

Steiker, Carol S., *Second Thoughts About First Principles*, 107 Harv. L. Rev. 820 (1994).

Sunstein, Cass R., *Order Without Law*, 58 U. Chi. L. Rev. 757 (2001).

———, *The* Dred Scott *Case*, 1 Green Bag 2d 39 (1997).

———, *Foreword: Leaving Things Undecided*, 110 Harv. L. Rev. 4 (1996).

Thomas, Clarence, *Why Federalism Matters*, 48 Drake L. Rev. 231 (2000).

Thomas, Clarence A., *Civility*, 4 Race & Ethnic Ancestry L.J. 1 (1998).

Treanor, William Michael, *The Original Understanding of the Takings Clause and the Political Process*, 95 Colum. L. Rev. 782 (1995).

Tribe, Laurence H., *Taking Text and Structure Seriously: Reflections on Free-Form Method in Constitutional Interpretation*, 108 Harv. L. Rev. 1221 (1995).

Van Tassel, Emily Field, *Antimiscegenation, The Moral Economy of Dependency, and the Debate Over Rights After the Civil War*, 70 Chi-Kent L. Rev. 873 (1995).

West, Robin L., *Constitutional Scepticism*, 73 B.U. L. Rev. 765 (1992).

INDEX

abortion, 76, 170

Abramson, Jill, 30

Ackerman, Bruce, 79, 130, 140, 192n. 2

Adamson v. California, 142

Adarand Constructors, Inc. v. Pena, 20, 24, 28

affirmative action: policy arguments regarding, 28–29; Thomas's position on, 23–24, 28–29

Age Discrimination in Employment Act (ADEA), 63–64

Alabama: Constitution of 1901, 12, 123–25, 127–28, 148, 158, 161, 165–66; racist origins of its 1901 Constitution, 123–25, 146–48, 149, 158, 165, 166; Reconstruction Constitution, 123, 146, 165–66; and Supreme Court of, 12, 104, 146–47, 148

Alden v. Maine, 53, 68–71, 73, 75–76, 105, 157, 190n. 37

Amar, Akhil, 45–49, 67–68, 133–34, 174n. 28, 198n. 1, 200n. 34

Americans with Disabilities Act (ADA), 64

Anderson v. Creighton, 46–47

Anti-commandeering. *See* Federalism

Anti-federalists, 134–35

Antimiscegenation laws, xi-xiii, 114, 170, 175n. 6, 182n. 11; effect of Fourteenth Amendment on, 15–24, 43, 130

Applebaum, Harvey M., 177n. 16

Arizona v. Hicks, 44

Article I. *See* U.S. Constitution

Article III. *See* U.S. Constitution

Article V. *See* U.S. Constitution

Articles of Confederation, 157, 175n. 9

Baker, James, 78

Bank of the United States, 156

Barr, Bob, 79

Bell, Derrick, 128

Bennis v. Michigan, 175n. 4

Berger, Raoul, 18, 176n. 13, 177n. 18

Bill of Rights. *See particular amendments*

Black, Hugo, 142

Blackmun, Harry, 3–4, 106, 117, 172n. 11; opinions in *Croson* and *Webster*, 3–4; opinion in *Lucas*, 36; use of recognition in constitutional interpretation, 1–3, 172nn. 11–12

Board of County Commissioners v. Umbehr, 2, 171n. 1, 172n. 6

Bork, Robert, 109, 170, 174n. 24, 176n. 13, 179n. 36

Brady Handgun Violence Protection Act (the Brady Act), 53, 72–74

Brennan, William, 117–18, 120

Breyer, Stephen, 57, 80, 189n. 14

Bridge on the River Kwai, 108

Broward County, 94, 96

Brown v. Board of Education, 39, 81, 114, 143, 179n. 36

Bryant, Donna, 193n. 21

Bunch, Kenyon, 138

Bush v. Gore, 6–7, 77, 79–106; and contest phase of Florida election challenge, 86–99, 100–101; definition of fundamental rights, 82; equal protection rationale, 81–95; failure to assess state interests supporting recount order, 84–86; and federalism, 95–106; and interpretation of Florida statute, 95–106; likely outcome of hypothetical recount under majority rationale, 94–95; majority's effort to limit reach of equal protection reasoning, 90; as maximizing favored election outcome of the majority, 80–81, 93–96; as smoking gun showing inconsistency of originalist justices, 7, 89–90, 106–7, 166–67; unquestioned error of law committed by trial judge, 99

Bush, George H. W., 28

Bush, George W., 86–89, 94, 96, 171n. 5; selection as president of the U.S., 13, 89

ABOUT THE AUTHOR

Samuel A. Marcosson is an Associate Professor at the University of Louisville Louis D. Brandeis School of Law. He began teaching there in 1996, after spending eight years working in the Equal Employment Opportunity Commission's Office of General Counsel in Washington, D.C. Professor Marcosson received his J.D. from Yale Law School in 1986 and a B.S. from Bradley University in 1983.